WILL THE **REAL YOU** PLEASE STAND UP?

Also by Fran Harris

Books
The Intentional Millionaire: Winning the Wealth Game with Spirit
Summer Madness: Inside the Wild, Wacky World of the WNBA

Audio Products
Six Figure Speaking Secrets
Guestpertise: How to Explode Your Income as a Radio
    & Television Expert
Fast Track Internet Marketing Series

Home-Study Courses
Turn Your Expertise into a Multimedia Empire
Women Entrepreneurs & Millionaires Challenge

WILL THE
REAL YOU
PLEASE STAND UP?

*7 Spiritual Strategies to Help You Discover
Your Purpose and Live It with Passion*

FRAN HARRIS, Ph.D.

Health Communications, Inc.
Deerfield Beach, Florida

www.hcibooks.com

Library of Congress Cataloging-in-Publication Data

Harris, Fran.
    Will the *real* you please stand up? : 7 spiritual strategies to help you discover
your purpose and live it with passion / Fran Harris.
      p. cm.
    Includes bibliographical references and index.
    ISBN-13: 978-0-7573-0549-8 (hard cover : alk. paper)
    ISBN-10: 0-7573-0549-0 (hard cover : alk. paper)
    1. Spiritual life.   2. Self-realization—Religious aspects. I. Title.
BL624.H328 2007
204'.4—dc22

                                    2006035110

Publisher: Health Communications, Inc.
            3201 S.W. 15th Street
            Deerfield Beach, FL 33442-8190

Cover photo by Michael Graham
Cover design by Libby Piscareta
Inside book design and formatting by Dawn Von Strolley Grove

Contents

Acknowledgments

Acknowledgments

*T*hank you, God, for all that I am and will become.

To my agent, Matthew Carnicelli, for your editorial direction on this project and those to come, as well as your enthusiasm for my talents and genius—thank you.

Thank you to Michele Matriciani, editorial director at Health Communications, Inc., for your belief in this book and its place in the world.

To those of you who have supported me from a distance, bought my books or courses, attended my seminars, or sent an e-mail or words of encouragement, thank you. Continued blessings to each of you.

To Daddy—John W.—for being a wonderfully loving and emotional man and for being such a shining example of "realness."

To my family and friends—you know who you are—I love you all.

❧ What Would Happen If You . . . ❧

- *stopped listening to all of the negativity you hear at home, work, church, or school?*
- *stopped investing in the opinions of others?*
- *gave yourself a "Get out of Jail Free" card from whatever emotional, religious, mental, physical, or financial prison you're serving time in?*
- *freed yourself from the chains of lack, limitations, and scarcity?*
- *stopped believing the lies that you've been told about who you are and what you can become?*
- *didn't vilify those who offend you or seek to do you harm?*
- *decided that you'd meet every challenge with love, forgiveness, compassion, acceptance, and laughter for the rest of your life?*

What Would Happen If You . . .

- *retired your ego?*
- *embraced your spirit?*
- *accepted your greatness?*
- *let go of the illusions?*
- *yearned for righteousness?*
- *overcame fear with faith?*
- *unleashed your genius?*

Know what would happen? You'd become the real you!

Preface

T he summer I retired from the WNBA I was at a major cross-roads. I was coming off of the inaugural championship season with the Houston Comets. It was 1998, and I was deciding what I wanted to "do" for the next phase of my life. I'd played for the Utah Starzz that summer and hadn't had the most joyous of experiences with that organization. Yet because I believe every experience carries both lessons and blessings, I was able to walk away from that time in my life with greater self-awareness, fond memories, and more important, a whole new set of friends whom I truly love.

The biggest takeaway from my minicrisis, which I now affectionately call my "Salt Lake Days," is a book that I conceived during one of my "keep my sanity" meditation sessions while looking out over a majestic set of mountains in Park City, Utah. The book, at the time, I called *What on Earth Am I Doing Here?* It was precisely the question I was asking myself at the time. I had no idea what the book was going to be about, but I was definitely digging the title. One night as I packed for a road trip, I got inspired to work on the book. I jotted pages and pages of notes on various topics as the information came to me. Who was I, really? How had I come to be the person I was, and more important, was who I'd become who I wanted to be? My life felt like a giant jigsaw puzzle with more than a million little pieces. It was clear that I was on a journey of self-discovery, which I didn't mind, but the answers weren't coming to me in a neatly wrapped package, as I'd hoped. The answers were coming at me the way sand flies into your eyes on a windy afternoon at Venice Beach—from every direction and faster than I could keep up with. I found myself asking, "Why, of all questions, is God asking me to answer 'Who am I?'" The answer I repeatedly got was: because to do the work you were born to do, you need to know who you are. So I bought a *WOEAIDH (What on Earth Am I Doing Here?)* journal and started to record the details of this new journey.

The premise of the book was going to be about self-exploration and spiritual awareness; that much I could tell. I would go to bed writing and I would wake up writing. I would be standing on the sidelines during practice thinking about THE question: who am I?

On the plane to our game versus the New York Liberty (a long flight from Salt Lake City), I wrote a book proposal and started to churn out the details of the content. I was sure I could get the book sold fairly quickly, but then, as it has a tendency to do, life got crazy, and the book project got tossed aside. It became like that pair of pants we buy "because they're on sale," but we never end up wearing. Still, I never forgot about it. And the question "Who am I and why am I here?" stayed with me. I kept the proposal tucked neatly in my filing cabinet in the "great ideas" folder, where it stayed for three years.

In March 2001, I participated on a panel of successful businesswomen and international leaders via satellite in the Second Annual WomenFuture.com global businesswomen summit that was aired on PBS. After a long day of energizing and encouraging 200 women and men of various ages, professional disciplines, and socioeconomic backgrounds to step into their purpose and passion, I looked out into the eager faces and posed what I believed to be a simple question: "How many of you are truly living your life's purpose?"

It seemed like a logical enough question, but immediately a hush fell over the previously raucous room. So I posed the question again—this time in Italian, since it appeared that either I'd asked a really difficult question or I'd asked it in the wrong language! The audience laughed as I continued to speak to them in Spanish, broken German, and pathetic French in an attempt to get a response. "C'mon, let's see a show of hands,"

I continued. Nothing. "Then just what are you doing with your lives?" I asked. They were speechless. On that day, I realized I wasn't the only one who needed to answer "the question." It was also on that day the book began to truly take shape. It was clear that I had to write a book about purposeful living. A lot of people were struggling with discovering their purpose. This book, I believed, would help them.

As I sat on stage looking out into the faces of people who by most standards had achieved phenomenal success and amassed incredible financial wealth, it became apparent to me that as much as we've evolved as humans, a vast majority of us are still roaming the earth in a zombielike state. No passion. No purpose. No joy. No light. "How did we get here?" I asked myself. Oh, it wasn't rhetorical. I knew exactly why the audience had been so silent. I could look at my own life and answer that question! The audience's silence was confirmation. Now, everything was falling into place.

There's something to be said about the time you spend alone with God. As I look back on the blessings from my Salt Lake Days, I realize that that was exactly where I needed to be to learn some of the lessons I'll share later on in the book. I knew that my spiritual walk was going to take an accelerated turn for the better when on my first Sunday in Salt Lake, I drove to the shopping mall only to discover that it was closed on Sundays. That's when I started going to the mountaintop, literally. And that's when I realized how spiritually lethargic I'd become.

I had been allowing my ego to dictate my life that summer so it shouldn't surprise you to learn that I found myself in some precarious situations on more than a few occasions. I was engaging in some serious spiritual aerobics with the Utah Starzz management and coaching staff over things that I was never going to convince them to see differently. My fear was that if they didn't see things differently (read: the way I saw them) that I was going to have a hard time surviving in Utah, and, therefore, have a miserable summer. Well, they didn't budge and neither did I. And the very thing I feared happened. They stood their ground, I stood mine, and I ended up having a miserable summer! Sound familiar? No? Keep reading.

Like many of you, even in my fear during that fateful summer, I sought a deeper connection to God, to myself, to my family, to the world, to my reason for living. And, like many of you, I wanted to seek answers from my spiritual community. I'd learned as an adolescent that church was a building where people went to "be fed" spiritually, yet what I saw in church were contradictions to the things we were taught in the sermons. As a twelve-year-old, I can remember vicious emotional warfare going on between church members. I saw blatant unkindness and disregard for human life. I saw people who lifted their hands in reverence to God in one moment, and then use the same hands to point their fingers in judgment and condemnation immediately after the service was over. And this wasn't just at my church. This was in every "church building" I stepped into. As you can imagine, I was a very confused adolescent. I thought church was supposed to be a place of love, acceptance, and spiritual nourishment. What I saw was anything but the Christ-centered love we learned about in Sunday school. One of my favorite Bible verses growing up was, "You will know they are Christians by their love." I wasn't seeing a whole lot of love sometimes on Sunday!

I wasn't satisfied with what I saw in church, so I began to seek out God—and spirituality—for myself. I began to read books on enlightenment and spirituality, although I had no idea what the words meant. I began to introduce myself to other spiritual paths besides Christianity. I wasn't looking for a substitution but rather an expansion of my faith.

I had been trained to believe that it didn't matter what you did on Monday, Tuesday, Wednesday, Thursday, Friday, or Saturday, but on Sunday your butt needed to be in church. And it was. It was in church all day on Sunday, from sunup to sundown. Yet as much as I was physically in church, there were things about church and God that I still didn't get. I enjoyed the stories and metaphors. I loved the singing and praising. I could recite the books of the Bible faster than an auctioneer reels off the bids at Sotheby's, but I still didn't get the relationship between how God wanted us to treat each other and how we were *actually* treating each other. I couldn't comprehend the often-conflicting messages about abundance. Was it okay to be rich as long as we gave God a percentage? I didn't understand why some people were upset that certain people drove certain cars. Or how much chatter there could actually be around a "good" teenage girl who mysteriously ended up pregnant. My teenage years were confusing enough as it was, and the dynamics of "church folk" made it even more confusing.

Still, nobody questioned what was taught at church. And if they did, they did so in private. The Bible was the most important book in existence, and we were told that if you wanted to know the answer to something, the Bible was the place to look. This didn't stop me from having a zillion questions. Since I can remember, I've always had a zillion questions. I have a curious nature.

I remember once asking one of my Sunday school teachers why most of the books of the Bible were men's names. "Because that's the way God made it," she answered. Hmmm. I didn't buy that. I still don't. But that's what I mean about questioning what you've been taught. Did they really think that a kid who questioned every decision (mostly in my head) that my parents made would actually buy that God, the Divine, the Spirit, who loves us all the same, would actually sign off on a book that discriminates against half the population? Come on! I was young, but I wasn't dense! And, thus, my journey to truth, spirituality, and the real me began.

I'm convinced that going to college was my University of Spirituality because it is there that I truly saw the vastness of God and how important spirituality was to people from all over the world. I attended and played basketball at the University of Texas at Austin, a 50,000+-student metropolitan college with a huge international population. Diverse cultures and ethnicities spread over the campus like lava. It was amazing. And with each of these groups came their respective "takes" on God and spirituality. It was like a spiritual Baskin Robbins—31 Flavors on campus!

I'd been raised in a traditional Baptist church that followed a Christian doctrine that taught that Jesus had died for my sins. Sins? I thought I was a fairly decent child. I was a bit precocious at times, but a *sinner*? That didn't add up for me. Anyway, as I was saying, college opened my eyes to many things, chief among them was the fact that I'd been led to believe that Christianity was the be-all and end-all and that anything else was just plain nonsense. Again, it wasn't adding up. God wouldn't want me to be confused and conflicted about divine messages, as I had been feeling for so long. There had to be more.

In college, before each game, we gathered in a circle and prayed to God. Not to the Christians' God. Not to the Muslims' Allah. Not to the Jews' God. Not to Jehovah. But to God. To Spirit. The Oneness that united us all. Because of these prayers, in my freshman year in college (when we think we know everything anyway), I figured it all out. God wasn't a man, even though we prayed to the Father. The Lord's house wasn't a place to deify men—although there was, and still is, a lot of that going on, but God was Spirit. Infinite. No beginning. No end.

It was that year, at seventeen years old, that I noticed how people responded to the word "God." It was also that year that I learned that God is called many things, depending on who's talking. Why were people so triggered by God and spirituality? Why were people so upset when someone spoke of The Divine, rather than using the word "God"? That year I learned that there is rampant ego (fear) among religions. No wonder our world was in such a mess! Every religion wanted exclusive rights to God! That's when I truly started to learn about spirituality and God's love. I learned that God was not watching over just me, but the entire world. That God didn't favor me over my non-Christian teammates. And most important, God wasn't waiting for me to screw up so that I could be punished with a plague of locusts. God was love, nothing but pure love. Were I and the little girls and boys at the campus nursery the only ones who got that?

I wish I could say that my life was transformed at the ripe old age of seventeen, but it wasn't. That was only the beginning of the journey to my personal spiritual enlightenment. The first thing I had to get used to was *not* going to church on Sundays—a trek that was about to be filled with some interesting plot twists and turns. It was a major adjustment. You see, college was not anything like high school. We had basketball practice on Sundays, and I would soon learn that not only were we going to be practicing on Sundays, but we might even play a few games on Sunday, too! I don't know why this seemed so farfetched. I'd grown up watching the Dallas Cowboys every single Sunday during NFL season. The concept of sports on Sunday wasn't new; however, missing church was a concept I'd have to adjust to. Because even though I'd watched football on Sundays, I watched the games after I got home from church.

I remember the turmoil I experienced as that first Sunday during my freshman year at UT loomed closer. I had to face the fact that I wasn't going to be sitting on somebody's pew listening to the parable of the fish and loaves because my coach had some silly notion that basketball players need instruction and conditioning.

My other church-going teammates and I researched the area and found a church that held an early service. Phew! I was relieved. And even though the service did little to stimulate me, I was glad to be in the midst. We'd arrive at the church in bunches of threes and fours. And everyone knew who we were because, as most of you know, athletes are rock stars on college campuses. Most of the people in the congregation always looked impressed that we were in church. I always found that kind of funny. We'd participate in the services like the other congregants, and as the clock neared practice time—12 noon—we'd tiptoe out the side door, stop by McDonald's or 7-11 for something we had no business eating, and zoom down the street toward the gym. Even though we might have gotten to be in service for only thirty minutes, we felt so much better about ourselves. At least we were "there," we'd say. God rewards us for being "there," we thought. We had a lot to learn.

Then one day I was talking to one of my teammates who never went to church except for funerals and weddings. She asked me why going to church was so important to me. She couldn't believe that no matter how late I stayed up on Saturday night, I always dragged my tired butt out of bed to go to church the next morning. Our conversation took an interesting turn after she asked me why I went to church "only" on Sunday. Wow! What a great question. I stared at her for a moment. She was genuinely interested in my answer. She admired my diligence and commitment and wondered if we got some special bonus for attending church on Sunday. "It's what I do," I said. "On Sundays I go to church. That's what I've done all my life."

She nodded as if the answer made sense. After all, there were things she'd done all of her life, too—played sports, gone to the Grand Canyon every summer, watched cartoons on Saturday morning. She understood. She got it. But I didn't. Why did I go to church every Sunday? This was another question I'd need to answer.

My friend's question stayed with me the entire semester. I continued to go to church like a robot. I was programmed to get out of bed every Sunday, rain, shine, sleet, hail, or snow, and make my way to the Lord's house. Then one night I kneeled to pray. Yes, kneeled. I'd been conditioned to believe that somehow kneeling got me extra points. Anyway, I asked God if I needed to go to church, and the answer I got was, "Do you?" You see, God doesn't answer questions we need to answer for ourselves. That baffled me. I expected—and wanted—the heavens of my dormitory to open up and show me some indisputable sign that what I was doing was the right thing to do. But why? Why was it the right thing to do? This answer, I was sure, would be my Holy Grail. It would unlock the door to my questions about spirituality and God. So I prayed and prayed and prayed some more, hoping, pleading for a sign. And then one spring day, I got it.

Our basketball team was very visible in the community, and, thanks to our coach, very civic-minded and community-oriented. It was customary for us to speak in elementary schools, serve food at homeless shelters, donate old uniforms to auctions, and visit assisted-living homes. One Sunday after practice we were invited to visit the Ronald McDonald House, a hospital for kids with terminal illnesses. As I walked from room to room talking or playing with kids who had shaved heads and oxygen tubes sticking out of their noses, I got the sign I'd been praying for since freshman orientation. I had asked for an unmistakable sign, and there it was staring me right in the face.

God is about service. Not services. Spirituality isn't found in the pages of a book but in how we coalesce with other souls during our time on earth. Every house is the Lord's house. Things started to become crystal clear. It didn't matter if I went to church. Not to God. Church attendance is high on the list of Ego's concerns. Church was just a place that humans built to gather. God's presence was everywhere, not just in that building I went to every Sunday, Monday, Tuesday, Wednesday, Thursday, Friday, and sometimes Saturday! Now spirituality made much more sense to me. Because God is not human, God does not bother with the cares of this world. God is all about how we treat one another. How we honor the earth. How we take care of one another as a human race. I'd asked the answer to be revealed, and there it was—in the faces of every child in that hospital. From that day forward, I went to church because I wanted to be around like-minded, like-spirited souls, not because I "had" to. The people I grew up with made it appear as though God was keeping some elaborate scorecard in heaven—one that rivaled anything I'd ever seen in the most famous gymnasiums or on any football field. God's scorecard had to be enormous, I thought.

After all, there were so many things that had to be accounted for: honoring our mothers, honoring our fathers, tithing, church attendance, feeding the hungry, clothing the naked, visiting "the sick and shut-in," as we called it at home. Boy, that was some scoreboard God had! There was probably one that was reserved just for religious-themed actions, like how many times we prayed or how often we repented or Hail Mary-ed.

Boy, was I relieved to discover that God isn't concerned with the "systems" we've put into place on earth!

My discovery meant that I was free to experience God as this magnificent, loving, and accepting Spirit who loved me without question or footnotes. For the first time in my life, the concept of God made total sense to me. I was starting to have some inkling of what it meant to be real.

This discovery changed my life on the spot. My spiritual sensibilities were always supercharged. I can remember staring out in the distance on one of my grandmother's visits to our house one summer. I had to be about seven or eight, and all I remember is staring into nowhere, and just as someone was about to tell me to snap out of it, my grandmother said, "Leave her alone. She's got something." She told them not to bother me, but to allow me to come back to earth on my own time. I'll never forget that. We're all connected to Spirit, yet some of us come to earth with a very different sense of Spirit. We all come here with special gifts. Some of those are spiritual gifts, some physical gifts. A few months ago I asked my Godmom, Jean, whom you'll meet later in the book, how she learned to play the piano. "I walked over to the piano, and I started to play." She was just a young girl, no more than six or seven, and she walked over to the piano and started to play? I understood. There are things that are innately in us. I came to this earth already having a deep understanding of what it means to be real—even when I didn't know how to express it. It was there all the time but was convoluted by a litany of human-made rules and interpretations. What I was now learning was that Spirit had a grander purpose for my life and everyone I came in contact with—a purpose that included greater service, success, and even financial riches.

Even though I'd had a great high school academic and athletic career, I hadn't yet seen the full spectrum of blessings that were headed my way. On the day of this discovery, this opening, it became apparent to me that my journey to the real me could help and inspire others to discover their "real" selves. I was ready. Or so I thought.

❧ The Real Deal ❧

I believe there's a great life out there for you. And I believe
there's a great life in you. No matter who you are, where you came
from, or what anybody's ever told you, your life can be as magnificent
or as miserable as you choose to make it. Wherever you are today
is the result of the choices you've made and the beliefs you claim as
truth. Whatever you become tomorrow will be no different.
It will still be about your choices and beliefs.
This moment right now can be the saddest day you'll ever have.
It can be the happiest day you'll ever have.
It can be the brokest day you'll ever have.
It can be the most joyous day you'll ever have.
It can be the most painful day you'll ever have.
Or it can be the most exciting day you'll ever have.
Either way, your choices will explain and determine your life path.
This moment right now is what you are making of it.
That is the real deal.

❧ The Real You ❧

The mask you've worn for the past week or twenty years is
probably not the real you—or at least not all of you.
Each of us has the potential to be more of who we are—the soul that
was given life to make a contribution to the world; the spirit
with no concept of fear, rejection, betrayal, or doubt; the person
who gives without need for recognition, lives without the need for
approval, and loves because it is its own reward. That is the real you.

Introduction

Introduction

*I*f I met you today, I'd need to spend only three minutes with you to be able to tell you what's stopping you from having the life you want. I could tell you what excuses you've told yourself all of your life. I could tell you which illusions you've allowed to steal your joy. I could determine which newsletter of lies you subscribe to and which truths you avoid. If I asked you a series of questions, your verbal responses, as well as your body language, would tell me everything I need to know about you. Three minutes, that's all I need. Three minutes with you, and I'd see you. I'd see past your face, I'd see past your color, I'd see past your status, I'd see past your persona, and I'd see you—the real you. That's not a fluffed-up claim; it's true. It's a gift. I wouldn't know these things because I'm extrapsychic. We're all psychic, by the way. No, I'd know these things because I know what used to hold me back and I remember too well the lies I used to let rule my life. I've spoken to hundreds of thousands of people, and I listen to what they share about which roadblocks have gotten in the way of their path on the way to the real them. I'm willing to bet that I would see you in some of their stories.

We all have gifts that we came into this world with. One of those gifts is the ability to be transparent, authentic, and real. Many of us lose that realness before we're five years old. We don't intend to lose it, it just happens. It happens because it is methodically and systematically stripped away by our parents, our friends, the media, our religious affiliations, and ourselves. Yet even though the authentic you might disappear from the surface, underneath, it's still there. Even when it's not detectable by the human eye, it's still there. Beneath all of the layers of limited belief systems, unrelenting judgment, self-hatred, and an insatiable need for approval, lies a real person who is honorable, open, and highly intuitive. Underneath all of the rubbish is real genius. Beneath the rubble of self-doubt, self-abuse, and self-denial rests the power to change the world.

In the pages of this book, I'd like to share my secrets for becoming the real me because I know that these keys will also help you unlock the door to the real you. These are recurring principles that I have shared in my exclusive business- and life-coaching practice, as well as in seminars across the world. People from all walks of life continue to tell me that these principles have changed their lives. These seven principles are powerfully transformative because they allow you to uncover the truth about who you are and why you're here. They will allow you to see a soul that is powerful, brilliant, and loving. These principles and their subprinciples make it possible for you to uncover and rejoice in being the real you. The *you* you were meant to be. The you you are ready to become.

Here's an undeniable truth: We all want to transform some area of our lives—not because we're broken or incomplete, but because there's always something we desire to change, heal, or move to another level. We want to be better—maybe better parents or lovers or teachers or servants. We simply want to be better. We want to be more. And there is nothing wrong with wanting to love better, nurture better, or serve better when it's coming from a place of love and respect.

Athletes talk about bringing their "A" game. Spiritually, we have an "A" game, and when we're on our "A" game, we're kind, compassionate, creative, and loving individuals. Like the world-class sprinter who desires to shave seconds off her time in the 200-meter run, we all strive to reach our fullest potential—to run a little faster, close more sales, love more completely, pick up the kids on time more often, understand more fully, remember to call Grandma on her birthday, or forgive more honestly. We want more. Yet sometimes we encounter obstacles on our way to becoming more. And when we get to this juncture, instead of turning inward, we tend to look outside of ourselves for the answers. Unfortunately, it's on the outside where we get diverted farther away from our true selves. When a situation at work doesn't go the way we want it to go, we think Happy Hour is the answer. When a relationship doesn't work out quite the way we envisioned, we think another relationship is the prescription for our seemingly broken heart. We look outward for solace when the answer is always inside of us. And the answer is always love. Always.

Instead of loving ourselves, we continue to run around in the same circles like a mouse in the maze, rarely reflecting on the lessons right in front of our eyes. Why does this keep happening to me? I don't know how I ended up here again! We are constantly given opportunities to learn new lessons, but we keep wanting to learn the same ones. The most difficult challenges we face are those that give us insights into who we really are—the real us. The path to becoming more of yourself is a path that leads you to greater love in all areas of your life. *Will the Real You Please Stand Up?* will illuminate what you need to address to move closer to who you really are. And once you get on the path to the real you, you will transcend your circumstances in a miraculous instant.

It feels like I've been a teacher or coach all of my life. That's why I was born—to help bring people from all over the world into the reality that they are powerful beyond their imagination. That's my purpose. I'm no longer confused about why I'm here. Teaching, healing, coaching, that's my call. But before I could answer that call, I had to overcome the biggest hurdle I'd ever faced. My hurdle had nothing to do with learning a new skill or earning a different degree. My biggest opponent was inside of me. I suspect that in many ways the biggest hurdle you'll ever have to clear is inside of you, too. That's where everything starts. That's where everything ends. The challenge we face as spiritual beings is allowing ourselves to be guided by the one thing that is real: love. Rather than being guided by the one thing that is not real: fear. Or Ego. The question is then, can you truly know and live your purpose if you're only allowing 10 or 20 percent of the real you to show each day? Can you truly know your full potential if 80 percent of the time you're wearing a mask?

I'm intimately familiar with the challenges you may face today, even though we may never meet. I know you because I know me. We're all connected by the same needs; therefore, we are infinitely connected by the same challenges. We all want to be loved, respected, and appreciated. And, likewise, we all experience frustration when things don't pan out the way we'd like. We're all disillusioned when someone we think we know does something that we perceive to be out of character. We're all saddened when someone we love dies. We're all the same.

Each day we bypass opportunities to love ourselves and others more deeply. We forego these opportunities to live out our fears. Mainly our fear of dying. Yet our greatest challenge is not adding years to our lives but rather adding more life to our years. I believe that our greatest fear is not that we won't be loved, but that we won't know real love when we see it. In general, as a society, we've done a horrible job in the love department. The cost for not truly knowing how to love ourselves is enormous. Yet until we can have the courage to let go of our human needs, we will never know the kind of love the Divine truly has for us. Our greatest charge today, then, is not to become simply more but to become more of who we really are. Only then can we know who God really is.

I believe God's desire for us is pure and simple: love each other; be real; be kind to the earth; and honor Spirit and all that is greater than you. That's it. No fine print. No disclaimers. No warning labels. No assembly required. None of the stuff I grew up thinking really mattered. God is not complicated. But I understand why some people are so outraged by organized religion and anything having to do with spirituality. Many traditional religious beliefs have ingrained archaic and oppressive thoughts into our minds and hearts, and, as a result, many of us can't get to the real "us." We're too busy trying to live up to everyone else's idea of us.

I now know that much of what those listeners at the WomenFuture.com conference were experiencing in 2001 is exactly what happens to all of us in some shape, form, or fashion at some point in our lives. The world sends us a message: hide your light. It's a message that we hear at home, at school, at church, on television, and every place in between. We are to be conformists at all costs. We are not to be individuals. We are not to aspire to fly. We are to fit in. Move to the beat of the dominant drummer. In other words, be anybody other than who you really are. The bad news is that most of us listen to this nonsense and never know the sheer elation that comes from living your life in and on purpose!

I challenge you today to listen to your own voice and the voice of God, which will always have your highest good in mind. I urge you to consider experiencing God, not as a person or a warden, but as a loving Spirit wanting nothing but bliss for you. I encourage you today to see yourself as a big ole juicy artichoke, and peel back every single layer until you get to the real you.

I'd like to introduce you to a system that changed my life. A system that has brought me closer to God and who I really am. A system that will also move you closer to the real you. Each of the seven principles in *The Real You* system builds on the previous, and I encourage you to take each step in the designated order because mastery of one is necessary for the full embodiment and mastery of the next.

When I reignited the flame on my spiritual path seven years ago, I experienced something that happens to most of us. I experienced momentary paralysis—a moment that lasted about three weeks! If we're even remotely awake spiritually we all come to a place in our lives where we yearn for something deeper and something more. Yet when most of us reach that crossroad, few of us have the courage to walk into the unknown. Few of us walk in faith and silence the voices outside of us that have told us to be content with who we are and what we have. We've listened to those sentiments because in many cases they've come from people who love us: our parents, teachers, siblings, lovers, and friends. Few of us are willing to ask ourselves the hard questions. Why have I stayed in this unhealthy situation for so long? When will I stop lying to myself about who I am? When will I have the courage to change my major to something I'm really passionate about? Why do I always lie about how I'm feeling or what's going on with me? These are hard questions for most of us. And if your question wasn't mentioned, ask yourself a hard question today and see if you can answer it with integrity and truth.

The truth is that few of us are willing to believe that God has a larger vision for us than we have for ourselves. This belief keeps us from our real selves. There's a fish in Japan called a koi. If you put a koi in a cereal size bowl, it will grow to that size. If you put it in a five-gallon aquarium, it will grow to that size. If you put it in a tank the size of a football stadium, it will expand to fit the stadium. We are like the koi. Our vision for ourselves is sometimes so small that we limit our growth. We have to continuously put ourselves in a larger fish bowl so that we can see the real possibility in all areas of our lives. If we continue to get into relationships with people who don't challenge us to grow emotionally or spiritually, we'll remain spiritual munchkins. If we continuously seek out job opportunities that don't stretch us, we limit our intellectual and financial possibilities. If, when faced with a tough decision or difficult conversation with a loved one, we bail without expressing our true feelings, we miss the opportunity to go to the next level of personal development. What would you do today if you knew beyond a shadow of a doubt that failure was not an option. Someone once said, "It's the stop that keeps people from starting." Or to paraphrase what Marianne Williamson says, "It's our light, not our darkness that frightens us."

For those who are brave enough to let their light shine, to lift their voices, and step out of the shadows of their past or away from the lies that they've bought into for years, a whole new world awaits them—one that is bursting with possibility and filled with multifaceted spiritual rewards. This is the central message of *Will the Real You Please Stand Up?* The new journey I describe in this book begins with discovering your purpose and ends with living it passionately, authentically, and unapologetically.

I called this a book earlier, but in reality this is not just a book, it's a companion—a fellow traveler written to nurture your unique spiritual exploration and to encourage you to incorporate Spirit into every facet of your life so that you can give birth to the real you. How different would your life be if you made decisions based on what was best for you spiritually? I think drastically different. Many of us wouldn't be with the same lovers, work in the same professions, live in the same neighborhoods, or befriend the same people if we were led by Spirit. What if you had a set of spiritually oriented factors or questions that you checked before you took a certain path, before you accepted the job offer, before you said yes to the date or the marriage proposal?

Will the Real You Please Stand Up? gives you the opportunity to clean out your spiritual closets and gives you permission to have a "fire sale"— to throw out what does not work for you. Sound radical? It's not really. Fire sales are a necessary good, and I recommend one in every area of your life—from your clothes closet to relationships that are not serving you well.

Recently, at a popular sold-out self-development seminar in Los Angeles, a fellow volunteer asked me about the church I attend—Agape International Spiritual Community. "I visited Agape a few weeks ago," she said with a childlike enthusiasm. "There were no pictures on the walls or anything. How do you know who you're worshipping?" We both laughed.

It was a beautiful prelude to this book. "That's precisely why there are no 'images' on the walls at Agape," I answered. "God is infinite, and there is no way to 'capture' God in a painting. God is Spirit. If we painted God, what would it look like?"

My new acquaintance, who was Catholic by the way, echoed the sentiments of most people in the world, regardless of their religious backgrounds—people who have put God in a box, people who can't conceive of a God who doesn't wear a special uniform or a God who isn't judgmental. They can't wrap their brains around a God who isn't jealous if we look at another God, or who doesn't get angry when we screw up. No wonder we have such a difficult time getting to our real selves. On some level we believe that we're not even good enough for God! Or worse, we've been brainwashed into thinking that God is a tyrant we must obey. I asked a friend about his plans for moving to New York to pursue his dream of being on Broadway. "Can't," he said.

"What do you mean you can't? Pack your bags and get in the car," I replied.

"The last time I disobeyed God I paid for it," he said sipping his coffee.

I sat there in wonder. He actually believed that God had punished him for a decision he made five years ago. My friend went on to share that a few years back he'd taken a job that "God" told him not to take. As a result, he said, "I had a terrible career with the company."

"Isn't it possible that you had a terrible career because you *wanted* to have a terrible career?"

He became irate. Apparently I struck a chord. "Why would I want to have a terrible career, Fran? That makes no sense at all!"

"Sure it does. If you'd had a great career you wouldn't get to tell me this sad story right now and you wouldn't be sitting here holding yourself back, avoiding the next level of success. Clearly, New York is the next level of what God has for you, but, now, you're blaming God because you're afraid to take the plunge. Makes perfect sense to me."

If my friend hadn't been such a kindhearted man, he probably would have doused me with his Ethiopian blend. Instead he did what any self-respecting Christian would do. He closed his eyes and prayed for me! On the spot! Prayer to-go. I love it!

What my friend shared is similar to what I hear every day in my coaching practice from people of all spiritual walks. On one hand they claim to believe that their Higher Power wants infinite blessings for them, but then they're afraid to receive those infinite blessings. And rather than saying so, they blame God for holding them back or not wanting them to experience the good life by saying things like, "God doesn't want me to have that." We forget that God desires what is best in us, as well as what's

WILL THE REAL YOU PLEASE STAND UP?

best for us. We'd do well to stop blaming God for our unwillingness to fly.

We must come out of our spiritual comas and start to lead lives full of purpose and passion. I believe it is the absence of such passion that has caused such rampant spiritual apathy. It is the absence of this truth that keeps you from knowing and becoming the real you.

THE REAL QUESTION

Will the Real You Please Stand Up? Of all the titles I could have chosen for the book, why this one? Henry David Thoreau said that most people lead lives of quiet desperation. I think we lead lives of *acute separation*—separation from our true selves; separation from real joy; separation from real love; separation from real truth. Separation from our real selves.

Right now, the real you is likely to be in one of these five positions.

- Sitting down
- Lying down
- Hiding behind _____ (fear, doubt, etc.—fill in the blank)
- Pretending to be someone else
- Standing up only three-quarters of the way

If you're already on a path to becoming more of who you are, then the real you is potentially already standing. But even if you are already walking in truth and realness I know that there is room for more realness, and that's why I know that you will stand a little taller after reading these next few hundred pages. Ready? Here we go.

WHO IS THE REAL YOU?

As the title of this book asks the "real you" to stand up, I'm clearly making an assumption that the real you is not the one you show every day. The real you is that person who knows no boundaries; the person who lives life fully and unapologetically; the person who is loving and compassionate; the person who has no need for jealously or envy; the person who knows that there's an infinite amount of abundance; the person who lives each day as if it were your first. You thought I'd say as if it were your last, didn't you? That's one of the biggest bloopers of humankind—living as if today were our last instead of the first.

If today were your first day on the planet, what would you do? How would you feel and act? You'd be curious, excited, and adventurous, wouldn't you? You'd be boundless, outrageous, and uninhibited. The journey to the real you starts with this simple yet critical shift in your consciousness. That's why I want you to start living your life as if it were your first, not your last day on the planet. If today were your last day on earth, you'd likely be running around trying to right your wrongs, saying good-bye, tying up loose ends, and cleaning up your damage. What a colossal waste of time! Life is to be lived!

Will the real you please stand up? We arrived here full of excitement about the newness of it all. So I want you to go back and get that exuberance you had on the first day of your life. Go back and get that freedom you had to just be you—all of you. If it's been too long since you felt sheer joy and love of life, take a field trip to your local day-care center or playground. There you will see what it means to be real. You'll see no ego. No boundaries. No ulterior motives. No agendas. No politics. Instead you'll look into the faces of real people. And if you look long enough, you may even catch a glimpse of you many, many years ago, when being real was all you knew.

What Happened to the Real You?

Most of us remember what it was like to be carefree, but we've now resigned ourselves to the fact that those days are behind us. We're in a constant state of grieving for that time in our lives, yet it's right here. It's with us every single moment of every single day. For many of us, our real selves are tucked away in a chest like a precious keepsake that we pull out only a few times a year. For others, their real selves are being held hostage by fear of rejection, success, or failure. Either way, it's time to access the power of the real you. No more faking. No more deferring to everyone in your life to make them feel good. No more squashing your passion, your joy, or your excitement about who you are and what you want to become.

YOUR PERSONAL COVENANT

A covenant is a promise or an agreement that we make with someone. Each of us has an agreement with ourselves, whether we know it or not. We've entered into a sacred contract, and each day we live out that contract. We stand in the mirror and we consummate the agreement. Today I'm going to be authentic, or today I'm going to be someone else. Nine times out of ten we choose the latter. We grab our backpacks and briefcases and we head out the door. Another day of faking it.

Today, I want you to enter into a new covenant with yourself, one that honors who you are—who you really are. Not the person you've become based on what other people have told you about yourself, but one that is deeply connected to your soul, your spirit, your essence. That's the real you. No two people will have the same covenant. The covenant I have with myself is very different from the one you'll have with yourself because each of has unique lessons to learn during our time here. Each of us has a divine assignment to carry out. Your assignment is your purpose. It's wrapped up in your covenant. By being the real you, you are honoring your agreement with yourself and with God. By being the real you, you will undoubtedly complete your divine assignment. And while your personal covenant may change focus, it's at the core of who you are. In other words, today's covenant may be to walk in greater integrity around money. Once you've mastered that covenant, your new covenant may be to stand taller in your personal values. So you see, the covenants are there to facilitate the unfolding of the real you! Go ahead, enter into a new covenant right now.

Understanding Integrity

When I was growing up, I don't actually recall hearing the word "integrity," but as I got older I realized that the values that my mother instilled in her kids were all about integrity. She encouraged us to be truthful, and, yes, we were punished when she found out we hadn't been truthful. She talked to us about being "our word"—doing what we said we were going to do, or at least letting those depending on us know that we weren't going to be able to come through. This is what I learned when she said, "Be home by 7:00, or call if you're going to be late." This was integrity.

I remember one evening I came bursting through our garage door, crying. "What's wrong?" Mom asked. I could hardly get the words out. My mom, afraid for my safety, asked again, "What's wrong?!"

Finally, I mustered up enough strength to tell her that the neighborhood bully had pushed me.

"Pushed you? Why?" she asked.

"Because she heard that I said something about her," I said, out of breath.

"Well, did you? Did you say it?"

I nodded. "Yes."

"So what happened?"

"She asked me if I said it, and I said, 'yes.' That's when she pushed me."

My mother, never one for long speeches or explanations, wiped my face and kissed me. "Go on out and play."

"But I'm scared."

"Scared of what?"

"Scared of her!"

My mother looked deep inside my teary eyes. My heart was beating faster now at the thought of going back outside where "the bully" surely awaited me. Mom took a deep breath and smiled. "No, you're not. You're not afraid of her."

"But, Mama . . ."

"You did the right thing. Now, if you said it, you have to stand by it. Now, you can go outside, or you can go to your room and read a book." What an alternative—a book or a beat down!

I stood there for a moment, not sure if I'd just heard right. Did she really expect me to go back outside where potential danger lurked? Surely she hadn't heard a word I'd just said. Mom went back to cooking and singing as if I'd just told her that I'd made a new best friend. She never looked my way again. But just as I was about to walk out the door she stopped me. "Don't ever say something about someone that you aren't willing to say *to* someone, okay?"

I wouldn't really understand the gravity of those words until I was a teenager. Mom was full of words of wisdom that I couldn't appreciate in the moment. My mind was on the bully in the middle of the street, who up to that point in time had not proven to be someone you could reason with. She was the one who called the shots in my neighborhood. I was the new kid on the block. All of the rules had been in place for years, and all of the other girls and boys seemed to be on board. If she said "jump," the kids on the block responded, "Broad or long?" She was like Robert De Niro in *Analyze This*. She was the Godmother of Oak Cliff. Who did I think I was standing up to her? Apparently I didn't value my beautiful teeth very much. A million thoughts raced through my head as I peeped out the door, only to see her standing there waiting on me! After what seemed like an eternity (maybe ten minutes), I headed back outside. There she was, standing in the center of the street like she owned it. Like if cars drove by that they'd have to go around her. The funny thing is that she wasn't that tall. In fact, I was several inches taller than she, but somehow because of her confidence, she seemed to tower like a monument. So there we were. Face to face for what I was sure would be my last day on earth. All of the other kids were standing around in a semicircle the way kids do when there's an impending beat-down. "Well . . ." she said. "Didja say it?"

I looked into the eyes of the girls and boys who seemed to be hanging on waiting for my answer. We all knew that this was a moment of truth for us all. My eyes turned back to the bully. I remembered what Mom had just said about owning up to your words. I took a deep breath and answered, "Yeah."

She pushed me again, and the last thing I remember is picking up one of the barrettes I'd had in my hair. It all happened so fast. Strangely, though, I remember feeling much better after the fight. The butterflies I'd felt just fifteen minutes earlier were gone, thanks, in part, to the punch in the stomach probably. But it was more than that. Of course, I didn't know it then, but I was reaping the rewards of standing up for myself. And a funny thing happened after that fight. The bully and I became the best of friends.

Years later I'd understand why this was such a great lesson in integrity. It had to do with being honest, being true to who I am. Being real. And although the short-term effects included a few scratches, it was well worth the lesson. I'd made a covenant with myself, and I didn't even realize it. Honesty was important to me even when it meant I might have to eat a knuckle sandwich.

Integrity is something we all have to come to on our own. On your journey to greater authenticity, you'll be faced with numerous situations that will challenge you to make a stand for integrity. Where do you stand today on the topic? Are you honest within yourself? Do you have a core set of values that you live by? Are you able to stand by those rules of integrity even when it's not popular or when it means that something potentially painful might happen as a result? Take a moment to establish or revisit your own personal covenants. They pave the way for a rich and real you.

THE REAL MOM

I remember the last time I saw my mother alive like it was an hour ago. The luggage guy tagged my bag at the American Airlines airport terminal at the Dallas/Fort Worth airport. She'd just dropped me off for my trip as

WILL THE REAL YOU PLEASE STAND UP?

an exchange student to Mexico. I was sixteen years old. As I was completing the luggage identification tag, Mom drove back around. "Everything okay?" I asked. "Yep," she answered. "I missed my exit out of here. Love you."

If I could have that moment back, I'd rush out to the car, hug and kiss her all over again, and tell her how much I appreciated her words of wisdom that seemed like meaningless "mother talk" until I got old enough to understand. My mom enjoyed hugging and kissing as much as I pretended not to as a teenager. Who would have thought that would be my last time to kiss her? I watched our burgundy car disappear around the airport exit bend, and that was the last time I saw Mom alive. I know exactly what she was wearing that day. How she wore her hair. I can still hear her coughing as she drove toward the end of the tunnel. Mom always had a nagging cough—something about bronchial asthma. She had medicines for everything.

Two hours later, I boarded the plane, excited about what awaited me in Cuernavaca, Mexico, where I was to stay for a month through the Gifted Students Institute program. The night before I left, we'd had a meeting at the GSI office, and I vividly remember seeing my mother's face in the waiting room as the directors of GSI went over what the twenty-one American kids would be going through over the next four weeks. My little brother, Chris, ten years my junior, was doing what six-year-olds do—getting into everything in sight: reading magazines, zooming around with his toy car, jumping off chairs (he was in his Superman stage), and making crash sounds as if he were in a demolition derby. I admonished Mom to "deal with him," but she just sat there silently.

This was not the mother I'd grown up with. The mother I'd grown up with would have shot Chris "the eye," and he would have instantly taken a seat and never moved again. But on this night, she was different—calm, almost otherworldly peaceful.

After the meeting, we picked up dinner from Burger King and headed home because I still had to pack a few things. We talked about me being a senior in August when school would start, but mostly we just sat at the dinner table eating our burgers. "You excited about your trip?" she asked me. I was sixteen years old. Sixteen-year-olds are cool, they're not excited. So I nodded yes and picked off the onion I'd told them not to put on my cheeseburger. She smiled at me, watched a few minutes of an episode of *M*A*S*H*, which was playing on the television in our den, and then gathered her food, planted a kiss on my forehead, and retired to her room. "See ya in the morning." The next time I saw her, we were loading the car for the airport.

The family I'd been assigned to in Mexico City was a couple with two small children. I had my own room, but that morning as I got ready for school, I noticed that they didn't have a phone. I said my good-byes and headed down the hallway to catch the school bus. When I got to school there was already a volleyball game in progress. Volleyball was one of my favorite sports. I quickly put my bags down and headed over to the court. The game was intense and fun, I noticed that the two directors were staring at me. I couldn't figure out why, so I continued to play. About five minutes later, they called me over to the sidelines. "Your brother called. You need to go home. Your grandmother's sick."

"Huh?"

"We'll take you to the airport."

All the way to the apartment, my heart raced. I wasn't buying the "grandmother" story at all. And as I packed my bags, I wished I hadn't studied those Spanish tapes a month before leaving for the trip because what I heard as the Mexican mother and her daughter stood in the doorway of the guest bedroom nearly incapacitated me. The little girl asked her mother in Spanish why I was leaving. The mother answered—in Spanish—that my mother had died.

I was devastated. The night I'd gotten there, I'd had a dream. I don't know what the dream was about. I just remember waking up and running to my Mexican parents' bedroom door requesting to use the phone. "I need to call my mother," I told them. They answered, "No hay tele-

WILL THE REAL YOU PLEASE STAND UP?

fono." I had not noticed this primarily because it had been a long day and I was getting acclimated to my new surroundings. That night I'd cried myself to sleep, but I had no idea why—until I was packing my clothes that next day.

To say that July 7, the day my mother died, was a day that will live in infamy for me is putting it mildly. It was one of my defining moments. On many levels, it was one of the truly spiritual moments in my existence. From having the "warning" that my mother was dying in the precise moment that I was trying to reach her to thinking back to her serene disposition the night before my trip, to being grateful that I had her for sixteen years. I'd gotten a glimpse of who I believe was the real Mom the year before she died. She and my father were headed toward splitsville, and for the first time in her life, Mom was more than someone's wife and mother. She put herself through school, earned her GED, graduated from cosmetology school, and opened her own beauty salon. For the first time in her life, she was doing what made her blissful. No more dependence on my dad. No more wondering what on earth she should be doing with her life. I'd seen her happy, but never *that* happy. And I'll never forget how the real Mom walked. How she talked. How she laughed. I'll have that with me forever.

THE REAL GUARANTEE

I believe that we were all born with everything we need to become more of who we already are. Sometimes we just need to be reminded of the power that lies within each of us. Sometimes we need a fellow warrior to look over and mouth "you can do it," or "you're not alone." Sometimes we just need to turn the volume down on all of the things that do not serve our highest good.

I wrote *Will the Real You Please Stand Up?* to help you peel back the layers and uncover the most authentic and real "you." The you that only a handful of people (if that) get to see. The you that maybe you haven't even seen yet. The you that you haven't seen since you were seven years old going to the neighborhood park every day in the summer. The you that used to laugh until your side hurt. The you who wasn't afraid to let someone see you cry. The you who forgave and made up at the drop of a pin because it was the right thing to do. Remember that person?

Most of us can barely catch a glimpse of our authentic selves anymore. It's been far too long since that person's been out to play. Most of us locked that person away many, many years ago in exchange for a faster, more shut-down version; a version that must win every argument, always have the upper hand, never admit our shortcomings, rarely show any signs of vulnerability, and never, ever, ever, ever admit that he or she is wrong. Seen that person lately?

Until you experience on a consistent basis the adrenaline from being totally authentic and transparent, you will never fully appreciate what it's been like to be "someone else" all your life. Most of us go through our lives as impostors. We're faking it. We're background actors in our own movies. Wallpaper in our own homes. We go to the schools our parents want us to attend, accept the jobs that everybody "craves," live in the neighborhood everyone "wishes" they could live in, vacation at the spots only the "elite" populate, endure in relationships that neither honor nor empower us, and, yes, toil for years in a religion or church that does not nurture our growth. And we call that living.

I believe once we find our truest selves, then and only then can we live the passionate and purposeful lives we all desire and deserve. It's not until we are courageous enough to question what we've been taught to believe about everything—including God—that we can truly experience and know God, or our true selves.

Will the Real You Please Stand Up? was written for anyone interested in the marriage of spiritual enlightenment and uncommon success principles. For the next 200 or so pages, I'm going to challenge you to stretch yourself in every single area of your life—emotionally, physically, mentally, financially, and spiritually. You'll be charged with developing a deeper and wider spiritual walk regardless of your religious affiliations.

Spiritual expansion isn't just for good Catholics, sanctified Christians, devout Sufis, or enlightened Buddhists. It's for anyone seeking a deeper and more enriching experience with their Divine connection.

Ask me what I believe, and I will answer, "I believe in the oneness of God." I believe God is infinite. I believe that there are many ways to experience the Oneness of God. To say that one path is the only path limits the infinity of God and Spirit. So you will hear me use several words interchangeably. If you find yourself stumbling over words like Divine, God, Spirit, Creator, and The One, I urge you to ask yourself: Why am I limiting God's reach? Why am I allowing my ego to put God in a box? Why am I so unwilling to allow other people to experience God or Spirit in a way that works for them? We have to let go of our need to control everything! When we master that skill, we will finally create a University of Love on earth.

This book will open a space in your life for you to experience new levels of connection to yourself, to your Source, and to the world. It's not an attempt to convert you to another "religion." Religion is something mankind created, which makes it subject to the limitations and biases of human thought and perception. Every book that was written as the basis for any religious doctrine or spiritual path was written by the human hand. That makes every single piece of spiritual or religious literature subject to interpretation. Never forget that. God exists outside of the human landscape, so there's no way to put a leash on God. There's no way to define what God or spirituality means for anyone but ourselves. Most of us seek something, some One greater than ourselves. Call it God, Allah, Yahweh, Buddha, the Divine, Spirit, the One, whatever you feel comfortable with, but it's all about a presence greater than our human existence. And guess what? It's not a presence that lives up there or out there. It's already within us.

Will the Real You Please Stand Up? wasn't written to provide a roadmap for you to become more devout, more self-righteous, or more "insert your religious doctrine" here. It's not about perfection (which doesn't exist, by the way). It's about completeness. I wrote this book because like you, I am committed to a path to increase my awareness as a spiritual being. I want a life sprinkled with miracles and deep appreciation for my gifts, as well as those around me. I aspire to a greater understanding of God, greater compassion for my fellow warriors, and a greater acceptance of my divine assignment on earth. Those are not things that can be explained or comprehended by us humans. They require a voyage to the spirit world.

So this book is as much about me supporting you on your journey as it is about me continuing down the path of spiritual enlightenment, unfoldment, enrichment, and transformation myself. And I believe that through the principles and insights that I share, you, too, will experience your own unique spiritual awakenings—if you're open.

We are spiritual beings on a human expedition, not a body that occasionally has a spiritual experience. Everything emanates from energy and spirituality. That which is now physical originated in the spiritual realm. That's why in a book about "the real you" there has to be a frank discussion about spirituality. To become real, we must acknowledge our spiritual existence and origins. We can't become our real selves without knowing that who we are is not who we look at in the mirror each morning. That's not all of us. That's the physical manifestation of who we are. As spiritual beings, we must know that there is always more "than meets the eye."

Will the Real You Please Stand Up? provides prescriptions for purposeful and passionate living that encourages you to incorporate more love, Spirit, and joy into your daily life. As you become more of who you are, as you step more enthusiastically into your divine assignment, I dare you not to experience new levels of delight, mastery, peace, harmony, and riches. I dare you! These things are mere byproducts of being the real you. They will overwhelm you on a momentary basis. That's the beauty of real living. So fasten your seat belts, we're about to take the first step toward becoming more of the real you and trust me, it's going to be one heck of a ride!

❧ When You Were Real ❧

I want you to take a trip to the past with me. Go ahead, close your eyes.
Think back to a time when you didn't know what cyberspace was.
When typing classes were taken with actual typewriters.
When a MAC had something to do with a hamburger.
When the "Net" referred to a sport of some kind.
When you were actually shocked when a kid killed anybody.
Go back even farther. Before Xbox and Sega.
When restaurants were a place where people ate, not talked on the phone.

I'm talking way, way back . . .

When the worst a neighborhood gang would do
is maybe break a window and run.
When kids respected adults and each other. When a miniskirt was worn
by adult women and not ten-year-old girls. Think back even farther.
Before it was cool to wear your jeans so low that the world had to see your
underwear. Before metal detectors were installed in schools.
When kids rarely feared for their lives when they went to class.
You've gotta go back before MTV and reality TV.
Go back even farther. To summers playing "Old Maid" cards
or kickball or dodgeball. To Simon Says, Red Rover, or Freeze.
When you had to be home for dinner with your family.

Think back to the excitement of the first day of school.
Or the ultraexcitement of the last day of school.
Remember lemonade stands to raise money for your baseball uniform?
Bike races, school field trips to the zoo, running like the wind
when you heard the ice cream truck getting closer to your neighborhood?
Remember when a penny actually bought you something?
When an eleven-year-old drug dealer was unimaginable and
the thirty-year-old who got him into the business
wouldn't have even considered him a viable "employee"?
Remember those days?

What about when big decisions were made
using the Rock-Scissors-Paper method.
Or the first snow or your best birthday party or opening a gift—
only to get what you thought you weren't going to get.
Remember how nervous you were when you found out
that the girl or boy in first period class thought you were cute?
Do you remember how adorable you looked when you lost your two front
teeth? Probably not. But guess what?
You were real back then. And you're real now.
Let's go back to that time in our lives
when we didn't know how to be anyone but ourselves.
If you would allow yourself to experience that level of openness,
your world will change right before your eyes.
So, how about it? Let's go back.

Spiritual Conditioning

REAL YOU BASICS

*B*efore we get into the seven strategies, it's important that you get the proper conditioning to be able to make the kind of changes necessary for bringing about the kind of transformation you desire in your life. And we all desire changes, right? So consider this your Real You Boot Camp and consider me your Spiritual Coach.

Real Love for Yourself

You're probably tired of all the books and CDs that tell you that the true path to success, fulfillment, and enlightenment is through self-love, right? But if there weren't such an epidemic of self-loathing and self-betrayal, we wouldn't keep writing about this stuff! You see, most people think they love themselves, but they don't realize all the levels on which they do not love themselves. When you languish in a job that puts food on the table but does little to feed your soul, you're not loving yourself. When you stay in a relationship that is abusive on any level—emotionally, physically, sexually, spiritually—you're not loving yourself. When you put harmful substances into your body, you are not honoring yourself. When you fail to nurture yourself daily with positive and affirming thoughts, you are not appreciating yourself.

If I asked you to jot down the activities of your life for a twenty-four-hour period, I guarantee you'd find more than a dozen ways to love yourself in a deeper, more profound way. You see, sometimes if there's an absence of the overt forms of abuse some of us fall asleep and think we're doing just fine, when in reality, we're doing much more destructive things to ourselves. In other words, you read the checklist above and you think, "Nope, that's not me." You go to the next one on the list. "Nope, I'm not in any physically abusive relationships." But if you'd look deeper, you'd discover that there are many ways to deny yourself love. Do you pass up a chance for a promotion because deep down you're afraid of leading people? Do you drive a fifteen-year-old car that breaks down constantly because you're afraid that if people know that you have money that they'll ask you for it—and worse, you won't be able to say no? Do you constantly take on too many tasks in the church because you've become known as the one who can "get things done," even though you'd rather spend your time doing something that truly makes your heart sing? These are just a few of the ways we deny ourselves love on a more spiritual level. Let's continue to crystallize this topic so that it's real for you.

Signs That You're Not in Love with Yourself

"I love you but I'm not in love with you." Ever heard that one? Ever said that to someone? Let me turn the question on you. Are you in love with yourself? I'm not talking about the kind of narcissistic, ego-laden, self-centered affection that makes you want to be the center of attention at all of the parties or the kind of self-centeredness that turns every conversation into a diatribe about you. That's not love, that's insecurity. When I talk about self-love, I'm talking about an abiding love for yourself that is natural because you're a child of God. The kind of love that is not predicated on how you look, how much money you have, or the kind of car you drive. Think you love yourself? Answer these two questions.

Are you currently in an abusive relationship with someone? Abuse can come in many forms. We're bombarded with messages about domestic violence and sexual abuse, yet emotional and spiritual abuse are as disruptive and destructive as being beaten or sexually assaulted. Being in a relationship where someone is constantly projecting anger, fear, and insecurity your way is also abuse. Or even if you find yourself in a relationship where you just don't feel that you can be all of who you are because your spouse or lover will feel less of who they are, this is also a form of abuse from within. You hold yourself back for fear of overshadowing someone else. That's not about them, by the way, that's work you've got to do for yourself. To become the real you, you have to be free to explore who you are. Participating in an abusive relationship impedes this process.

Are you currently in an abusive relationship with yourself? Are you constantly berating yourself, putting yourself down, second-guessing yourself, or sabotaging your own growth? This is classic self-abuse. And let's not leave out the other ways we abuse ourselves—drugs, alcohol, food, sex, exercise, and other addictions. All of these are impediments to becoming who we really are.

We create abusive relationships with ourselves because we believe we deserve the abuse, plain and simple. We believe we deserve to suffer. No pain, no gain? Right? Wrong! We believe there's something wrong when nothing's wrong. In the absence of drama, we create it. In the absence of abuse, we seek it out. Even if there's no one outside of us to inflict the pain on us, we find a way to do it to ourselves. Again, let's think for a moment in less graphic terms. Ever had a project that you needed to get done but you waited until the last minute to do it? That's abuse. That's drama. I've done this many times.

Let me back up for a second and define what I mean by abuse. It's a given that when someone smacks you upside the head or calls you names or forces you to do things against your will, those things are abusive. But abuse, in my view, is anything that we create, endure, or participate in that does not serve our highest good. So back to the example of overextending yourself and why this is abuse. When we take on more than we can handle, we are giving birth to a dramatic and potentially abusive cycle of events. Here's how it goes. You get a project. You have a target date. You procrastinate as the deadline lurks around the corner. You start to stress because you know that it takes more time than you've allotted to complete the task. Yet instead of doing the project, you procrastinate more, thinking that you will pull it off in time to look like a pro at the end. Now, here's where the abuse comes in. The moment your mind acknowledges that you are up against a wall, your body responds. Your internal systems get the memo and they start to react to the stress you've just put on yourself! The body is very sensitive to stress. In more ways than most of us realize. But you're on a mission. You've slapped the "S" on your chest and you're headed for the next tall building. You've got to get it done so you start to engage in other abusive behaviors such as worrying, over- or undereating, smoking, drinking, or even just staying up until three or four o'clock in the morning to make up for lost time. Do you see what I'm talking about? This isn't healthy behavior. And what's worse, it was all avoidable.

So, why do we do these things to ourselves? Why do we constantly find a way to invite drama into our lives? It's simple: Because we think we need it. Nothing can be farther from the truth. When I finally got quiet and looked at how good my life was and how much better it could be if I exterminated all of the drama coming from other people and then all of the drama I was creating in my own laboratory, my life did a 360. It simplified everything. Now, when my coaching clients are asking me to "tell them what to do" about all of the drama in their lives, I turn it back on them and ask, "Why do you feel that you need all of this drama in your life?"

Listen, you were born to flourish and live a life free of drama, disease, and deprivation. Yet many—make that most—of us don't believe this to be truth. Into each life some rain must fall, right? No! That's a cute little story someone weaved many years ago that a lot of people bought into. It's not possible to have it all, is it? Gotcha again! No, no, no! It is possible to have a life full of love, passion, abundance, money, and fulfillment, and if your life is not reflective of these things today, it's because you don't want this reality. Don't believe me? Listen to this.

One of my most requested keynote presentations is called "Are You Feasting At Life's Buffet . . . or Settling for the Crumbs?" I get this request several times a month. During this forty-five-minute speech, those within the sound of my voice are admonished to take a look at what's on their plate. Literally. I have my assistant pass out paper plates and then over the next forty-five minutes to an hour, I have them examine their lives—emotionally, physically, mentally, spiritually, and financially. Then I have them look at their plate, complete with what they have said is "on their plates," and I tell them in no uncertain words: what is on your plate is exactly what you have ordered. If you don't want it, send it back.

Like clockwork, the audience erupts into applause and knowing glances. On some level, we want exactly what we're getting in our lives— good and bad. We want it. Because if we didn't want it, we'd change the cause that brought us the effect. The life you're creating right now is the life you picked when you walked up to the buffet line.

It's that simple. Yes, it's that simple. You can make it hard, but it's that simple. It may take some planning, it will take some adjusting, but everything that's on your plate is there because that is precisely what you ordered. Remember, everything that's shown up in the physical dimension started in the spiritual dimension. And if it's no longer what you want, send it back! Get a new dish. Try something new.

Why People Aren't Being Real

When you're unhappy, you've forgotten who you are. When you're feeling unfulfilled, you've forgotten who you are. When you're worrying about what people think, you've forgotten at the core who you are. You come here with everything you need to create the life you want. That's why in my book *The Intentional Millionaire: Winning the Wealth Game with Spirit,* I boldly proclaim that we're all millionaires regardless of the amount of money on our bank statements. If you have a million dollars or a thousand dollars, it's because the propensity to create wealth was already there. It's there! Like a plant, it needs certain things to help it grow but it's nevertheless in there. If your natural gifts and talents aren't nurtured, they atrophy, plain and simple, but they are still there.

The Seven Things You Must Give Up to Become the Real You

Being real doesn't require any massive effort on your part. It just requires that you allow yourself to "be." Most people aren't being real for two reasons. First, they don't know that they're not being real. They think they're being authentic. The second reason people aren't being more real is because they perceive it to be so hard. They think they have to give up too much to become real. And to some degree that's true. You do have to give up some things but not things you'll miss. You have to give up the need to be right. You have to give up fear. You have to give up all of the things that do not serve your highest good. Are these good sacrifices? Absolutely! Here are some other things that you won't need on this Real journey.

False Sense of Control

You don't control anything except your own actions. It's a fundamental truth that we know *intellectually,* but emotionally we keep forgetting. That's why we keep falling on our behinds. We try to control everything around us. Our kids, our lovers, our friends, our parents, the driver in front of us, the pizza delivery guy, even the speed of our computer! Don't think you're a control freak? Every time you attempt to guide someone's life, no matter how gently you may think you're doing it, you're attempting to control it. The difference between offering your perspective and attempting to control someone is subtle but obvious.

Here's a simple test. Ask yourself how attached you are to whether people follow your recommendations. My brother Alonzo is one of the most generous people I know, but when he gives you good advice, he wants you to follow it, darn it! It's very funny to hear him talk about how upset he is that people are not following his advice. "If he'd only done as I suggested," he says. He truly wants to make a difference in their lives, yet it's not always easy for him to see that people have their own journeys, their own pace, their own cadence. They have lessons they need to learn.

That's why sometimes we have the experience of telling our friends something over and over again that we think they're not getting. Sometimes it's not time for them to learn the lesson, and sometimes the message needs to come from a different messenger. About five years ago a friend of mine called me so excited about a breakthrough. She'd just come from a spiritual retreat and she was on fire. As she shared her process and all of the things she'd learned over the weekend, I found myself saying to myself, "I told you that three years ago." When our conversation was over she said, "I know I've been talking the entire time, but I just got so excited by my growth. This weekend was transformative. So, what's new with you?" In that moment I got a great lesson. Even though I'd shared some of the same insights with my friend on numerous occasions, it wasn't time for her to hear them yet. I was not the Messenger for her breakthrough. Has that ever happened to you? Weren't you just dying to say, "I just told you that yesterday!" In these instances, though, the lesson we need to learn is to give from our hearts and detach from the outcomes or acknowledgment. That's so hard for us sometimes. We need to release our need for recognition and rejoice that those we love have so many opportunities to grow. We aren't always the teachers. Sometimes, we're the students.

You came to the planet empowered. My special gift lies in my ability to help people tap into the power inside of them. That's why I call myself an in-powerment coach. As an in-powerment coach, part of my role is to tell my clients what I hear and what I see in their lives and their businesses. I tell them what I discern. I tell them what I think. I am not emotionally attached to what they decide to do with their businesses or lives. Neither have anything to do with me. They don't pay me to tell them what to do (although lots of them think they want me to). Sometimes they exclaim, "I don't like you right now! You're not telling me what to do!" We laugh and then I remind them that they hired me to assist them in next-level living or next-level business. You see, it's really not my job to tell them what to do. My job as coach and mentor is to reflect; to be a mirror and to challenge them to create the lives they "say" they want.

When I hang up the phone after a session, I'm done. When the session's over, it's over. I don't wonder if they're going to follow my counsel. I don't wait for them not to follow it so I can say, "You should've listened to me." That would be about control. This is a skill that anyone can develop. It's a skill that I wanted to be sure I had before I started coaching in any arena, sports, business, or life. We must respect the path that people walk on and not try to make it the one we want them to travel even when we think we know what's going to happen if they travel their own way. We still have to let go. When you learn how to allow people to walk their own path without any emotional investment, you have given up control. You are walking in their genius.

Need for Acceptance

We want people to like us, agree with us, and accept us. This makes us feel special, smart, and significant. Yet it also puts us in the position to be controlled by things outside of us. The real you has no need to be accepted. The real you knows that by being true to who you are, there's nothing to accept or reject. As children we share our lunches because we want to make friends. Sometimes we associate sharing with being accepted. There was a kid in my third grade class who used to bring food to some of the kids in the class. He was a gangly little boy who stayed to himself but always tried to make the class laugh. He wanted to be liked and accepted so badly. I ached for him even though at seven years old I didn't quite understand the dynamics of approval and acceptance. I did, however, figure out that he wanted people to like him. One day I saw him buying a box of Blow Pops from the candy truck that stopped in the parking lot every morning before the school bell rang. He was counting the suckers to make sure he had enough for everyone. That day in class he went around the room passing out suckers. He looked very proud of the fact that he'd gotten all of the "important people" covered. He looked into the box and realized he had one sucker left. Our eyes met. He headed over to me and placed it gently on my desk. I handed it back to him. "I already like you." And I gave him his sucker back.

To this day, I don't know what made me say that to that little boy. Intuition, I suppose. But I never forgot that day. As he grew in confidence the gift-giving slowed down and eventually stopped altogether. When you're a kid, the last thing you want to feel is left out or like you don't belong. As adults, we never lose that sensation of being the new kid in school, yet we have the opportunity to walk in a new light when it comes to needing acceptance. We must replace anxiety with peace during those times when we are feeling like we need to be liked and accepted.

Need to Vilify

When someone does something that you perceive to be hurtful to you, what's your first course of action? For many of us it's usually to vilify— either yourself or the other individual, right? We either say, "I'm so stupid for putting myself in that position!" or we say, "I can't believe he did that to me" or "She's such a horrible person!" See what I mean? Instant villain. And it doesn't matter who the villain is. We just need a villain to complete our story. Every good movie has a villain, we're told, so in the absence of one, we create one. To become the real you, you must let go of your need to make somebody "bad" when things happen in your life that you don't like. We have to stop projecting our own stuff onto people we don't agree with. I remember a few years ago I was speaking at a large entrepreneurs' conference in my hometown Dallas. After the event a woman came over and thanked me. "I appreciate that you weren't afraid to use the word God. Some people talk about a 'source' or a 'higher being.' It's God!" She was so triggered by this topic so I said to her, "I appreciate your words, but why are we so angry?"

At first she didn't get it. She didn't think she was angry so I role-played with her on the spot. I traded places with her and let her hear how she sounded. "Oh my God," she said. "I'm coming across in such an un-Godly manner. I don't know why I'm so defensive about that."

Does God really need defending? I don't think so. We need to stop vilifying people who don't see things the way we see them. This is killing our world. So, the real you doesn't need to vilify anyone anymore. Every person brings you a combination of lessons and blessings. Every single thing around you today is necessary. And when you see things, people, and situations as necessary to move you to a new level of spiritual awareness, trying to make them a bad person seems a little silly, doesn't it?

Guilt

Did you forget to call your mother until late on Mother's Day? Guilt. Did you not give as much to your church this month as you did last month? Guilt. Were you unable to get your son the $600 bicycle he wanted for his birthday? Guilt. Were you too sleepy to make love with your spouse last night? Guilt. We carry an enormous amount of guilt around with us each day because, as I alluded to earlier, we want to bring the pain! We don't know how to live life without pain. In the absence of pain, we create it. We want to feel guilty. We enjoy the experience of beating ourselves up over something we said or did. It makes us feel better! It's even conceivable that we do things that we know we shouldn't do so that we can feel guilty later. This gives us our dose of pain that we feel we deserve. And the cycle continues.

The real you doesn't need pain. It doesn't need guilt.

One day one of my cousins and I were marveling that it had been twenty years since my mother's death.

"I bet your Dad has a lot of guilt about Aunt Bessie," she said.

"Why would he feel guilty?" I asked.

"Well, things weren't the best between them when she died."

"And . . . ?"

"And I would just think that he'd feel guilty about that."

What my cousin expressed is what most of us believe we "should" feel. It is true that my parents were no longer in their honeymoon phase when Mom died, but what good would it do Dad to feel guilty about that? The sad part is that my Dad did (and probably still does) feel guilty for whatever part he played in the demise of their relationship. He probably feels bad that he was in an awful place in his life when she died, and I'm sure if Mom were here and Dad were dead she'd feel the same. The saddest part is that Dad doesn't need to feel guilty. Yet he does so because he thinks he should. Just as we all do. We think that guilt makes us honorable. It doesn't. Guilt keeps you from the real you because it usurps the energy needed for you to be fully present in this moment. Guilt is an emotion that keeps you living in the past. If you have twenty gallons of emotions to get you through the day— today—why would you expend two or three of those gallons on something you did yesterday? If you want to do something productive with your guilt, let it go. Make a different choice today that will keep you from producing the same results you got yesterday. There's no need for guilt. Whatever you did is done. Want something different? Do something different.

Self-pity

The next useless experience you have to give up is self-pity. This is a perennial favorite. People luuuuuuuuuv to be the victim. A few years ago I had a blowout with someone who I was fairly close to. We both said some things that were not in our highest good or the highest good of our friendship. We blasted e-mails back and forth, pointing the finger and reprimanding the other for being so cavalier with the relationship. We were like two gladiators—neither giving up, neither giving in. In the middle of all of this, I realized that what I expected from this individual was not altogether fair, given his level of spiritual maturation. I was the spiritual senior in our relationship. I should have taken the highest good road, but instead I allowed my ego to drive the car.

Upon this realization, I crafted a sincere apology and e-mailed it. Within a few days, I got a response. The apology was warmly accepted, but he went on to share with me how hurt he was by the things I'd said, how devastated he was, and how he didn't know if he could recover. As I read the e-mail, I found myself being filled with ego and disbelief, and before long I was screaming at the computer at the top of my lungs, "Can you be any more of a victim?"

It was as if I had been the only one to send unkind words through cyberspace. I had the e-mails to prove that I hadn't gone to battle by myself! Why was he wallowing in such self-pity? I was furious! Why was he feeling so sorry for himself? I wasn't expecting an apology or anything. I'd had enough history to know that he wasn't great at apologies, but I must admit, I didn't expect him to play the "victim card" either. Are you a card-carrying member of the National Society of Victims? Are you reading this book feeling oh-so-sorry for yourself about something someone's "done to you"? News flash! No one's done anything to you. What we do out of unkindness, jealousy, fear, and doubt, we do to ourselves, not to those we project those things onto. All of the incendiary words I used in my e-mail were about me not my friend. I was projecting my fears about not being appreciated onto him.

In return, I got projections of fear of abandonment. Neither of us was right and neither was wrong. We cocreated the results we got, and as a result of that experience, we had the choice to become more of who we truly are, or less of who we truly are. That's also your choice today and every day. You can either become more real and authentic, or you can continue to wear the mask that you and everyone in your life have grown accustomed to seeing. I recommend a new approach to life, though. No more "poor me." The next time you get ready to tell someone anything that resembles "life has been so hard for me," stop yourself. You're engaging in a game of "Poor Me," and, honestly, nobody really cares. Most people care only about what's happening to them. So, no more self-pity parties; you're wasting your time.

Underactualization

Some people call this "failure to live up to your potential." I call it underactualizing—not fully realizing all of you. The reasons we underactualize are deep and wide. We blame our spouses for our underactualization. "My wife doesn't think art's going to put food on the table, so I gave it up after college" or "My husband wants me to stay home with the kids, so I stopped teaching a few years ago." We blame our children for our underactualization. "When my kids go to high school, I'll start writing again." We blame our parents. "If my parents had encouraged me to take more risks, I wouldn't have stayed at the plant for thirty years." We blame the church. "I didn't hear my call to ministry for ten years because I was brought up to believe that women couldn't be ministers." We blame our circumstances. "I grew up in the worst part of town; we never had anything." We blame God. "If God wanted me to be rich, I'd be rich." We blame society. "They'll never let a 'fill in the blank' hold that position." All of these statements are nothing more than our excuses for underactualizing. None of these factors are enough to keep you from the real you if the real you is truly who you want to be. Who are you blaming today?

The Need to Be Recognized

Life offers us many rewards during our time on earth. We get to take in the beauty of the creation, including nature, oceans, mountains, animals, and of course, a diverse population of people. Yet we are so afraid that people will forget about us or overlook us that we crave recognition like the air we breathe. Do you crave acknowledgment? Ask yourself these questions:

• If I send someone a birthday gift and they don't send me a thank-you note, what's my first reaction?

- If I remember our anniversary and my mate forgets, what's my initial response?
- If I work for this company for ten years, and they don't reward me with a commemorative plaque, how will I feel?

Recognition. We crave it. We need it. It tells us that we're doing okay. Without it, we don't know how to exist. It's a challenge to rid ourselves of this need, but it can be done. I learned not to depend on acknowledgment in what some would call the most brutal entertainment field today: stand-up comedy. Read on.

SILENT NIGHT, UNFUNNY NIGHT

One of my covenants with myself upon moving to Los Angeles in 2004 was to "go for it." I wanted to challenge myself to become more of who I am. I wanted to live a 100 percent, no-limits life. So I decided to truly stretch myself and take a shot at stand-up comedy. Most of my friends and family laughed when I told them about my plans. This was a good start. My audience was already responding to my work! Shortly after my announcement I went to do a live show in Culver City where I live. My three friends attended and laughed during my set like I was Robin Williams. I appreciated that. A few weeks later I did a show in North Hollywood. Prior to this show, which they were videotaping, I'd practiced my set at a tiny coffee house in Santa Monica and had gotten pretty good response, so I felt ready for a bigger show. That's the best thing about being a newbie, you don't subscribe to any rules. There was nothing for me to unlearn. I was simply following my gut. On the way to Hollywood, I practiced my jokes, certain I would bring the house down. The show started and the first few comics were good. One guy was incredible with his impersonations. My humor is more observational. It's more about the insanely funny things we do each day, like the way we overexaggerate our silent hand and mouth gestures when we're asking someone in the car next to us if they'll let us over into their lane.

When the emcee called me to the stage I realized immediately how comfortable I was just talking about life. I'm not a pretender. I'm not an actress. I'm real. This was going to be all me, and either it was going to get laughs or it wasn't. The clock started ticking, and I launched into my set. The crowd was rolling. They were laughing about things I hadn't planned for them to laugh at! It was great. A new career was born, I told myself. I was already planning for my Comedy Central special. I did my seven-minute set and left to thunderous applause. I was flying high.

A few weeks later I met some comics who were also just starting out. They invited me to do a show at the World Famous Laugh Factory. I'd just come off the North Hollywood show so I was feeling pretty confident that I'd be able to show the Laugh Factory crowd the funny as well. So I did. Again, the crowd appreciated the humor, and I was flying high. More shows followed and more laughs, too. Then one night I did another show, a bigger one, at The Comedy Store, or as we comics call it, The Store. It was packed. The crowd seemed to be very generous with their laughs, and I was preparing to tear it up. So, I go on stage and launch with the same line I'd used a dozen times before, knowing that I'd have folks in stitches within seconds. Instead the room was silent. And not just your basic silence. The "somebody died" silence that none of us are crazy about. So, I moved on to the next topic. Nothing. I think there was one lady in the far left corner who chuckled, but I later learned she had actually been clearing her throat. It was brutal.

Finally, my comic friend let out a huge bellowing laugh. It was the signature I'm-laughing-because-I'm-your-friend laughter and not the you're-hilarious laughter, which made it ten times worse. Thankfully, the clock was merciful, and I was getting "the light" to get off stage. I made the short but oh-so-long trek to the back of the club and tried to maintain my I'm-oblivious-to-your-approval stare as the next comic took the stage. But I wanted nothing more than to walk—make that crawl—out of the club before the lights came up. But I didn't. I stayed and cheered on the final comics. On my way home, I realized just how attached I'd been to the crowd's acknowledgment. As long as they were doing what I wanted them to do, I felt great. When they yanked their approval away, I felt awful. I've never felt that way since.

I share that story for two reasons. First, so you can be sure to laugh if I'm ever playing at a club near you! And second (and seriously), so that you'll take a look at the areas of your life where you are expecting acknowledgment or recognition. Don't get me wrong, applause feels much better than silence, let's be real. But we have to constantly check in with ourselves as to why we do what we do. I played basketball because I loved it. I played my heart out when there were only thirteen people in the stands and half of them were family. If I'd never gotten paid one cent to do it, I would have still played basketball. I love speaking. I love writing. I love a lot of things that I don't get paid to do. When I started doing comedy, I did it because I love telling stories and I love to laugh. That was my only reason for doing it. But along the way I got addicted to the cheers. That never happened with basketball or the other things that I do, and it was kind of strange to suddenly notice an audience's response to my work. So, the silent treatment I got at The Store that fateful Saturday night is exactly what I needed to bring me back to a reality that I hope will touch you as well: Do what you love because you love it. Recognition comes and goes but the joy you get from being who you are and doing what you love is enduring and everlasting.

THE STORY OF YOUR LIFE

Right now you're writing your biography and the screenplay for your life's movie all at the same time. Some of you think that the family you were born into has determined the ending of your movie. It hasn't. Some of you think that outside forces can throw a wrench in your plans for greatness. They can't. Somewhere deep inside you may think that you have to be diabetic because your grandmother was or that you have to be psychotic because your dad was. You don't. Some of you think you're

WILL THE REAL YOU PLEASE STAND UP?

destined to be doctors because your mother was or a construction worker because your father was but you don't, not unless you want to. There's nothing wrong with being a doctor or a construction worker if that's your desire for your life. But you're the writer of your story. You're the star of your movie. You call the shots.

In 1999, I set out on the journey to become a screenwriter. I've always loved film and theater, so writing a movie seemed like a natural progression for my writing talents and sensibilities. I enrolled in some online classes, bought a few books, and attended several seminars. I learned early on that the elements of a great screenplay are also the elements of a powerful personal story. You and I are writing our own stories right now. We are producing, writing, and directing our own movies. We hire the crew, we recruit the cast, we even edit it. I challenge you to use this powerful analogy for your life from this day forward. Know that everyone in your life plays a role in your movie. Each person has a significant part in the development of your story. So, if you can begin to see people as your "cast of characters," your spiritual growth will be ignited. Your lessons will come faster than you could ever imagine. Your denouement won't take ten years. It won't take you six months to figure out "why this person is in my life."

Based on the archetypes I'm about to share with you, you will know why every single person is in your life. And because you'll know, you will grow. And when you grow, you'll move closer to the real you. It's vitally important that you understand that characters make our lives more interesting. These archetypes provide the necessary thrills and challenges for us to move to the next act of our movies, the next level of our life stories. They are neither good nor bad; they are simply characters.

The Hero

This is you. You are the main character in your movie. You come equipped with many virtues as well as flaws. The story revolves around the lessons you came to this earth to learn. It revolves around the work you were put here to do. The Hero's in the movie to complete a divine assignment.

The Coach

This person has entered your life to aid you on the journey. They are there to push you, to challenge you to become the real you. They have insights into your growth that sometimes you can't even see. Spiritual coaches—the ones you need in your movie—do not require you to see things the way they see them. They are not invested in whether you follow their counsel. Be leery of coaches who become angry when you make a decision independent of their advice. Their egos are too involved in your movie.

The Warrior

This might be a best friend, a spouse, or both! They are your spiritual peers. They challenge you to commit to a spiritual path. They walk beside you on this journey. They encourage you to see the spiritual elements of a situation that might be eluding you.

The Ally

These people support from nearby or from a distance. They aid you. They are on your side. You may encounter difficulties, as in all relationships, but this person is on your side. You may never actually meet your allies, but they surround you with unconditional support. They sometimes work behind the scenes for your edification and good.

The Rascal

The rascal keeps the journey light. This is the person in your life who reminds you that humor is necessary on this journey. Their role is comic relief. When you appear to be taking life a bit too seriously, the Rascal will say or do something that cracks you up and brings everything back into perspective.

The Chameleon

This person's role might fluctuate across archetypes, but his or her role is to keep you on your toes. This person may or may not be a friend. You don't necessarily know this person. He or she appears to be one person but is actually someone else. This might be someone in your office who you "just can't figure out." Don't try. He's a chameleon. She's in your life to remind you that as much as you know, you know nothing.

The Messenger

The Messenger's only role in your life is to bring you important messages. He or she may be in your life for a quick season. It may be a complete stranger. They show up, deliver a message, and leave. Or they may show up at those precise moments when you're at a crossroads and you need a sign, a message about which road to take. Messengers are powerful characters in our movies. They can be human, animals, nature, or inanimate objects, so don't miss a message because you're looking for a human messenger. See the symbolism in your life.

The Mirror

This person's role is to reflect, in a very direct way, what you're putting out into the world. They hold up a mirror to your life. If you're wondering why you can't seem to shake a cold, the Mirror shows you that you could be infecting some area of your life with something that does not serve your highest good. Something or someone you need to shake!

The Herald

This may be an older person or mentor—someone whose role is to warn and challenge you to expand spiritually or in other areas of your life. It could be a parent but doesn't have to be. They may be either a positive or negative herald. They provide motivation for you to become more of who you are. Look out, your herald could also be your fifteen-year-old son!

The Shape Shifter

This person exists to make you think about the decisions you're making, the roads you're taking, and to reflect what you might not want to see. This individual might appear to always be questioning you. Don't get angry with the questions, simply embrace the experience as a chance to learn a new lesson.

The Shadow

This person's role is to wreak havoc in your life. He or she will attempt to get you to lead with your ego and to take you away from the real you. This can literally be anyone in your life. It can also be a world issue or a life circumstance like traffic. Yes, traffic.

So, those are the characters in your movie. There are no enemies, just teachers. They are the people and situations that will help you get closer to the real you, or take you away from the real you. Now that you have names for the characters on your journey, no more calling people jerks, witches with a "b," or any of those other words that we love to call people. They are mere characters in your award-winning movie. Teachers in your university of life. This small shift in your consciousness and attitude will literally transform you on this journey to greater personal growth and freedom. And since transformation is the order of the day, I know you'll leap into this voyage with adventure and passion. Let's get started.

❧ The Platinum Rule ❧

Do unto others without expecting them to do unto you.

—*Fran Harris*

$\mathcal{R}$etire Your Ego

You can turn your head off . . . you don't need it here.
—*Sedona Soul Retreat Leader*

WHAT IS EGO?

Our greatest opportunity is to travel on this journey with a spiritual awareness that transcends the cares of the ego. The ego is the part of the mind that houses self-awareness—not the kind of awareness that brings you closer to who you are—the kind of awareness that makes you self-conscious and self-absorbed. That's the simplest and best definition I can offer for the ego. This isn't the self-awareness that is steeped in spiritual exploration. It's more of a self-centeredness that robs us of the essential elements of realness and innocence that bring us clarity about every situation in our lives.

Because we have an ego, we think that God does.

Ego attempts to persuade you to believe that you are what you look like, what you own, what you wear, what you do, what job you do, what position you hold, what neighborhood you live in, what ethnic group you belong to, and what others think about you. That's ego in a nutshell. Your ego is that part of you that believes that you are not significant. This belief leads you to spend your entire lifetime trying to be "important."

Importance is more of an "outer" term. Something that is created, sustained, and fueled by external factors—opinions, agendas, and other egos. You are significant because God created you. Importance is what the world tries to get you to strive for. Ego wants you to tie your value to your "importance," which is often tied to those external factors again—money, titles, cars, things, and opinions. But if we were only valuable when we had those things, we'd lose our value when those things were no longer in our lives.

Significance is about "meaning" or "worth." Words that I believe are particularly God-centric. Some people say that ego is an acronym for "edging God out." That's not possible. God is infinite, therefore, God cannot be edged out or otherwise eliminated from anything. God is in everything.

If you're old enough, you'll remember the famous Eggo waffles commercial where two people would stand over a toaster fighting over a waffle. Both would reach for the waffle and one would exclaim, "Let go of my Eggo!" Today, I want you to let go of your *ego*. But to do that, we have to acknowledge a few things: where the ego comes from, why it exists, why we think we need it, and how to retire it.

WHERE THE EGO COMES FROM

When a baby is first born, she is real. She is the purest form of realness. She has no clue about how to be anyone but who she is. She has no personality and no persona. She doesn't know anything about acceptance or rejection. She knows only love, joy, and her interpretation of pain. She knows love because she is a full expression of God's infinite love. She knows joy because she has no concept of anger, jealousy, revenge, or rejection. She doesn't know what pain is, but she knows what pain feels like, at least on a physical level, so she responds to that physical experience. From there, a baby starts her journey to the ego, led by the person who is raising her, usually a parent or guardian.

The Wonder Months (0–6 months)

In the first few days, a baby is the apple of Mom and Dad's eyes. Everything he does is cute, precious, and adorable. If he gurgles, people "ooh and ahh." If someone catches a glimpse of a smile, they take pictures and rush to the phone to call other people. "She smiled!" Months pass and the adoration continues. If someone even thinks they hear a decipherable word, they go bananas. "He said Mommy! Did you hear him? He said Mommy!" You get the picture—the new baby is a precious gem who receives mostly love and affection. As he approaches his six month birthday parents start to get anxious. He hasn't attempted to stand himself up using the furniture. In fact, he's looking like he might be a slug! Oh no! "He's not even attempting to walk?" someone asks with an undercurrent of worry. So what does the parent do? The next time he's awake, Dad attempts to prod the little guy along. "Are we gonna walk? Is today the day we walk, son?"

To understand how devastating the world is to a baby, we have to remember where they've been for the past nine months. They've been insulated from the

The ego attempts to seduce you with the past and entice you with the future . . . which takes your attention off of the present.

ego. Under normal and healthy circumstances, the child has been utterly and completely nurtured. He's been loved, fed, and held. He arrives to the "outer" world and has to meet strangers, be subjected to the stares, and most important, be subjected to the energy of those present at his birth. Not only is he subjected to their energy but also to their desires and wishes for their lives. The child knows. He intuits the emotional and spiritual currency in the room. He knows that things will never be the same. He has entered the "Ego Zone." It's also during this phase that we start to put pressure on our children to live up to our standards for their lives. We start priming them to walk and talk. "Say Dah-Dah." We stand the child up, hold their hands, and expect them to take a step. Children this young don't even know that they have legs! How are they going to know what to do with them? As well-intentioned as it all sounds, this is nothing more than ego. Many parents even go as far as to set goals for when they're children will walk or talk. "She's going to talk any day now," I heard one woman say on her cell phone while I stood in line at a local coffee shop. "I can tell she wants to say something." This Mom sounded so proud. I wondered how the little bundle of joy in the stroller was feeling.

The Age of Innocence (6–12 months)

It's during this phase of a baby's life when those raising it begin to plant the seeds of fear, doubt, and insecurity. These are scary months because parents start to feel more insecure about *their* roles and their ability to control their child's existence in the world. They start to worry about what could happen to their kids. During this phase, it's not uncommon for a parent to stand over a sleeping child for minutes on end—even hours. They are overwhelmed by their love for the child, yes, but they're also often engulfed by all of the "what ifs" that surround parenthood. What if he doesn't wake up in the morning? What if I lose my job and can't take care of her? What if she chokes on her oatmeal? What if he gets sick and I'm not here? What if she doesn't start walking as early as her brother did? Will she become an addict? Will he get a tattoo? What if she doesn't get into Berkeley? What if he flunks out of Duke? What if? What if? What if?

It's also during this phase that parents begin to lay the foundation for acceptance and approval. If a baby acts like he's not hungry, what do parents say? "Be a good boy and eat just one more bite for Mommy" or "You gotta eat this if you want to grow up to be strong like Dad." We're already telling the child how to "be loved and accepted" by us . . . and the world. We don't realize this, but this is exactly what we're doing. And even though we think the child doesn't discern what's being said, children are extremely intuitive. Words are merely extensions of the energy we carry and transfer to those with whom we come in contact. A child knows what you're saying! They feel it. When we say, "Be a good girl" to a toddler, we're laying the foundation for a lifetime of approval seeking.

The Make-or-Break Years

During the first four years of a child's life, the pressure to perform is heightened. The pressure to conform also goes to another level. Why? Because parents are ready to see some results! They've fed you, burped you, clothed you, bought you toys, and sent you to the best preschools. Where's the return on investment?! Children in this stage are at the apex of imagination. They're full of curiosity and self-discovery. Ironically, as the child's need for independence escalates, so, often, does the parent's desire to control the child. This is a train wreck waiting to happen!

Before the child is born, parents talk about how much they're going to encourage individuality and how much they'll nurture the child's innovation, but the moment the child begins to exhibit what is innately normal, everything the parent "planned" goes out the window. I could have also called this phase the "Who's the Boss?" years because it's during this time that the parent and child fight over who's running the show. The child doesn't understand why he can't be free, and the parent lies awake at night thinking of ways to harness the child's free spirit.

A classic example is when a parent and child are walking in a store, and the parent tries to hold the child's hand. The parent doesn't understand why the two-year-old can't appreciate her need to protect him, and the two-year-old can't understand why the parent insists on stifling his freedom.

The parent, equipped with a full-blown ego, decides to take things into his own hands and pick the child up, signaling again "who's the boss."

Now, don't misunderstand me, our children need us to love and care for them, yet there are ways to be good caretakers without allowing our egos to take over. This shift in approach is mainly in the way we talk to our kids and the words we use. I was in the grocery store the other day when I saw this exchange between a mom and her toddler. The child ran down the cereal aisle because I assume he saw his favorite cereal. By the time the mom got to the end of the aisle, she kneeled down to her son and said, "How would you like to never see Mommy again?" The kid looked perplexed. He turned to the colorful cereal boxes. "Do you want to see Mommy tomorrow?" she continued. Her son turned to her and nodded yes. "Then don't run away from Mommy like that because someone could take you and then you would never see Mommy again. Do you want that?" I looked around for the cameras. This had to be a video production of the things "not" to say to your kids. But it wasn't staged. It was real. I shared this story in a recent seminar and a parent asked a great question: "Why is this ego?" This statement is steeped in fear. It's ego because it inspires insecurity rather than confidence and love.

The Indie Years

Over the next few years of adolescence and on into teenage-hood, parents become more disillusioned by their fears. They start to think that they must control their kids more now than ever. I've often heard parents say, "I'm just afraid I'm gonna lose her." What this parent is really saying is that he's afraid he's not going to be able to control her. The more independence a child asserts, the tighter a parent typically holds on to them. I once saw a casting notice for a popular talk show that read, "Do you want to regain control of your kids? We're looking for parents who have out-of-control teens who want to show them who's the boss." I smiled. They probably got tons of responses to that ad. How funny is it going to be when they all find out that no parent has control over his kid. Kids do exactly as they please. And if they're not doing it in front of their parents, there's a good chance they're doing it when their parents are not around. My parents had many, many rules. Or I should say my mother had many rules. She made her rules very clear to us. Some I followed, some I did not. And I guarantee you that if my mother were alive today she'd be shocked by the rules she thought I was following that I actually wasn't following! It's no different with any other kid out there today. Kids do exactly as they please. So, don't think just because your kids appear to be obeying your rules, that they are. That's not

WILL THE REAL YOU PLEASE STAND UP?

to say that all kids are breaking rules but it is to say that the goal shouldn't be to control our kids but to do our very best to equip them with the tools they need to lead healthy, productive lives. That's all we can do. Challenge them to think for themselves. Encourage them to tap into their true gifts. And then love them regardless of who they become.

This is a tall order for most parents, not because they're bad parents, but because many parents lead with their egos. They become so invested in how their kids will "turn out." This isn't a spiritual concern; it's an ego-based concern. If our kids don't turn out to be model citizens, we feel responsible for what and who they become, and we fear what people will think about us. We project these fears onto our children. "Comb your hair, son. People are going to think I didn't raise you right." As parents become more centered spiritually, they can begin to let go of the world's stamp of approval on how their kids turned out. It's an arduous journey to enlightened parenthood, yet it's certainly one worth traveling.

One week while caring for a friend's daughter while she traveled, I learned a wonderful lesson about parenting: most parents take their child's behavior and decisions too personally. This isn't the most spiritual approach to child rearing, as most of you know.

My friend's daughter, Tiffany, was seven years old and just beginning to come into her own about her fashion preferences and identity. (Seven is a great age, by the way.) On this day, she picked out a pair of pink pants and a red, green, and yellow polka-dot top. It had become one of her favorite blouses, and she wanted to wear it to school. When Tiffany got out of the bath tub, she called me to her room to check out her outfit. She had it all laid out on the bed. The polka-dot number alongside the pink pants.

I have to admit I laughed silently. Not because the outfit was funny, but because I knew that Tiffany's mom cared way too much about what people thought. She was going to fall over when she got a load of that outfit when she picked her up from my house the next day.

"Can I wear it?" Tiffany asked.

"Sure," I replied. "You're gonna look great!"

When my friend arrived at my house, she was wearing a warm smile—a smile that quickly faded when she saw her daughter's outfit. "Uh, hi, sweetie, is that what you wore to school today?"

Tiffany beamed. "Yep!"

The moment was priceless.

"Go upstairs and grab your book bag, okay?"

Tiffany dashed away as only a seven-year-old can.

My friend turned to me with a frozen stare.

"Doesn't she look cute?" I asked.

"Cute? Cute? No, she doesn't look cute. She looks like a clown! I can't believe you'd let her go to school like that. I wouldn't let your future children go to school looking like that!"

"Look, she wanted to wear that outfit. It's time to start letting her find out who she is and what she likes. She's stepping into her identity," I said. "This is a good thing. She doesn't need to like everything you like or the girls at school like."

This little Enlightening Parenting Moment wasn't going over so well. You see, my friend at the time appeared to be vying for the Approval-Seeker-of-the-Year Award. She cared desperately about what other people thought of her and, therefore, cared desperately about what people thought of her daughter.

As long as our kids are not in danger, what's the harm in letting them explore who they are? None, if you ask me.

I remember when my youngest brother Chris was little; he had a pair of ivory-colored cowboy boots that he adored. He didn't just "like" them; he loved those boots! The only time he took them off was at bedtime. I'm not joking! He'd wear them with jeans. He'd wear them with tennis shorts. He'd wear them to church. He had no concept of which clothes "went together." Those were cares of the ego, and at five years old, he didn't have a clue that the world expected him to care about what he looked like.

We would lay clothes out on the bed for him, and he'd put them on

WILL THE REAL YOU PLEASE STAND UP?

and then march right to his closet to grab those boots. We tried to out-smart him by hiding them on shelves, but he'd just go get a chair and search every closet until he found them.

Because he loved them so much, the boots quickly went from ivory to beige to taupe and eventually to a color I'd call "dusty smut." And even when they were on their last leg, Chris wore those boots until the "wheels fell off." Then it was on to the Superman cape, which you'll meet later in the book.

MY SOUL'S ADVENTURE

I have a slight uneasiness with heights. There's something about climbing a 100-foot mountain that makes me a little queasy. In December 2003, though, I had a stirring in my soul. I was going through a major transition in my personal and professional life, and I was seeking some answers. I needed a spiritual awakening, and I needed to be held by God.

I had gone on many retreats for business—the Tony Robbins-like weekends, Mark Victor Hansen's inspirational seminars, and other big events designed to fire you up. I love being in those environments, but this stirring was different. I wasn't lacking "motivation," I needed sustenance—spiritual electrolytes, if you will. And I needed them in an environment that was pure God—no additives, no preservatives. So I logged on to the Internet and typed "spiritual retreat" into the search engine. That's what I needed. My search turned up several results. One of the early entries was Sedona Soul Adventures. I liked the sound of that—"Soul Adventure." I had no idea what I would find once I got to the website, but I excitedly clicked the link to find out. When I arrived at the site, I read some of the testimonials and navigated around the site trying to get a vibe. I liked what I saw and felt. This was it. It was done. I'd head to Sedona for two weeks before I headed to Dallas for the holidays.

As I flew over the mountains into Phoenix, I was filled with a mixture of apprehension and anxiety. What exactly was a "soul" adventure anyway? I closed my eyes and reminded myself of my commitment: to be open to what awaited me on this "adventure." Whatever it was was exactly what I needed, I told myself. Whatever it was, it was ordered.

The drive from Phoenix to Sedona was long and, of course, hot, but also exciting. I felt the way I felt before big games. Adrenaline was flowing, and I couldn't wait to get to Sedona. I checked into the resort where I'd be staying. I drew my curtains and got a peek of the breathtaking mountains that smiled back at me from across the way.

Later that day I stepped outside my room to take a stroll and to breathe in the cool air that would soon be replaced by a brisk wind. The next morning I'd meet my first Soul Adventure teacher. Day One was all about surrender, according to the agenda in my welcome packet. Great, I thought. "Letting go" wasn't my strongest suit at the time.

Around 9 o'clock in the morning, we stood at the foot of a mountain that seemed to be a stairway to heaven. It was that high. "We're going up there?" I asked, hoping she'd say "no." Instead she started up the mountain. Super. Not only do we work on an area of emotional vulnerability for me, but we also expose my fear of heights. Funny, isn't it? Fear is never about the event; it's about the possible result of experiencing the event or situation. My fear wasn't of heights. It was of plummeting down the mountain to my death! I took a deep breath, and up I went. "Just keep climbing," she said. "Don't look down."

There was no chance of that. Finally we arrived at the top of the mountain. The view was astounding. I nearly lost my balance. I had actually climbed to the top of a mountain before. This wasn't a first. I'd lived in Switzerland and Italy—two places with mountains so beautiful they made you cry, and here I was in Sedona, climbing my first real mountain. Even better was that I was staring out onto an incredible vista. Across from me, nothing but mountains and sky. The view was humbling.

My soul leader invited me to come over to sit next to her on the ledge of the mountain. I didn't think so. "It's okay," she assured me. "You're safe here." Reluctantly, I walked over to her and slowly sat down, careful not to look down, lest that creepy fear of mine get the better of me. She looked out over the engulfing space with a knowing smile—more like a peaceful gaze. Then she glanced my way.

"Turn your head off. You don't need it here," she said softly but confidently. I'm sure you can understand why I'll never forget those words. They knocked me over like a ton of bricks. She had me pegged. Always thinking. Always questioning. Always figuring it all out. She had read my mail in a matter of five minutes. This adventure wasn't going so well. My soul adventure teacher then took me through a series of prayers, declarations, affirmations, and exercises that invited me to know God—Spirit—on a level deeper than I'd known. One that was without ego and all of the trappings that accompany an ego-centered life. This chapter was born on that mountain, and I left the adventure with one sole question: Do I really need my ego?

Do You Need Your Ego?

People think that it's their ego that protects them. Other people believe that it's their ego that helps them to make good decisions in business. Some think that you need a healthy ego to excel in sports, but do you really need your ego? No, you don't. You need your intuition. Intuition comes from a spiritual place. Intuition is a "knowing" that God gives you before you get here. It's part of the package. Your original packaging does not come with an Ego—you don't get that until later, as we talked about earlier. Ego comes from a place of fear—a fear that you will be replaced; fear that you'll become obsolete; fear that you'll be triumphed over. The real you has nothing to fear; therefore, the real you has no use for an ego. It's hard to escape the throes of our egos, yet while we all have an ego, we also carry the antidote for an ego-centered existence: love. When you find yourself saying things like "I'm the only one hurting here," or "I want to be right," remind yourself that you are walking in the opposite direction of love. Do a U-turn and head back down the path toward love.

THE HOUSE THAT EGO BUILT

Does this sound familiar? "He's going to be a doctor." "She wants to be an engineer." "He was walking before he was six months." "She said her first word before she walked." "I'm not going to be happy unless I get the highest grade in the class." "If I'm not the high-scorer, my season is a failure." "If I don't get this promotion, all this work's been for nothing." "If this relationship ends, I'll be crushed."

Sound familiar? Ever heard anything similar to these sentiments? Ever made any of these statements? Sure you have. We all have. How can we not when ego—the search for importance—is at every turn?

We learn to make ego the center of our lives from our parents, then our teachers, then the media, and finally our social constructs. Even before we physically emerge from our mother's womb, we are being conditioned to live from a place of ego.

Our parents paint our rooms a certain color, go to great lengths to name us something "powerful," and even decide what profession we'll probably go into after we graduate from the college of their choice. Once we arrive, the onslaught of egocentric messages goes to new heights. "She's so smart." "His IQ borders on genius." "She said 'Mom' before she said 'Dad.'" And so forth and so on. All of these things, though seemingly harmless, do nothing more than cultivate ego.

Instead of focusing on achievement, what if we raised children to be kind, loving, compassionate, and giving? What if we changed the way we approached life and stopped focusing on the "outer" and turned inward? Would that be weird to you? Or would it liberate you?

A journey to the real you must begin with a candid discussion about how you're living your life today. Are you driven by fear or love? Are you motivated to achieve because of how you will be perceived if you succeed (or fall short), or do you strive for your fullest potential because you know that in doing so you are fulfilling your divine assignment? I remember once hearing a sports announcer say during one Monday Night Football telecast, "An athlete has to have an ego. A little ego is necessary for success." For some reason those words hung in the air like a spider web. They really struck a chord with me as an athlete and now as an inpowerment coach. Many athletes and highly successful people often agree with those sentiments. They think that without an ego, they'd have no will to succeed. That's not true. When you're on a course to complete your divine assignment, nothing is more motivating than knowing that you are doing exactly what you should be doing with your life.

One summer a few years ago I was having a discussion with a few of my male professional athlete friends and I asked them all, "Would you walk away from a potential fight if a guy punched you during a game?" These were pro football players, golfers, and basketball and tennis players. They all thought for a moment, and then one by one, they all looked me square in the eyes and without hesitation answered. "Nope."

"Why not?" I asked.

"Because I wouldn't be a man." "Because you can never let that happen." "Because I'd never be able to show my face in practice." "Because in my sport the opponent feasts on your fear."

"Even if your team's future was at stake? You couldn't even walk away under those circumstances?" I asked, thinking at least one of them would change his tune.

"Nope. You have to make a statement." They all agreed.

"What statement is that?" I asked, knowing what they'd probably say.

"That you're a man," one guy responded as he sipped his drink.

I laughed. "You don't think he knows that."

The biggest of the guys answered, "He will when I bust him across his face."

Like my friends, we are constantly trying to prove or disprove something to someone. And it's not just in sports, it's in business and in everyday life. We don't want people to think we're wusses. We want to make sure people know we have an MBA. We need the guy at the car wash to know that we're a lawyer. We need the woman at the department store to know that our credit card was declined because the card has expired not because we have "blemished" credit. We need to let our friends know that we drive a pre-owned vehicle because we "want" to, not because we have to. Am I stepping on any toes yet? The need to prove—or be approved of—is a function of the ego. Am I putting your feet to the fire? Good! At least I know you're alive. Let's keep digging deeper.

Let's do a quick ego-check exercise. Take this quick test that will measure how dominant ego is in your life. Remember, growth requires next-level honesty. Go ahead, be honest with yourself. It really is the only way to experience a breakthrough.

A. When a situation arises between you and a friend or loved one, which of these is most important to you?
   1. That I make my point.
   2. That I show the other person that they're wrong.
   3. That I get in a few good jabs before we make up.
   4. That I bring up everything the other person's ever done to offend me.
   5. That I'm heard.

B. When you know that what you've done has caused someone hurt feelings, you . . .
   1. Let a few days pass to see if you really want to apologize.
   2. Find things that person's done to you so that you can justify not apologizing.
   3. Send a card, flowers, or gift—but no apology.
   4. Say I'm sorry, but add something that negates it, such as, "But you deserved it," or "You really made me mad."
   5. Make immediate contact with them and offer a heartfelt apology.

C. When someone accuses you of something that you know you didn't do, you . . .
   1. Charge back at them with your own ammunition.
   2. Defend yourself and vow silently to get back at them.
   3. Become hurt, never offer your side of the story, and retreat.

4. Say nothing at all.

5. Listen until they've finished and then offer an honest appraisal of your perspective, including the fact that you didn't commit the act.

D. When you hear gossip about a friend or family member, you . . .

1. Say nothing, do nothing.

2. Add to the gossip.

3. Call the people being gossiped about and start your own gossip about the others.

4. Call no one but instead stew inside, allowing thoughts and feelings to eat away at you.

5. Say a silent prayer or affirmation for those involved.

E. When you're playing a board game with family members and there's a questionable call that will determine which team wins the game, you . . .

1. Stage a full-fledged trial, explaining why your opinion is accurate.

2. Throw a temper tantrum.

3. Share your perspective but say, "It's only a game."

4. Say "It's only a game," but inside seethe because deep down you want to win.

5. Say nothing even though you may be the only person who knows what really happened.

F. You read or hear about a big deal that a friend lands, a deal that will take his or her career to the next level. Which response is most likely for you?

1. Say nothing. After all, it didn't happen for you.

2. Say nothing until the friend contacts you and tells you personally.

3. Call or e-mail and say something like, "I had to read about your big deal in the paper? I thought we were friends."

4. Send a congratulatory note, flowers, or gift because it's politically correct.

5. Immediately call or e-mail with genuine congratulatory sentiments.

Take a quick look at your answers above and remember, no judgment; this is just an assessment. Assign each response the point value of the number preceding it, and add up your score. Scores above 15 indicate that your ego might not be the captain of your ship after all. That, or you avoid potential conflict. If you scored 14 or below, you're probably letting your ego run your life, thinking only of how things impact and serve you. It's time to send your ego on an extended vacation.

A New Day

Every single day, we have the chance to create something new and powerful. Each moment, we have the opportunity to become more of who we are. I once saw an interview with Academy Award winning actor Tom Hanks where he talked candidly about his rise to stardom. The interviewer asked him how he was able to snag such great parts early on in his career. Tom's response had such spiritual resonance that I wrote it down on a napkin because that was all I could find at the time. "It's simple," he said. "I wasn't self-conscious. I could walk into an audition and totally be myself." Wow! Those words came at a time when I needed them most. I was about to audition to be the host of a fitness-related show on Lifetime Television. I knew that the producer was looking for someone with a clinical nutrition background, which I don't have. I'm a sports nutritionist and a certified personal trainer, but I'm not a clinician. Yet after hearing the wisdom of Tom Hanks, I decided that I was going to just "be me." And when the cameras rolled, that's exactly what I did. A few days later, the producer called. "We've decided to go with another host because the client really wants someone with a clinical background," she said.

"I understand," I said, still feeling good about my audition because it was more of a spiritual triumph for me. I'd been the "real me" in the audition.

"But," she interrupted. "We liked you so much that we've created a role for you on the show. We want you to train the women. Would you consider doing that?"

"Of course!"

Within weeks I was on the set of a TV show with a great crew and wonderful women who were on a path to losing weight and becoming more of who they were. It was miraculous and very affirming.

By being more of who we are, it's impossible for us to lose. Losing isn't even a concept that Spirit recognizes. It's a term that the ego constantly throws our way, though. *You're such a loser. You can't be all of who you are, they'll think you're crazy. If you're too energetic, they'll think you're on drugs.* Ego wants us to believe that if people saw who we truly are then they'd reject us. Rejection to many people is a form of death, therefore, to be avoided at all times. Had I not been "me" in that audition, there's a good chance the producers of that show would not have created a space for me on the production. Had I succumbed to the pressure from my ego to be what I thought they'd want to see in the audition, who knows what would have happened? That's why I'm always amazed and inspired by performers who appear to be totally transparent on stage.

I recently traveled to Las Vegas to see Celine Dion in concert at Caesars Palace. Her show, "A New Day," was one of the best performances I've seen in a long time, and I was amazed to watch her transform that stage into her own unique world. As I got lost in the experience, I realized that we, too, have that same opportunity every moment of our lives. Through authenticity we get to change the world by showing people what it looks like to be all of who we are. Through this process people become less afraid to become who they are.

Like Celine we get to choose the characters, select the music, change the setting, pick the props, and adjust the lighting to our liking. Each song she sang had a different background and a different feel. We were transported through time as we listened to her melodious voice on songs like "Because You Loved Me" and "My Heart Will Go On," the theme from the blockbuster movie *Titanic*.

As I sat in that palatial setting, in seats that were akin to fifty-yard line tickets at the Rose Bowl, I realized that each day is a new day for me. We should never have the same day we had the day before. That's a tragedy.

With all that the world has to offer us and us the world, we should live each day anew. We must seek new ways of loving, new ways of trusting, new ways of living. Only then can we begin to know that we don't need our egos to be our real selves.

The ego nurtures sameness. It attempts to hypnotize us into a false sense of security through habits that don't feed us spiritually. It persuades us to stay in jobs and relationships that don't serve us. It tries to convince us that there's safety in keeping things the same when spiritual apathy is the reason the world is where it is today. We have to fight the desire to live routine lives. We aren't routine beings. We're dynamic and complex, yet what moves us forward in the world remains simple: love.

THE DECONSTRUCTION OF THE EGO

Okay, so I've gone over how your ego is born and built, now let's talk about the retiring process. First, let me warn you: your ego is going to kick, scream, and curse at the thought of you even entertaining the thought of retiring it. You cannot listen to it. There's no place for ego in the life of someone whose true desire is to be authentic. Now, I must tell you something else important. And you must follow this prescription to the letter. There can be no freelancing or thinking you know better; you must follow this process. If you are willing to surrender to this process, you will see immediate changes in your life. Make that instant—you will see instant changes in your life. Ready?

Step 1: Go Back to the Beginning

Babies are almost always in a state of glee as long as they are what? Fed, dry, and held. They don't know anything about expectations, validation, or recognition. They learn those things in due time, but when they first arrive in their physical form, they are ignorant to the things that drive most humans. That's why it's been said that babies cry when they leave their mother's wombs. Their pure souls recognize the new landscape, and they are sad! I think there's probably some spiritual truth here, and for this reason, we have a lot to learn from babies and children in general.

First, babies are neither afraid of what's in front of them, nor do they have any concept of being ashamed of what they've done. They are the poster children for "being." They haven't yet learned to be a "doer." The world will cram that down their throats by the time they're walking.

Are you dry? For babies "dryness" means that they're physically nurtured. So, what's eating at you? What's synonymous with a wet diaper in your life? Is it a nagging relationship? An unfulfilling job?

Are you held? When it rains and thunders it's always fun to have someone to snuggle with, but the kind of "held" I'm speaking of here has more to do with your heart. What holds your heart? Try not to think outside yourself. So, don't think in terms of another person physically holding you but rather of an experience that is more of a spiritual nature. The rain holds me. The sound of children's laughter, my father's voice when he hears my voice on the other end of the phone—these things hold me and give me great joy. What holds you?

Step 2: Surrender to the Process

You are a masterpiece in progress. To recapture that which you've lost in the real category, you must be reborn. A baby is born with a supreme intuitive IQ as well as intellectual IQ. What it doesn't know yet is how to fake, how to pretend, how to be inauthentic. It simply doesn't know how to be anyone but its real self. Isn't that amazing? So, we've all been without our egos at one point in our lives, that's why I know it's possible to be there again. It's only because we are now conscious of our ego's existence that it's difficult to surrender to the process of letting it go. Make sense? Surrendering to that which is innately you will illuminate all that is beautiful and astonishing about you. Your strength, wit, intelligence, and charm will all peak in the absence of ego. It's your childlike nature that makes you real. That's what I'm encouraging you to tap into—your inner infant. The brand-new you. When you were born you were brand new.

You were a blank slate. Let's go back there and become a blank book, an empty glass, or a gigantic sponge. We were open to new possibilities and experiences. The simplest things astounded us. We were curious and eager to learn. Above all, we were open, and only when we are truly open to learning and receiving can true transformation take place.

Step 3: Let Go of the Need to Be Right

When you remove the need to be right, you make your way toward becoming more real. When you release yourself from the need to prove the other person(s) wrong, you clear the path for the authentic you to step forward. When we give up our need to "make a point," the real you can lead you to deeper spiritual truth. Becoming the real you is not about becoming more enlightened so that you can be better at trying to change other people. We are not here to be the spiritual director of other people's lives. When you liberate yourself from this role, you will love more freely and judge less often.

Step 4: Get Ready for a New Reality

Watch what happens when you retire your ego. All of your relationships will change overnight. These will not be gradual changes, they will be startlingly different relationships. People will start looking at you like you're from another planet. They'll start saying things like, "What's wrong with you?" They'll squint and say, "You're different." This is good. This is supposed to happen. When I got back from my soul adventure in Sedona, I was different. Something happened on that mountain for me. I started the long journey to retiring my ego for good.

I learned that the ego cannot exist in a space where fear, arrogance, and control have not been invited to the party. When you replace fear with love and judgment with acceptance, everything and everyone around you will change. It's inevitable. That's the nature of love. And when love has dominion in your life, your ego will do everything in its power to extinguish love's flame. But guess what? It can't do it. Love is the most powerful resource in our human toolkit. It trumps everything. Give it a try. The next time you're in a battle of wills, instead of trying to get the upper hand, surrender to love. Respond with mercy, compassion, peace—all of which are shades of love—and watch what happens to you. You see, your love may appear to be doing nothing to or for the other person but even so, it's changing you. If you continue to respond with the shades of love eventually the people around you will also be changed. That's the power of love. I practice this in my personal and professional life and I am blown away by how much I can increase the peace by spreading love.

HEART-CENTERED LIVING

People have such low regard for their hearts. They think that when they fall in love and the relationship doesn't work out the way they fantasized that it's their heart's fault. "I just fell too hard" or "I love too hard." Baloney! It's nobody's fault! We place undue and unrealistic expectations on romantic relationships anyway and then we're completely disillusioned when our fantasies don't come true. These fantasies are created in the ego to begin with. The ego convinces you that your relationship has to be a certain way or else it's a failure, right? Your ego tells you that you should forego being individually whole in favor of being in a relationship that doesn't support you. That's why some people feel so alone when they're single. Because the world has fed them a bunch of crap about why "twoness" is better than "oneness." Yet many of you reading this right now can attest to the fact that even when you're in a relationship it's possible to feel alone, right? Of course it is. No one can nurture your heart better than you can. Living a heart-centered life isn't about making decisions that don't support you in a positive way. Heart-centered living is love-centered living. I believe that the heart—not the physical heart—houses a Mecca of love. The heart is that true essence of who we truly are. Think of your spiritual heart as the ocean. It's massive, it's endless, it's vast, and it's often engulfing. In other words, our capacity to give love and "be" love extends far, far beyond our intellectual comprehension. So don't try to understand or wrangle love. It's not possible, so stop trying!

A colleague and good friend of mine, Myron Golden, shares a story in his trainings that truly illustrates our need to let go of knowing how everything works. He asks his audiences, "Do you truly understand how an airplane gets off the ground, takes flight, and travels at incredible velocity without you feeling the speed at all? Do you truly understand how that happens?" The answer for most of us is no. We don't understand all of the intricacies of the flying bird but that doesn't stop us from traveling, does it? It's the same way with love. You don't need to understand "how" love transforms and heals the world to know that it does. So, lead with your heart and let love do what it does best.

FROM EGO TO LOVE

To move from ego to a place of love in our hearts requires discipline, minute-by-minute discipline. We spend an inordinate amount of time focusing on things that do little to move us closer to our real selves. We work all of our lives trying to be "successful" instead of trying to be more of who we are. Don't misunderstand me, there's nothing wrong with material gain. It is a natural extension of God's generosity. Get paid. Enjoy the fruits of your labor. Expand in all areas of your life. The goal is not to stifle your growth or try to limit your harvest but instead to lead with Spirit rather than ego.

Ego is synonymous with fear. And fear and love stand opposite each other. Therefore, the journey to the real you will be paved with great difficulty when ego is the navigator.

Transformation is not possible in the face of fear. Awareness is blurred in the presence of fear. We long for a life full of love, yet we can't achieve this state of awareness because we are blinded by fear. We look at children, and we marvel at their zest for life when they're young. We look at them with a sense of sadness, too, because we know what awaits them. We know that soon they'll join us in the fear-based world. We're saddened that they can't stay "little" all of their lives. We mourn their innocence, yet we also participate in indoctrinating them into our fear-based reality.

We love them and want them to cling to their zest for life, but how? How do we do it?

We must first do within our own hearts what we wish to teach our kids, friends, loved ones, and neighbors: To lead with love rather than ego. Whether we are willing to admit it or not, we're all secretly longing for a more loving existence. We watch the news and read the newspaper, and we shake our heads in judgment at the horrors in the world, yet we do little to create more love and harmony in the part of the world we live in: our homes, schools, churches, and communities. We long for the days of old, yet while they're gone, we can still create a different level of peace and love in our own hearts and minds. It may not look the way it looked twenty years ago, but it at least is the love we can create right now. And that's a start.

We watched the terror on September 11, 2001, and we hated the people who did that to "us." We wanted to retaliate and kill those who had robbed our kids of their future, and snatched our mothers, fathers, grandmothers, husbands, wives, and children from us in one vicious act. And while the devastation of that day still reverberates today, we've done little to change the world around us.

Although those who send out the terror alerts would like for us to believe different, the world is no more violent than it ever was. We've created the illusion that it is, but it's not. The ego tells us that because we have more "toys of evil" the world must be a more evil place, but the reality is that what happened on September 11 is no more tragic than what happened in Auschwitz or Rwanda. The ego creates these pictures to drive us deeper into a fear-based consciousness and away from a love-based consciousness.

It knows that as long as it can run our lives, we will be immobilized. The ego knows that real love is not a possibility as long as it is anywhere on the premises. It knows that there can be no healing of ourselves or our world as long as it's around. It seeks to dominate our lives so that we won't morph into our full spiritual selves but instead will remain spiritual "minis."

RUNNING TOWARD LOVE

The journey away from ego toward love is shorter than most of us realize. It's truly a matter of choice. It's a matter of remembering who we are and why we're here. If we were to access the power that lies in each of us to transform the world, we'd never experience fear again. If we decided to be authentic in all instances, our ego would not survive, and the world would instantly become a more real place to live. The real you responds to everything in its path with love and compassion. Your ego tries to get you to respond to everything and everyone in your path with indifference, suspicion, and doubt. That is not the real you. The real you knows an impostor when it sees one, so there's no need to fear anyone. Equipped with a knowing of who you are, you'll intuitively know what's and who's going to serve your highest good.

TEN SECRETS YOUR EGO
DOESN'T WANT YOU TO KNOW

As you read this book your ego's probably working overtime to get you to be distracted. How many different things have you thought about doing since you started reading this book? Laundry, e-mail, chores? Your ego knows that if you continue to absorb the principles in these pages that it will be history. It knows that you will be a more powerful, passionate, and purpose-driven individual if you turn your back on all of the fear that's dominated your life up to this point. So, there are a few things your ego wants you to remain in the dark about. Here are ten of them:

Secret #1: You Don't Need Your Ego

If you're experiencing challenges on your spiritual path, it's probably your ego trying to preserve its place in your life. The ego is not interested in your becoming more spiritually enlightened, more emotionally stable, or more financially rich. It knows that as you move closer to wholeness and completeness it won't get to put you through the rinse cycle every week. When you commit to personal development, the ego cringes. It's not a big advocate for personal or professional evolution because it knows it can't run your life if you grow. Your ego is like a stubborn stain. Like ink on a leather sofa. If you don't know the secrets to getting ink out of your leather sofa, you can spend hours, days, weeks trying to work that stain out. You become more frustrated because all of the products you're using don't seem to make the stain go away, and even when you see some improvements, you can still see hints of the ink, right? But when you discover that hair spray or nail polish remover are excellent choices for removing ink from leather, you rejoice knowing that if you ever get ink on your sofa again that you've got the answer. The ego is like ink. It's a formidable opponent only because we don't use the right "treatment" on it. But now that you know that love is the kryptonite, the perfect antidote to ego, you don't have to fight with it any more. Just spray it with love and keep moving closer to the real you.

Secret #2: Anger Is Not Hurt, It's Fear

Some things we accept as truth. One of the things we've heard is that anger is hurt in disguise, but actually, anger is usually an expression of fear. We fear that someone is going to hurt us. We fear that someone is going to overwhelm us. We fear that someone is going to expose us. So we project anger. When someone doesn't do what we want them to do, we say, "You hurt my feelings," but actually what they did was to bring up our insecurities about being safe in the world—that's not hurt, that's fear. The problem is that we're relying on something outside of ourselves to provide safety in a world that is already safe. And the only reason we perceive that it's not safe is the ego.

I maintain that anger is nothing more than fear in a sweatsuit. For example, if someone cuts us off in traffic, we honk our horns and sometimes get angry, right? Why? Because we didn't like what they did? Sure, that's part of it. That's level one. But if we delve deeper we are actually angry because we fear that their cutting us off will kill us, and we fear dying. That's why we got angry. Not just because they're driving recklessly but because we are afraid of what their reckless driving will mean for us. Next example. You're in a relationship and you learn that the person you're dating is also seeing another person even though you've agreed to be monogamous. You get angry. Why? Because you don't like being lied to? Sure, that's part of it. That's level one. But at the soul level you're afraid that you'll be alone—not just left alone by this person—but alone forever. That's probably why you're angry. Next example. You learn that your bank has made a horrible mistake and depleted your account by 75 percent. You call them up and you're so mad you could scream. Why are you angry? Because your mortgage is due and the check won't clear? Sure, that's part of it. But the real reason is that you are afraid of the deeper implications: that you won't be able to take care of yourself; that you will be destitute; that you will be homeless; and potentially that you'll suffer financial death. Those are the fears behind the anger. Now do you see why anger is fear? I could go through at least fifty more examples and show you how your anger—no matter what you think or say it's about—is steeped in fear.

We're so afraid to admit we have fears that we'd rather convince ourselves that our anger is righteous. It makes us feel more powerful to say, "I'm angry with you." We think that keeps us in a position of power over the other person or the circumstance. In reality, acknowledging what's at the core of your anger empowers you more than being angry. Energy and medical studies have proven that when we're angry our bodies undergo severe physical and physiological stress. So, while you may think you're punishing someone by being angry with them, you're actually punishing yourself, literally! Your body, mind, and spirit pay the heaviest taxes for your anger. So let it go.

Secret #3: You Don't Have to Continuously Learn the Same Lessons

I'm not a big fan of learning the same things over and over. If I start to see an unhealthy or nonsupportive pattern developing in any of my relationships, I say, "Hold on, this is feeling very familiar." The ego steps in and tells me, "No, really, this time it's different. You haven't been here. Keep doing what you're doing. You'll see. It'll be different." So, what do we usually do in that circumstance? We stay. In the relationship. On the job. In the situation. The ego wants you to think that you have to keep repeating the same grade. You don't! Get the lesson and move on to new lessons! The ego doesn't want you to advance to the next spiritual grade. It wants you to be in kindergarten all of your life! If you stay in elementary school, guess what? It gets to be your principal all your life!

Secret #4: Judgment Isn't Necessary

The ego is like a parasite that lives and breeds on indifference and separation. It wants you to judge everything you see in yourself and others. It knows that where there is judgment, there can be no love. When love is absent, there can be no peace, no reconciliation, no harmony, and no growth. That's why the ultimate desire of the ego is to keep love at bay. It knows that if you surrender to love you will instantly have everything you want in your life. It knows that it will have no choice but to become extinct.

At the end of most of my e-mails is a company signature followed by a "thought for the day." Last year I decided to use several thoughts for the day, including one about judgment. I chose this one because I was starting to realize all the many ways we judge ourselves. We criticize our looks, our intelligence, our financial situations, everything. I figured I'd see how other people felt about judgment so I changed one of the quotes at the end of my e-mails to a question: What would happen if for one day you didn't judge yourself? The response was overwhelming. People wrote back saying, "Loved today's thought for the day." Or "I never realized how hard I am on myself until you asked this question."

Why do we judge ourselves so often and harshly? Because we've been taught well. We've been taught by our spiritual communities, parents, and all the way down to the media that we must constantly scrutinize everything in our path. Judgment is another form of abuse, which we've already talked about. We judge because we believe God judges us, and since that is the teaching of most spiritual dogma, we follow the model with ourselves as well as everything around us. That's why I asked you earlier in the book to consider experiencing your Source as pure love. By knowing a loving God, judgment is not a natural part of your psychological anatomy. For most of us who've been raised believing that at the end of our lives we'll be "judged," the process of criticizing every single thing we see is automatic. It is as natural as breathing. But guess what? It's also reversible. You can change your beliefs about judging and being judged.

Today I want you to record the times you judge yourself and everything around you. Write it down, or at minimum make a mental note of how often you find yourself seeing the shadows in the light, seeing the negative instead of the positive. Check out how frequently you want to find something wrong with what your friends or loved ones say. You will be amazed at how much judgment you heap onto your world. Do this for a twenty-four-hour period and if it it's truly your desire to live a more authentic life, your life will undergo yet another transformation. Remember, I want you to notice all of the small and large judgment you put into the universe. Whether it's a nasty comment about someone's clothes or a belittling comment about your waistline, it's all judgment. Then, in the next twenty-four-hour period I encourage you to see how much love and positive energy you can put out in the world and watch how differently you feel. When someone says something you don't like, shoot back something affirming to them. When you notice something about yourself that you previously disliked, declare something positive in the place of something negative. You will feel differently. Continue to do this and it will become a habit. What you habitually do and say to yourself, you ultimately become.

Secret #5: The Real You Will Make It in the "Real World"

The ego is all about survival, by any means necessary. It wants you to think that the real you, the authentic you, is for weenies and religious zealots. It will try to convince you that if you buy into this "spiritual, real-you crap" you won't last a NASCAR minute in the real world. The ego wants you to believe that without it, you won't be able to make good decisions, you'll get eaten by the sharks and you'll miss out on all of the things it wants you to believe you need—money, fame, and prestige. All things you can still have with love as your guiding light. In short, the ego wants you to believe that you need it to survive in the world. You don't. Remember, you came equipped with every-thing you need to have and can become everything you want.

Secret #6: Forgiveness Is Something You Do for You

The ego has done a real number on us when it comes to forgiveness. First it's taught us that we must seek the forgiveness of others. Then, to complicate things even further, ego persuades you to believe that you won't get the forgiveness of others even when you seek it! This creates an interesting dance between humans that goes like this:

> You do something to someone that you know is offensive. Let's say you spread some vicious gossip in the office. You know that this is not in your highest good and you know that it's not supportive of the other person but you do it anyway. After you do it, you feel bad. You want to apologize, but you've been convinced (by the ego) that the person you've offended has already judged you for spreading the gossip and they won't forgive you. To avoid the pain of this perceived rejection, you decide not to apologize even though you know it is the right thing to do. That's Part I.
>
> Part II goes like this. The ego drives over to the home of the person you've offended to start working on them. Ego says, "You know Jimmy owes you an apology, right? He really hurt your business by spreading those rumors." You start to think, "Yeah, he did. Dude owes me an apology." Ego says, "How long has it been since he did what he did? Two, three days? He's had plenty of time to call you, don't you think?"

You think for a moment. "Yes! Come to think of it, it's actually been four days. . . . "

Ego jumps in, "Four days? That's unacceptable." You become furious. "You're right, it is unacceptable," you reply. "I thought he was my friend."

Now the ego's got you right where it wants you. So, it goes for the kill. "I bet he's not planning to say one word about what he did. He's just going to move on as if it didn't happen. As if *you* don't matter."

By now you're seething. The thought of your friend not calling you makes you boil, and the thought of him calling but not apologizing takes you over the edge. Either way, he can't win. Your ego has worked you into such a frenzy that you actually believe that you need an apology and that you hold the keys to forgiveness.

You don't. None of us do. Yet that's exactly the way we've been taught to play the game. We believe that when someone does something that we don't like, they should apologize to us. We believe that everyone should see the world just as we see it. That's why human beings experience hurt feelings— because someone does something in our movie that does not follow our script. The only problem is that they're not reading from the same script! They're reading from their own script. Can we fault them for not seeing things the way we see them? Not as spiritual beings, no, we cannot. We get offended because we don't like the message the Messenger has delivered to us. We don't want to hear what the Shapeshifter is saying to us. We are upset because we don't like what the Mirror in our lives is showing us about ourselves. Remember, every person in our lives has a role in our life story.

We are called to love and harmonize even when we don't understand the behaviors of our brothers and sisters. Boy, this is so hard! I routinely call my sister Debra with one exclamation. "What is wrong with people?!" What I'm really saying is "I'm upset that people don't operate the way I'd operate." Well, guess what? I don't always behave in the way that they'd like for me to behave either. In relationships we must always be aware that we're producing one movie about our lives and the person you're in the relationship with is producing his or her own movie, too. It's not possible to see eye to eye on every scene of our movies. That's how we grow.

Ever felt like you were producing a love story and the people in your life were producing a horror flick? We have to learn how to heal without the actions of others. We must learn how to get closure in difficult spots without depending on others to rescue us or make us feel better for what we perceive they've done "to" us. That's the mark of a spiritual champion. When you realize that your healing happens inside of you, you'll walk this path with much more joy, passion, and clarity. When we're not waiting on someone else to tell us that we matter—which is essentially the function of an apology—we'll be whole.

Secret #7: Spirituality, Not Religion, Is Vital to Realness

Ego will keep you attached to rituals and practices that do little to lead you to who you really are. It will tell you that you should put your faith in the words of those sharing the word of God rather than God. I stopped caring about being popular more than twenty years ago. I know what I'm about to say won't win me any coveted awards, but that's not what's important to me. So here goes: Stop drinking the Kool-Aid. And if you don't know what this phrase is referring to, rent the movie, *The Guyana Tragedy: The Story of Jim Jones.* It's a story of a leader who started out with a benevolent mission but who ultimately spiraled into a deep abyss, taking hundreds of people with him . . . to death. They drank the Kool-Aid. Stop being spoon-fed religion and seek truth and God for yourself. Established religion is the result of someone's interpretation. "Divinely inspired" reminds me of the line "This film is inspired by actual events" that you see on the screen before a "fact"-based movie begins. It's subject to the interpretation of the writer or filmmaker, plain and simple. So, if you've been living your life based on someone else's interpretation of spirituality, you've been severely limiting yourself and your spiritual growth.

Secret #8: Healing Is Essential . . . Pain Is Optional

Ego's motto is "no pain, no gain." If it's worth having, it's worth hurting for. That's why we stay in abusive relationships with others and ourselves. We think we must endure pain. We think it makes us special to tell people what we've endured in the name of love. There's nothing honorable about staying in a relationship that does not serve your highest good. I'm always amazed that when someone says they've been married for lots of years that people applaud. Why are we applauding? We don't know that those have been healthy years. They could've been terrible years, yet we applaud without knowing anything about the relationship. Even people who have actually been in long-term relationships that are abusive are sometimes drinking the "longevity Kool-Aid." One woman at a seminar told me, "I've been with my husband for fifty-two years." I said to her. "Wow. Were most of them good years?" She flashed a slight smile. "Well, now, that's another story," she said. "I can say that of those fifty-two years I may have had one good *day*, baby." How many people do you know who are languishing in a relationship without "one good day" behind them or in front of them? It's time to heal, ya'll.

Spirit has a way of reminding us of what needs to be healed in our lives. That's why we keep attracting the same people, places, and things. It's not a coincidence that the employer you work for today is exactly like the one from the previous job. It's no accident that the person you're dating talks to you in the same way as the previous lover. It's no fluke that you're reading this book instead of another one.

Something inside of you needs to be healed or ignited. It can be a tiny wound or it can be a huge gash. Only you know what needs to be healed inside of you. And the reason you haven't healed before now has nothing to do with "God's time," it has to do with your ego's persuasive powers. Your ego tells you that you don't need to heal that part of your personality that keeps you on a path to self-destruction. "You don't need to address the fact that your mother is still trying to control your life. That'll upset her." That's the kind of stuff that ego tells you. "If you ask for a raise, you could lose your job." The real you knows that you must ask for a raise because your contributions are worthy of reward. The real you isn't attached to whether you actually get the raise but it knows that the journey to the real you must address your issues of self-worth.

Secret #9: You're Not Separate from the Rest of the World

Separation is an interesting concept. If we can maintain our separateness, we can justify our crimes against each other, against the earth, and against nature. We're all an extension of Oneness. Ego says that at all costs, you must separate yourself from the rest of the world. It tells you that you're different from those not like you; therefore, it's okay to vilify them, stereotype them, and hurt them. That's the great seduction of separation and why we must never think that we are separate from those with whom we share this planet. If you start to feel in your heart that you are not like "those people," you're cultivating a spirit of separation, which will ultimately lead you to project negative spiritual energy into the world. Remember, what we do to others, we do to ourselves.

Secret #10: You *Can* Have It All

If you decided once and for all that you were going to have a life full of emotional stability, spiritual depth, and financial prosperity, ego would attempt to convince you that there's something wrong with wanting those things. When it comes to love, it will tell you that your relationship isn't as good as you think it is. It'll tell you that spirituality is for people who aren't logical. That if you can't see it, smell, it touch, hear it, or taste it, it's not real. It'll tell you that you shouldn't aspire to have more money because you can't handle it. It'll tell you that being real will scare people away. It'll tell you that the real you just isn't possible. The ego has no interest in you having it all because if you had it all, you'd have no use for the games it attempts to play to keep you in a perpetual state of lack, emotional servitude, and spiritual chaos.

Not only can you have it all but you should attempt to have it all.

What's wrong with having loving relationships, a thriving family, great health, unimaginable wealth, and every good thing in between? Nothing! So don't think for one second that your time on earth has to be full of lack and drama at every turn. We have those things in our lives because we believe they are necessary. They are not, so go for it!

THE TAO OF PROJECTIONS

If we are to lead truly spiritual lives, we must stop projecting our fears onto everyone we meet or encounter. Ego has trained us to approach every situation as a wounded, victimized, angry, unloved, and frightened being. It's either "Poor me" or "Look at how bad I'm hurting" or "I'm scared" or "They did this to me." There was a time when you didn't need to be a victim. There was a time when you didn't need to hide behind your fears of loving and losing. There was a time when you weren't a factory of projections. That's the place we all want to go back to. If we can rid ourselves of some of our most common projections, we'll immediately see pieces of who we were the day we got here.

One year I hired a new employee to work in my office. The moment I met her I knew she and I were going to be a great fit. And we were right up until the last day of our journey together. My employee was bright, full of energy, and funny. She caught on to things very easily, represented my company very well, and basically was a great extension of me. A few months into our working relationship she started to have some personal challenges. We all have personal challenges, right? But her challenges started to affect her ability to do her job well. I called her into my office and asked her to be straight with me. I shared with her specific instances regarding a few work items that had not been done, things that put me behind schedule. I told her that unless the drama was behind us I was going to have to look for a replacement. She assured me that her personal issues would not interfere with her job. I accepted this and we finished the next few days without incident. Then one night I needed to go to an event and I asked her to meet me at the office at a specified time. Because of the unpredictability of the Los Angeles traffic, I told her that our departure time was not negotiable. She was late arriving and I had to go. I sent an e-mail from my phone telling her that I couldn't wait for her and that she could have extended me the courtesy of a phone call to let me know if she was going to be late. I told her that this was not an unreasonable or unrealistic request. The next day she sent an e-mail to me that was full of projections. "I don't need a speech from you. I called you but you didn't answer." There was no accountability whatsoever in her response.

Now, here's what happened next. My ego said, "Shoot her an e-mail, girl-friend! You know you can write a serious e-mail!" I laughed in Ego's face because I've grown to the point that I can have conversations out loud with Ego so that I can hear just how ridiculous it wants me to be! So, Ego and I went about two rounds in the ring. It wanted me to attack her personally and bring up all of the old transgressions from our time together. Ego wanted me to fight projections with projections. An eye for an eye. A harsh word deserves another harsh word, right? Wrong. So, I called her but she didn't answer. I asked her to meet me at the end of the business day. I realized that her e-mail of projections had nothing to do with me. She was going through a difficult time for reasons that I may never know fully. It would have been unfair of me to be unkind to her or to add to an already heavy heart even if she hadn't been the model employee as of late. When she arrived at my home that evening I vowed to be kind and respectful no matter how she acted. And that's what I did. Was it easy? Actually, yes it was. But only because I'd had that time to walk myself through a love-based, heart-centered response. That's what I encourage you to do. When your ego invites you to tango, to engage in ego-based warfare with the people in your life, just talk through it. Commit to love and you will see mind-blowing results.

"Poor Me"

People who talk this way are the Walking Wounded. They lead with their cuts and scars. We don't even have to ask what happened, they'll find a way to weave their sad stories into the conversation. Here are some of the famous lines:

"My mother was emotionally abusive."

"My father was physically abusive."

"My manager doesn't recognize my talents."

"My kids never say thank you."

The list goes on. The ego delights in these statements because it knows that when you're mired in depression and self-pity that its place in your life is secure. You're not going anywhere near spiritual enlightenment when you're a member of the Association of the Walking Wounded.

"Look at How Bad I'm Hurting"

I love this one. This one will get you a good solid ten minutes of airtime from most people. It's like that accident on the highway that we try not to look at. Some of us can't drive by without turning to look, while the rest of us keep moving.

I'm not interested in the accident. My mind is on what's ahead for me. I say a prayer for those involved, and I keep driving. And that's exactly how I am with people who want to get me sucked into their painful episodic television series. You see, it's possible to be compassionate with someone without having to endure a long story that is more about his or her need for attention and validation than it is about getting through the ordeal. We have to discern when we're seeking attention and when we need to walk and talk through a painful experience with those we love. The more spiritually aware you become, the less you'll seek to engage people in pity parties and the more you'll look for true spiritual support to move you to the next level of enlightenment.

"I'm Scared"

This one should be recoined, "I don't want to grow." That's what it means in spiritual terms. If fear is opposite on the scale from love, and love is what we seek, moving away from love is a confession that we don't want to grow. Fear is our number-one bailout emotion. When we don't want to grow, we resort to saying that we're afraid.

A year or so ago a friend and I had a misunderstanding. We both acknowledged our part in the experience and, I thought, had moved on. I started to notice that his e-mails weren't as frequent as they had been. It was a familiar pattern with him. Whenever his feelings were hurt, his feelings were almost always the only feelings that mattered. I e-mailed him and asked him if everything was okay. He e-mailed back saying that he was "afraid to trust again." He went on to write that he was fragile and although most women don't see men as such, he was also quite sensitive. He didn't know how to move forward after our "incident."

I remember being struck by the self-centeredness of it all. I know that doesn't sound very compassionate, but I didn't feel compassionate in the moment. I'd seen this maneuver too many times—in myself as well. And I know where it comes from. Growth is never easy, so we avoid it at all costs most of the time. So, I felt like writing him a big bold, multicolored e-mail that read, "Stop looking for excuses not to grow," but I didn't. Instead I reminded my friend that we are the directors in our own movies.

My friend was choosing to create a reality he couldn't trust because his feelings had been hurt. And I chose not to judge my friend for not wanting to grow. I blessed him and our relationship and proceeded to move forward as if everything was back in balance. About ten days later, he called and before I could say a word, he said, "I know you think I'm a chicken shit." We both laughed. "I wasn't afraid to trust, I was afraid to grow." I admire my friend's courage. He's one of the most honest and open men I know. His courage not only inspired me to be more open in my dealings with people but it also gave us the chance to have a deeper, more real connection with each other.

"They Did This to Me"

When's the last time you said, "I can't believe you'd do that to me. I'd never do that to you"? or another favorite, "I don't deserve this." Ever made one of those statements? We all have. The ego is turning cartwheels when it hears us utter one of those phrases. It's got us exactly where it wants us—wasting away in Victimville. I'm not going to talk about "giving away your power" because that's not really what being a victim is to me. A victim is someone who lives life as a "reactor." Everything happens "to" them. Likewise, they don't typically participate in the creation of anything they want in their lives. I coach men and women of all ages, ethnicities, and backgrounds, and there is one thing that is constant across all past and current clients. They approach their lives either proactively or reactively. There's no in-between. They're either seeking new ways of doing things, or they're waiting to see how things are going to be handed to them. For those in the latter group, they are always devastated by the decisions of others that affect them. I once spoke at a conference where a woman rushed over after hearing me talk about creating multiple streams of income. During my keynote, I'd ask the audience a poignant question. If your employer walked into the office tomorrow morning and announced massive layoffs, would you be able to maintain your current lifestyle? By a show of hands, more than 80 percent of the audience said "no," they would not be able to continue living the same lifestyle. Those folks in the 80 percent represent most of the human population. They react. Their motto is they'll cross that bridge when they get to it.

They don't see a need to prepare for the unexpected. The other 20 percent of the audience was already actively engaging in passive or residual income opportunities. They were proactive. When I suggested that the 80 percent were setting themselves up to be victims, I could hear a collective moan sweep across the room. No one likes to be labeled a victim. Yet we don't do anything to avoid having the experience of a victim. We don't want to think about the prospect of losing a job, losing a loved one unexpectedly, or losing our health. Those are the unthinkables. We'd rather continue going through life as if all is well, even when it is not. And just so we're not confused, I'm not talking about having a positive and affirming disposition despite your circumstances, I'm talking about setting yourself up to feel bad later on, about an experience that you can avoid.

We invite this experience because we want to be able to say, "Look at what they did to me!" Somehow this has become some kind of badge of honor when in reality it does nothing but highlight our need to be victims.

Freeing yourself from wanting to be a victim takes work and courage. It's less soothing to look at ourselves in the mirror and say, "You know what? I put myself in the position to have that happen. I can learn from that experience and move on." That's too painful for most people. Yet I find that it takes the judgment out of the equation. I don't have to judge the person who supposedly "did something to me," and I don't have to judge me for being a willing participant.

THE REAL CHALLENGE

Over the next twenty-four hours become more aware of how much ego guides your life. Notice your interaction with your friends and family. See if you can feel yourself wanting to be right in most instances when it really doesn't matter who's right. Become more aware of how much you judge even the slightest of things—the clothes someone's wearing, the way someone laughs, the choice someone makes.

Pay attention to your energy toward strangers. Are you impatient with the person in line in front of you? Do you wish they would have gotten their money out before they got to the front of the line? Do you find yourself getting irritated because you're hungry and your spouse is taking too long to get dressed? Do you find yourself sending the customer service rep negative vibes when they put you on hold? You will become acutely aware of the ego's role in your life.

If you've never been keenly aware of ego's presence before this book, it'll be extremely difficult for you not to notice it from now on. Our problem is not that we don't want to be more spiritual, we'd prefer to just take the pill for spirituality rather than doing the things necessary to step into our spiritual mastery. That's like saying you want to do a triathlon but you have no interest in learning how to swim. It's not going to happen.

The challenge is not to fight with your ego but to become more committed to spiritual fitness. It's time to make spiritual mastery more than an occasional trip to the "gym." Like champion-level athletes, we must exercise our spiritual muscles to actualize fully as human beings. Without doing enough "reps," we'll experience spiritual atrophy.

Our spiritual chops become dull, and nothing would please your ego more than to know that you've "let yourself go" spiritually. This would mean that the ego is again your personal trainer in this life. What keeps us from living our best life isn't all the stuff we think holds us back—lack of money, opportunity, or connections. What robs us of our fullest potential is the trickery of our egos. That's why we must retire it. Totally take it out of our game of life. Once we can confidently know in our hearts that the world needs us to become spiritual giants, the battle between love and ego will dissipate because ego will know that it no longer has dominion over our lives.

Ego knows that the real you is the Highest You. When you decide to become all of who you are, the ego will limp away with its tail between its legs. It will have sung its last song. The curtain will fall and there will be no encore.

WHAT'S ON YOUR SPIRITUAL MENU?

What nurtures you spiritually? Are you getting enough spiritual food each day to sustain you through the rigors of an ego-centered universe? Spiritual food comes in many forms. You can listen to CDs, read books, take a long walk, look into the eyes of someone you love, appreciate nature, pray—the list is endless!

If we are not careful, we will find ourselves run down by the cares of the ego. We've become so enamored with outer success and achievement that we forget to nurture ourselves spiritually. And when we hit the wall, we have the nerve to ask ourselves, "Why am I so tired?" Spiritual fatigue cannot be healed with a bottle of the hottest new sports drink. Spiritual exhaustion happens to all of us who are bogged down by the demands of our external world.

This is why there's always a collection of inspirational audio in my car. This is why I have a playlist on my iPod of nothing but spiritually themed music and content. This is why sometimes I have to take a break from the world and retreat to a quiet place where I can actually hear my own voice and intuition. When we monitor our spiritual diets, we become much more conscientious of what we're feeding our spirits and we become much more in tune with what we intend for our lives. Like a balanced nutritional food diet we must also have a balanced spiritual diet. This may include prayer, meditation, reflection, and communion in the ways that speak directly to your own individual spiritual needs. This is key. Just as no two people have the same bodies, no two people walk the same spiritual path. No two people will need identical spiritual nutrients.

If we were to take an inventory of our daily activities, we'd discover that most of the things we engage in each day feed our egos rather than our spirits. We must bring ourselves back into balance with spiritual nourishment. The time we spend nurturing ourselves spiritually prepares us for those moments when the ego will attempt to sneak back into our lives. That's why we must become spiritual athletes—individuals who practice heart-centered living on a moment-by-moment basis. The more we respond to our daily challenges with love and compassion, the less likely we are to fall back into our ego-driven mind-set. Finally, the only way to truly retire your ego is by aligning your intention with the desire to live a life based on faith rather than fear.

REAL QUESTIONS, REAL ANSWERS

As a corporate executive in a fast-paced company, I'm concerned that if I retire my ego, I'll be perceived as "soft" or less capable of doing my job. How do I deal with this?

It's the seduction of the ego that makes us think people won't respect us if we come from our hearts. That is one of the top-selling products from Ego Central. As you begin to replace heart with ego, you'll see an amazing shift in how people respond to you. Being a heart-centered leader doesn't mean that you lose the ability to make sound business decisions. Your intellect doesn't take a hike just because you replace previous ego-driven tactics with heart-centered principles. And guess what? Those around you will actually grow in admiration and respect because your heart-centeredness "disables" the ego, allowing for a much more open interaction and experience in all areas of your life. Try it.

I'm raising two teenagers who are always trying to get away with things. I find myself being very ego-based and not wanting to appear "weak" for fear that they'll run over me.

You are not alone in this fear. Most parents perceive that if their children don't fear them, they will not have any impact on their children's decisions. Nothing could be farther from the truth. First, consider changing your perception that your kids are "trying to get away with things." The only thing kids are trying to do is find their way in the world. It has nothing to do with their parents. They are attempting to answer the same questions we're all trying to answer: Who is the real me? Yes, it is important to create an environment such that your kids understand that your guidelines are in place to ensure as much safety for them as possible. When kids understand that you are "concerned" about their well-being and not just trying to "control" them, they respond in ways that surprise most parents. Talk to your kids and encourage them to share with you without the threat of punishment, and watch your relationship grow into one that is based on mutual respect and love, rather than authority and domination.

WILL THE REAL YOU PLEASE STAND UP?

Embrace Your Spirit

God, if you're out there, why can't I see you?
I guess you're kinda like the wind, huh?
—*Gregory, 7*

A man died and upon entering heaven was assigned his own private escort. His escort showed him around heaven, and they came upon a large contingent of people in a corner. The escort whispered in the man's ear, "Those are the Catholics. They're having their Wednesday mass." The man nodded and they continued to walk. "And see over there," the escort leaned in. "Those are the Baptists. Midday prayer service." The man looked intrigued. "Oh, and in that corner over there, the Lutherans. They . . . " The man interrupted, asking his escort a question, "Sorry to interrupt, but why are you whispering?" The escort pulled the man closer. "They all think they're the only ones here."

DEFINING SPIRITUALITY

I love when I hear people say, "I'm not religious, I'm spiritual," as if the two have to be mutually exclusive. The word "religion" has a black eye these days such that people prefer to let others know they aren't like "those people."

Mention the word "spirituality," and you may find yourself in a three-hour-long conversation. It's a term that has many meanings depending on whom you talk to. You're not likely to hear the same definition twice, but here are some of the more common responses to "What is spirituality?":

• That which renews, uplifts, edifies, comforts, and heals.
• An inner sense that one's existence transcends one's circumstances.
• An approach to living that emphasizes that which cannot be seen.
• An attachment to religious values, or to things of the spirit, rather than physical, human, or worldly things.
• A sense that there is something or someone greater than ourselves.

Spirituality isn't about the absence of material things; it's about losing one's "attachment" to those things. It's about recognizing that your identity isn't tied to what you own. Spirituality is beyond the physical.

If those are some of the elements of spirituality, what then is Spirit? When they hear the word "Spirit," many people tend to think of the supernatural. In religious and metaphysical settings, Spirit may be used to refer to God, the Creator, or the Divine presence. Spirit may also refer to the essential element present in human souls, through which we are all connected to the earth. That is why when we die, we are still present. That's why I can still hear my high school basketball coach's laughter even though he died twenty years ago. That's why I can catch a glimpse of my sister's essence when she leaves Los Angeles. We're all connected by Spirit. It is through Spirit that we commune with God because God is not human. What I love about the word Spirit is that it is infinite. It banishes any references to God as human. And while intellectually we all understand that God is not human, we tend to relate to God as if God were human.

In fact, most people relate to God as a grand, white male (probably bearded) with a thunderous voice. With this God we send up prayers (because for some reason we think heaven is actually a place beyond the sky) in hopes that those prayers will be looked upon favorably and

WILL THE REAL YOU PLEASE STAND UP?

answered. In fact, that's why many of us think that we drive the cars we drive and live in the homes we live in—because God, the great vending machine, has smiled on us and answered our prayers. If that's your perception of God, it is very limited.

When my agent was shopping the proposal for this book, one potential buyer responded by saying, "We are an XYZ publisher. We are not interested in more pluralistic views." Pluralistic views? Apparently this publisher saw only one path to God and saw this book as an attempt to encourage people to experience God as they choose so that they could get closer to becoming more of who they truly are. The potential buyer was right. That's exactly what this book is about.

I chided my agent for sending my proposal to publishers who believe that God can only be experienced in one way—their way. His response was that "he thought he'd give it a shot." My agent, a compassionate and open guy, didn't realize the extent to which we humans thrive on being "right" even when it comes to God—*especially* when it comes to God.

Having grown up in a neighborhood where "pluralism" was rampant, I had an appreciation for others' spirituality and religious beliefs, even when I didn't understand them, which was most of the time. I had sense enough to know that it wasn't possible for God to be seen through only one lens. In my neighborhood, there were Baptists, Jehovah Witnesses, Pentecostals, Muslims, Buddhists, Catholics, and a bevy of other spiritual tastes and preferences. I'll never forget one blazing summer day when I started to truly see how people used God as a tool to enslave and terrify people into "doing the right thing."

I was about eight at the time. My cousin Ron, who was two years older, was visiting me, and all the kids were on my porch talking about God. We were a spirited little group of about six kids, ranging in age from seven to ten. It was a Sunday and we were sharing freely about God and what we thought God was like and why things were the way they were in the world. An older girl, probably eleven or so, came over from down the street. She attended what we called a "holiness" church. Full Gospel Holiness Church was the name of it. Her mother was devout. They never wore pants. They were forever in church, and honestly, we barely saw the little girl except when she was getting in their car to go to church or getting out of their car coming from church. And when we did see her, she was always talking about the "evils" of the world, never about the kinds of stuff kids talked about. At eleven years old! On this particular day, she sauntered over and joined our God conversation. "The world's coming to an end, ya know," she blurted out. "If you aren't 'saved,' you're going to burn forever and ever." The crowd went numb. Burn forever and ever? She continued her tirade. "That means you and you and you," she pointed with conviction. Then she turned to Ron. "Do you wanna burn in hell forever and ever?" He started to cry. He was so cute. He shook his head "no." "Then repeat these words after me." I don't remember what happened next. The ice cream truck came by or somebody's mother called out to him or her, but for some reason she didn't get a chance to finish her sentence or terrorize us any longer, thank goodness. But I'll never forget that day. I'll never forget the look in her eyes as she spoke with authority about something her eleven-year-old mind couldn't have possibly fully understood. I can still hear the thunder in her voice as she talked about turning our lives over to God or being sentenced to eternal damnation. I'll never forget my cousin's bloodshot eyes and his trembling lips as she spoke to him. But mostly I'll never forget that I didn't buy one word she said. I don't know why. There was something not quite right about her "presentation." I had gotten various presentations of what and who God was over the years, but this was, by far, the most terrifying one of them all. It was all very confusing to my eight-year-old ears. But I never forgot it. I suppose I never will.

That little girl was doing what I'm sure she's seen someone else do. She was modeling behavior that she believed to be appropriate, but who really has the authority to tell you that what you believe is wrong? I don't have the authority to decide what is right or wrong for your life. No one does. I wrote this book to ask you to search your own heart to decide if what you believe about God and Spirit serves you. And if it doesn't, then it's time to have a fire sale! Time to toss out all of the ideologies that are steeped in fear rather than love. The only way to get to the real you is to clean out your spiritual closet. There are things that have never made sense to me, but rather than be angry about what humans have institutionalized, I asked God to reveal the truth to me about what is right for my life. What's right for me may not be right for you, and what serves best your mother or father's highest good may not serve your highest good. It's okay! It's really okay to leave the pack and explore your own spirituality. So many people are afraid to go against the "establishment." That establishment may not be your church or spiritual community. It may be your family, your culture, or your social group. It doesn't matter which "institution" is holding you back, you can walk away from it. All of our lives have been informed by the things and people who were around us as we were coming into being. There's no judgment about what those people taught us, but I don't have to believe what my mother believes about God or anything else for that matter. What she believed apparently worked for her. It may not work for me.

So, yes, there is danger in believing something simply because someone you care about says it is so or because you're afraid to "not" believe it. As frightening as it may appear to be, exploration is the only way you can truly know Spirit for yourself.

SET YOUR SPIRIT FREE

It's time for you to become a free spirit again—the way you were when you were about one week old. Remember when you were one week old? Don't laugh! There are people who even have prebirth memories. That was a time in our lives when we understood who we were. Before we became bombarded with all of the messages about who we are and who we're supposed to be.

I wanted to follow the ego chapter with one that challenged you to journey back to your innocence. When you were walking in the spirit of love, light, bliss, and joy. It's been so long since most of us walked in that space, it's hard to remember, isn't it? It's still possible, though. I catch glimpses of my own innocence many times a week, and when I'm there, it is truly an amazing atmosphere. One of the reasons we don't experience that level of joy as adults is that we believe that it has to go away once we hit a certain age. Not so. The giddiness and pure elation that you see in the eyes of children is still very much a part of you, we've simply silenced it. We've put it way back in the back of our cupboards of life.

When a kid gives his parent a Mother's or Father's Day sweater or a tie that he made with items around the house, do you think that kid cares how his parent looks in that outfit? Not at all. To him, they look like a million bucks.

This is the kind of innocence that draws us nearer to our spirituality. Yet when people think of becoming more spiritual, they often have visions of quiet rooms with lots of prayer, chanting, or meditation. Those are definitely activities that can support you on your spiritual path, but the level of spirituality I'm challenging you to explore in this chapter is Practical Spirituality—communion that you can practice no matter where you are. You don't need to be in a yoga studio or church or on a sandy beach on the coast of Fiji. Spirituality is a state of being. It's the space where you dwell regardless of where your physical body rests. It's not like cologne or perfume, it doesn't wear off as the day goes on. It's not just something you feel when you're in certain buildings or environments. It's a deep resonance and connection that affects the way you see the world, the way you move through the world, the way you respond to everyday events and the way you treat the world.

So now that we've begun the process of retiring our ego (we have begun that process, haven't we?), we can begin to truly appreciate what it means to lead a Spirit-driven life. A life that is all about walking in your higher purpose at all times. If we look at the five primary areas our lives revolve around: physical, spiritual, financial, mental, and emotional—together, they make up what I call the Wholeness Matrix. It's one of the tools I use to keep me on track.

THE WHOLENESS MATRIX:
FIVE BUILDING BLOCKS

I call this a "Wholeness Matrix" because the ultimate goal is to be whole in all areas of our lives. Wholeness, not perfection in the ego's terms, is that which helps us to keep our lives in "perfect" balance. You are not broken, and you're certainly not incomplete. We're all in varying stages of "development." Much like a house, you will go through phases where renovation is needed. Some of us will need a touch-up or redesign, while others may need a demolition crew to come in and build a whole new foundation! Wherever you are today is fine and exactly where you should be today. The amount of work to be done on your house will depend on how serious you are about becoming the real you.

At the center of our lives and the matrix—whether we acknowledge it or not—is our spiritual connection. It touches every area of our lives—relationships, career, purpose, bodies, and soul. It is placed at the center of the Matrix on purpose—to remind you that Spirit is at the center of who we are.

In the upper left hand corner is our physical self. Our bodies are the vehicles by which we get to travel through this amazing journey. It's our vessel, our instrument. In the upper right hand corner is the financial block, representing more than money and career. This block represents our connection to abundance, prosperity, and the tangible manifestation of our spiritual energies. Money is more than a physical currency; it's also a spiritual currency. But it's only one of the ways that we can be reminded of abundance. In the bottom left box is our emotional self—the place where we store our feelings. I see our emotional self as the motor for our being. Finally, in the lower right box is our mental self, the center of our intellectual prowess as well as mental health.

If you were to take a pen and draw diagonal lines from one corner to the opposite corner, you'd have what looks like an "X," signifying the inner connectedness of every single aspect of our Selves. Most important, you'll see that you can't draw the lines without passing through Spirit. Everything we see, touch, feel, smell, hear, or experience contains Spirit.

This is to remind us that not only is there is a spiritual component to all areas of our lives but that the answer to every challenge we face can be found by turning toward, not away from love and spirit.

Fran's Wholeness Matrix

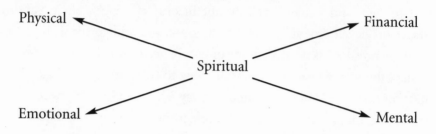

There are several other relational components that the Matrix provides. Let' s explore them briefly. First, draw four additional imaginary lines on the matrix.

1) One from Physical to Financial
2) One from Emotional to Mental
3) One from Physical to Emotional
4) One from Financial to Mental

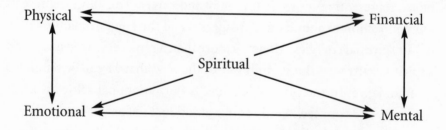

Physical to Financial: When we worry about money, does it affect our physical health? You bet it does. Finances are one of the top reasons that people have stress in their lives. When people are stressed out, what do they typically do? They seek to harm themselves either with food (or without food), drugs, alcohol, or death.

Emotional to Mental: When we feel emotionally safe in the world and in our relationships it has a profound impact on our mental health. The lesson is to maintain healthy relationships first with yourself, then with others, and, finally, the larger world. This balance will keep you emotionally and mentally nourished.

Physical to Emotional: I believe that what's on the inside manifests on the outside. Acne isn't something that starts because of something that's attacking your face from the outside. The problem must be addressed from within. When we address, work through, and heal our emotional wounds good health is the result. I'm amazed that most people don't make the connection between their emotional wealth and health and their physical fitness and wellness. They are inextricably connected. If you're noticing that you're gaining or losing weight, or just not feeling well, there's something going on inside of you.

Financial to Mental: If money is one of the primary reasons that people stress, consider the cost of continuous stress on your mental health. A crippled mental health will impact every single aspect of your life. If you don't feel psychologically balanced, you will have a difficult time functioning at optimal levels at home, work, church, or play. Where money and mental health are concerned we can do one of two things to improve the scenario. We can either stop worrying about money or we can improve our financial reality so that we remove the source of the stress.

Your Eternal Flame

Inside all of us burns a light. We come here with it, and throughout the course of our lives that light, that flame, either burns bright or it flickers. It can never be blown out without our permission. Even when it appears dark in our lives, that light is still there. Imagine, if you will, walking along a deserted path. In the distance you see a house. You can't tell if anyone is home, but you see the light. You are miles away, but you can still see that light. It's the same with our eternal flame. It is forever burning.

We allow this light to be blown out by our own fears or the illusions of those around us, but the light is still there.

In the daily grind of work, home, and play, the challenge is to let that light shine so that you can see the path that has been laid for you. Your heart houses your light; therefore, your light is safe from any outside forces that might cause it to flicker—the wind, the rain, the storms of indifference. None of these things can touch your light unless you open the door.

In the 2006 movie *Akeelah and the Bee,* an adolescent girl shows us what it looks like when we're afraid to let our flames burn bright. She attends an inner-city school where most of the outside world doesn't believe in the promise of the young minds coming from her neighborhood. In the midst of the low expectations she learns about a spelling bee. Then, with a bit of encouragement from some teachers, mentors, and friends, she decides to go for it and enter the school's spelling bee. As soon as she makes that decision she experiences the fallout of "letting her light shine." Kids start to make fun of her, her brother teases her, and her mother doesn't provide much support at first. Rather than fight for the right to be great, Akeelah decides to play small. The price of accepting her greatness is too costly for her. The discomfort she feels by allowing her gifts to flourish is emotionally unbearable, so she quits. You'll have to rent the DVD to see all of the steps that lead her back to the real Akeelah but essentially she learns that she is doing herself a great injustice by not unleashing her genius. Isn't that what we all go through at some point in our lives? No one wants to be ridiculed, least of all for our gifts. Yet the journey from hiding your talents to standing tall in them is one that is full of all kinds of rewards, as Akeelah bravely shows us in one of the best family films I've seen in a long time. Rent it; you'll be glad you did.

CONNECTING TO SPIRIT

It's my sincere desire to commune as closely with God as I possibly can. Staying connected spiritually is like having wireless Internet—it's always there. Sometimes conflicts arise in our lives that move us away from who we are, but we are always connected to Spirit.

When people speak of conflict, they typically think of an argument, a fight, or a disagreement, but conflict can be something simple as an idea that's contrary to your idea. We experience conflict many times a day—hundreds of times a day! And how we handle it reveals our true relationship with Spirit.

When life is good, it is easy to be with Spirit, to be spiritual. It's easy to be grateful, and appreciation is effortless. But when things get rough, sometimes we revert to being Earthlings, to our old ways. We go back to responding to circumstances from the ego rather than the heart. Though we're spiritual beings, we're all also human beings. The real you strives to see the world through spiritual eyes. That's what it means to embrace Spirit. To know that there's more to life than meets the eye. There's more to this journey than what we can see, feel, touch, hear, or taste. There's more.

Becoming one with your spiritual self is truly knowing peace. Those who go through the world approaching and explaining life only in physical terms miss the moments that transform. They miss the opportunities to transcend their circumstances.

For me, spirituality is about being consciously aware of the duality of our existence. To nurture a deeper and wider connection to Spirit, you must take the time to feel the connection. You are infinitely connected to that which is greater than you. This reality creates amazing possibilities for us to grow and expand in all areas of our lives. What will it take for you to feel intimately connected to Spirit?

One afternoon in early 2005, I had my first known near-death experience. I was returning from a consulting session with a production company for a show we were doing for The Learning Channel. I was on the 101 Freeway near Ventura, California, just outside of Los Angeles. At this particular juncture, the 101 Freeway is five to six lanes wide. On this day, a few yards ahead of me was an eighteen-wheeler that I noticed was swerving back and forth between two lanes. It was as if the wind were swaying it every few seconds. Behind me was a highway full of four-o'clock traffic. Suddenly a white compact car drove up beside me. A young guy who couldn't have been older than nineteen or twenty smiled as he passed me. And just as his car pulled in front of me to pass the eighteen-wheeler, the back of the truck clipped the guy's car. The force tossed the little car to the left toward a cement embankment. It bounced off the wall and ricocheted across three lanes in slow motion until it came to a complete stop one inch from the front of my car. The side of the small car was perpendicular to my car, which meant that the young guy and I were again face to face. His heart was pounding so fiercely that I could literally see his chest moving inward and outward. He looked so frightened. His dog was in the backseat barking like crazy. I rolled down my window and asked if he needed me to call anyone. He didn't answer at first. He was in shock.

He looked around his car for his phone and found it. Behind me were about fifty cars (across multiple lanes) that just sat still. Slowly the cars started to pull around my car and the young guy's car. The eighteen-wheeler had pulled off to the side. "You're sure you're okay?" I asked. He nodded yes, and I eventually pulled away slowly.

We've all had near-death experiences whether we know it or not. Some people are forever changed when something near-death happens to them. I was grateful that I had another opportunity to do the things I love because I know there'll come a day when my clock will expire. I did change that day, but not in the way most people speak of when they have a near-death experience. I didn't call all of my loved ones to tell them I loved them. I didn't go to a church service that night. I simply looked in my rear view mirror at the young guy as he and the driver of the eighteen-wheeler exchanged information, and I said, "Thank you." But after that incident I did have a greater appreciation for my life. It's a rarity that I drive on a freeway when I don't think about that day on the 101. There was something very spiritual about that experience. I believe that there had to have been an army of angels out that day because everything about that accident was too surreal. The fact that there were no cars traveling at high speeds on the highway until after the young man's car hit the embankment and slid in front of my car. The fact that I happened to be driving just the right speed to keep me from being too close to the young man's car or the truck ahead of us. When things like this happen I become keenly aware of the world we cannot see. When those kinds of things happen it's very difficult to ignore the spirit world we inhabit.

Becoming More Spiritually Aware

People who don't acknowledge their spiritual existence are nonetheless spiritual. Spirit doesn't rely on acknowledgment. It just is! However, the individual who is keenly aware that they are a human as well as a spiritual being will be able to tap into new levels of alertness, aliveness, and awareness that helps them to see the path to their real selves, their highest self.

The spiritually aware person knows that we can tap into the world beyond the physical. That's why we hear music after the radio is turned off. That's why we can smell someone's fragrance even though we haven't seen them in three years. That's why we can hear the voice of someone who's been dead for ten years. We can't see, feel, touch, hear, or taste any of these things, but they are still there.

Spiritually aware beings get beyond the physical and emotional layers that cloud the truth. As you continue on the path of spiritual alertness, you'll begin to live more consciously in the unseen world, both metaphorically and physically. In every situation there are spiritual forces at play. Discerning those forces will allow you to find greater peace and harmony in your relationships as well as in your professional and social lives. Spiritual athletes know that it is possible to approach or respond to all situations from a place of Spirit. It may not always be easy, but it's still possible.

Spiritual warriors know that there's no such thing as enemies—only teachers. As I mentioned in the earlier discussion on archetypes, we can no longer afford to see the people in our lives as villains even when it's clear that they don't have our highest good at heart. I've given you the tools to be able to understand their roles in your life so that you can stop the cycle of returning negative energy to those who send it your way. This one requires a great deal of discipline, especially since we've been programmed to see the characters in our lives as "good guys" versus "bad guys."

REAL STORY

I recently had an experience with a wonderful soul who played the role of Messenger in my life story. We were planning to work on a film together, and we were both excited about the process of creating something memorable, something we could both be proud of. His portfolio of work was solid and his ethic was impeccable. As with most partnerships, we needed to get all of the "paperwork" behind us so that we could move forward on the project. He sent over an agreement that was drafted by "his people." I was to review it and get back to him over the weekend. His agreement was a great start; however, it contained tons of deal points that weren't exactly appropriate for the kind of project we were working on— a documentary, a low- to no-budget documentary, on top of that. As I skimmed his agreement and began to "red-line" it, I made notes about the areas that I felt needed to change from my perspective. "I want to look at this and have my attorney review it as well, so let's talk about it some more. I have some ideas that I think will work for us both," I said.

I left his home that day feeling quite optimistic that we'd be able to craft an agreement that felt right for both of us. A week or so later, I presented him with an agreement that had been drafted by an entertainment attorney. One that was significantly different from the one he'd sent to me a week earlier.

When I woke up the next morning, around seven o'clock, I had an e-mail from him. It was one of those "we regret to inform you" e-mails. He was dropping out of the project because the agreement we sent over "insulted" him. He wished me well and told me that my materials would be available for pickup during certain hours. I was shocked—not that he'd dropped out of the project but that he chose to e-mail me rather than continuing to communicate with me in the open manner in which we'd grown accustomed for nearly three months. It was a strange shift in spiritual energy.

I immediately picked up the phone to call him. Yes, at seven o'clock! We'd developed a friendly rapport so I felt completely fine about waking him up (which I soon found out that I had done). When our conversation ended about an hour later, I learned that his sense of self-worth had been challenged by the agreement the attorney had drafted. The agreement didn't feel right for him and so he chose not to continue on the project. He wanted more financial assurances, assurances that weren't feasible from our view. What we offered was too low and what he wanted, we felt was too high.

The deal fell through, which is just part of the business sometimes. My Messenger taught me a great lesson: even in business it's difficult not to take things personally. I had not taken his agreement personally, although it had pretty much asked for a huge stake in my film. In my mind, an agreement is a piece of paper. There were things in his agreement that wouldn't work for me. When I read them I voiced my concerns, and we had an open conversation about retooling the agreement to reflect a more realistic view of what was possible, given that we were essentially producing the film on speculation (that it would sell). That's the process of negotiation. You talk, you pull, you push, you talk some more, and then, if you're really fortunate, you come to terms that both parties can live happily with. That wasn't possible with this deal because he was so triggered by the terms outlined in our agreement that he shut down. There was no negotiating. It was over. Pick up your stuff, have a great life!

My Messenger gave me a great gift and message that day that I was able to implement in my life immediately. I needed to start with the end rather than allowing months to pass before I initiated the "business" part of a project. So that's exactly what I did. I thanked my Messenger and moved on.

I let the project rest for a few weeks, and then I put a notice on a popular entertainment job board. Within a few minutes I had five responses. I met with one of the guys who responded and this time when I sent over the agreement, I added: "This is simply a starting point. Please don't take this piece of paper personally; it's not a commentary on your self-worth. It's a place for us to start our conversations. I'm open to what the final document looks like." From there, we were able to have honest and honoring conversations about working together, and I have my Messenger to thank. I entered into a great collaboration and the film is on schedule to be completed soon. The process has been positive and my working relationship with my new editor is awesome.

Who are the Messengers in your life? Are you so triggered by the Messenger that you're missing the message? Sometimes we get stuck on the package or the delivery of the message or the messenger, and we can't get the profound words of wisdom that they have for us. Think about the characters in your life today. What roles are they playing in your growth?

MAKING THE SHIFT FROM EGO TO SPIRIT

Every encounter, every interaction, and every experience carries a spiritual message—sometimes many messages. Don't miss those. The problem is that most of the time we don't want to pick up our messages. Ever know that you have a voice mail but you didn't want to listen to your messages? It's the same way with spiritual messages. Most of the time they are coming as trumpets in a band—loud and clear—but what do we do? We pretend not to hear it. Sometimes the message will come in the form of us not getting something we thought we wanted. But instead of being thankful for what we didn't get, we keep knocking on the same door. The spiritual warrior sees the physical world as an open field, fertile with opportunities for growth and learning, a field that can lead us to higher levels and frequencies of love, mercy, and prosperity. There are two shifts you can make today that will elevate your level of spiritual awareness:

shift from trying to make things happen to letting them be, and shift from a perspective of being separate from everyone else in the world to knowing that we are all bound together.

Shift #1: Making It Happen Versus Letting It Be

Nonspiritual beings focus primarily on steely determination and ingenuity to manifest things in their lives. Spiritual beings turn their attention toward creating a oneness with what they wish to manifest in their lives. Now don't get this twisted, spiritual beings don't have the luxury of sitting on their cans and "waiting" for things to happen. Nothing can be farther from how we operate. We, too, have to work hard, exert effort, sweat, and strategize to get the results we want. The biggest difference isn't necessarily in the physical steps we take but in our intention. We trust that we will get what is ours. In other words, the people who are supposed to read this book will read this book. Those who are not, will not. I'm sure my publisher is banking on there being more of you who are supposed to pick it up than not!

By embracing Spirit you release yourself from having to "make" something happen (as if you could, anyway) and you ease into a space where you relax in the knowing that what will be, will be. My motto is to do the work and let it be. Try this approach and watch how much better you feel in your heart. Oh, your head won't initially feel better because the head's the ego's lounge. Your ego will tell you that you have to force people to see things your way; that you have to be manipulative if you want to get ahead and that you must always be in the driver's seat. The ego does not enjoy "being." That's not its natural habitat. That's why you are now under new management.

When we are truly aligned with our highest self, we are spiritual giants who are focused on the transformative power of love. We focus on creating a harmonious and peaceful world. We are in a state of balance. The world teaches us that we must always be watching our backs and on the lookout for traitors. As we grow spiritually we discover that these people are characters and elements that the world wants us to include in our life stories. We always have the choice to reject them or leave them on the cutting room floor.

Shift #2: I Am Better Versus You Are Connected to Everyone

Those who do not embrace Spirit often feel that they are somehow different from or better than those with whom they share the world. This sense of separation nurtures an incessant level of narcissism and self-absorption.

When a person feels separate from others he or she may unconsciously create a paranoia that is based on fear about others. In other words, a person who is completely self-centered rather than spirit-centered may always feel that "those" people are not worthy or not as good as people like me; or they may feel that people are trying to usurp their perceived power, take over the company, undercut them, or "do me in."

As spiritual warriors, we know that what we do to others we do to ourselves. When we speak affirming words about others, we speak those words about ourselves. Likewise, when we spew venom in the direction of those with whom we are upset, that same venom comes back to us. And this is not the boomerang effect that many of us grew up hearing about—the notion that if you cheat someone, that someone's going to cheat you. It's deeper than that. We all breathe the same air. Therefore, what we put into the universe—literally or spiritually—is inhaled by us all. That's why it's important to take care with what you put into the world. The Bible says, "They will know you are Christians by your love." This isn't a quote just for Christians. This is a declaration to us all. The world will know that you are seeking the Highest good by what you blast into the world.

Everyday Spirituality

What I'm proposing in this chapter is simple but not always easy. I'm encouraging you to see the spirit in everything and everyone you see. If you could bring greater spiritual aliveness and alertness into your life during the next twenty-four hours, would you? Or would you continue to live a mundane and lifeless existence? The new level of awareness I'm recommending comes from "everyday spirituality," simply living life in-spirit, or in-spired. This approach to life will create a more peaceful and joyful existence for you, guaranteed. Here's how we get there.

Step 1: In-Joy

Are you enjoying your life? If you're not, it's probably because you are not in-joy. You may actually be attempting to force yourself to be happy with your current living situation, job, or relationships. That's not being "in joy," that's going through the motions. Pick one of the five cornerstone areas in the Wholeness Matrix and make a decision to in-joy that area of your life. How is this different than trying to force yourself to be happy with your life? First, I recommend starting with an area that's not the toughest. In other words, if you know that your physical house—your body—is in a condemned state and about to be repo-ed, don't start there! It's going to be hard for you to get in-joy physically. Start with an area that's not in preforeclosure! Let's say you are struggling with seeing how blessed you are financially because you're not where you want to be at this point in your life. The easiest way to in-joy what you have is to be around people who have less than you—and I'm not talking about a little less than you, I'm talking significantly less than you. So, today, if you're unhappy with your financial picture, I invite you to find the poorest neighborhood in your city and walk through it. Notice I didn't say that you should drive through it; you need to know what it feels like to walk those streets. I have done exactly what I'm suggesting that you do and it cured me of any whining about how little I thought I had. I immediately had a new level of gratitude for everything I had. I was able to be financially in-joy after that trip.

Step 2: Know

There's a peace that comes from knowing. Think about those things you know. Things you are certain of. For me, those things are God's presence, my family's love, and the content of my character. Those are the top three things I know. What do you know? What are you sure of? Make a quick list or mental check of what you know to be true. These can be things about yourself or about the world around you. Things that even if you question, you are certain of their existence or meaning in your life.

Step 3: See Beauty Every Day

When I was playing professional basketball in Switzerland, one of my bedroom windows faced the most magnificent mountains I've ever seen in my life. This enormous, lush emerald landscape took my breath away on most mornings. Each morning (or afternoon if I'd had a late night the night before) I got to see the earth's beauty by simply drawing my blinds. When is the last time you noticed the beauty around you? The flowers, the lakes, mountains, trees, sky, or ocean? It's humbling to know that we as humans had nothing to do with any of those things. We don't build trees or engineer flowers or manufacture oceans. They are what they are, with or without us. That's beauty. Make time to see it today.

Step 4: Practice Wholiness

It's sometimes difficult to be kind and compassionate when people project their anger and insecurities in your direction, isn't it? As you move toward a more whole and real you, this will become less of a challenge because you will acknowledge that their actions are about them and not you. Your response is your responsibility. A few days ago I was having trouble getting my wireless Internet to function, and the customer service reps were telling me six different things. I'd talk to one and she'd tell me one thing. I'd hang up with that one and speak with another and he'd tell me something completely different. It was frustrating. After the third "runaround" phone conversation, I took a deep breath and said aloud, "I am choosing frustration in this moment." And in that moment I decided to have a different experience. I was frustrated for ten minutes, and once I held myself accountable for the frustration, I chose to move on because frustration was not an experience I wished to continue having. Wholiness is that place where you choose peace in the midst of whatever is going on in your life. It brings you back to the center. Back to love. Back to the real you.

Step 5: Bless Each Day

When you wake up in the morning, bless the day. Announce that no matter what the day brings, it's a blessing. The first word out of my heart and mouth when my eyes open is "thanks." I get at least that moment. The day isn't promised, but that "moment" is mine, and for that, I'm grateful. So, bless each day and know that whatever awaits you brings amazing lessons and blessings to you.

SEEING SPIRIT

Once we acknowledge that we're spiritual beings, we can begin to approach each situation with more spirit. We can begin to see the spirit in others, which is not always easy. By seeing the spirit in others we can begin to see their highest good (love), even when they can't! Seeing Spirit doesn't mean seeing "ghosts," it means not allowing the ego to engage you in a dance that would take you away from love.

RECEIVING SPIRIT

When you're about to turn down a certain street and something tells you to take another route, listen. When you meet someone and something tells you that you should heed their counsel, listen. This is Spirit— that intuition that knows what we don't always know, sees what we don't always see, and senses what we don't always initially sense. To connect with this intuition you must be open to receiving it. That which we want wants us. What we don't want repels us, too. In my book *The Intentional Millionaire,* I talk about our currency around money. Currency is energy.

So we all attach a certain energy to the money we give and the money we receive. Right now, my dear friend is avoiding me because he "thinks" he owes me money. Does he owe me money? No, he doesn't. I gave him the money he needed but he thinks I "loaned" it to him. And because he carries an energy, an indebted-like currency about "borrowing" money, he's probably not going to call me (or return my calls) until he can give me back the money I "gave" him. The currency we attach to our money will determine its presence in our lives. If at the core you do not want money to show up in your life, guess what? It will avoid you like the plague. In my Millionaire Spirit Boot Camps someone always says, "You mean subconsciously? Why would someone not want money in their life?" Well, for the same reasons we don't want love or success in our lives: fear. But wait, why would we fear having money? According to the people in my workshops, lots of reasons, including (1) not wanting other people to know that they have money because they'll ask to borrow it, (2) not having the courage to say no to people who ask for money, (3) not being able to manage it appropriately, or (4) fear of losing it all and being poor.

LIVING IN-SPIRIT

Underneath all of the stuff that we think is important—prestige, position, money—is a consciousness that is built on peace, harmony, and love. We can't live in-spirit by simply announcing that we're going to do it. That's a great start, but it's not the end of the road for spiritual athletes. Embracing spirit requires that we consistently commune in a place away from the chatter of the outside world. This isn't a physical place; it's an inner sanctuary that allows you to escape the noise of the ego. This place reminds you that you were born to be great and to do great things through your service and gifts to the world.

SPIRITUAL RECHARGE

Getting quiet may mean prayer for some people, meditation for others, and a ride through the country for others. There's no right or wrong way to be in-spirit. Don't let anyone sell you that! However, your commune is perfectly well and fine. We need alone time with God, Spirit, ourselves. It's the only way the world makes sense to me sometimes. To maximize this time, though, we also have to let go of what we've been told we have to do with our "quiet" time. Every person is different. What nourishes the real me may not nourish the real you. Just because your grandmother spends forty minutes in silence each morning before her first cup of tea doesn't mean that you should do the same. Find what recharges you spiritually because we all need to be plugged in to our Source.

Think of yourself as a lamp. Most lamps have to be plugged in to a "source" to work. Others can run on solar power for a certain amount of time. Sooner or later, though, that lamp needs to be put on the "power up" cradle so that it can recharge. This is analogous to what happens when we indulge in prayer, meditation, nature walks, and quiet time. We get our batteries charged. Some of us require longer recharge times than others. Some of us can plug in for a few minutes and be ready to go. Some of us need longer recharge times. Your recharging may even change over the years. When I first bought my laptop computer, it would run for about three to four hours on the battery alone. The older the computer got, though, the less effective that mode of charging became. Eventually, I had to buy a new battery, and I suspect that I'll also need to buy a new computer soon as well. Spiritual beings are the same way.

What recharges your battery today may not work next year or even next month for that matter. Living in-spirit means being open to and finding new ways of reinvigorating your spiritual life. It starts with plugging in to your source on a regular basis.

A Quick Word on Prayer

Prayer is a form of meditation and affirmation. When we pray, we enter into a wholly communion with our Source. Prayer isn't about cutting a deal with God; it's an opportunity to communicate with God. Therefore, this communication can happen anytime and anywhere. It doesn't have to be on your knees. It doesn't have to be in a quiet room with candles. There's no designated length of prayer or any key words that a prayer has to include. In fact, no words are even necessary.

We've come to think of prayer as an opportunity to dump our problems at the altar so that God will "fix" them. We've come to treat meditation as a chance to share our extended wish list of what we'd like to see God "do" for us in the upcoming fiscal year. We've come to treat prayer as something that has to be done in the morning when we wake up and at night before we go to sleep. If we get in a few reps during the day, those are bonus prayers.

To get a good sense of how many of us view prayer, rent the movie *Bruce Almighty,* starring Jim Carrey. In this film, Jim's character is endowed with the powers of God. He can bless and he can curse whomever he chooses. One night, his godly duties included answering e-mails. It's a hilarious scene to watch as his inbox nearly explodes with all of the prayer requests. Yet it also reveals how we view prayer. He received billions of e-mails asking him to grant wishes that ranged from curing diseases to getting someone into Harvard to helping someone get approved for a loan. This is how we typically pray.

When prayer is something that we send "out," having faith that we'll get something back, we miss the opportunity to strengthen our connection with our Source. That's why I believe prayer is more of an affirmation of what we wish to show up in our lives than a 1-800 request line that we perceive to have been busy when our demands aren't met.

If we want to be in a loving romantic relationship, we must pray that we will continue to embody the love that we want to show up in our lives, rather than asking that the perfect mate be sent to us. If we desire financial riches beyond what we've ever imagined for our lives, we must affirm that we are good stewards of financial wealth. If we desire optimal health, we must affirm our body's systems throughout the day so that they will respond to our desire for a strong, vibrant body. We must become one with our prayers rather than simply sending them out over the proverbial heavenly airwaves in hopes of a favorable response. When we know and have faith that God desires what is righteous in and for us, guess what? Our prayers are already answered.

A Deeper Prayer

While we all have our own systems for praying, I've come to appreciate several exercises that have taken me deeper into communion and farther away from my ego.

I've found that it's much easier to get clear when the space around me is peaceful. Breathing is a powerful way to connect to Spirit, so I recommend taking a few deep breaths. As you breathe in love, power, abundance, compassion, prosperity, and peace, you simultaneously exhale everything that is not those things: fear, worry, doubt, lack, limitation, envy, insecurity, and condemnation. Inhale all that is good and exhale all that is not. Now visualize beauty, love, peace, and prosperity. Everyone sees something different. You may see an ocean or a sunrise while someone else sees the mountains or the trees. Allow your own creativity to take over. As you sink deeper into love and more into your heart, you may start to feel your body relax and you may even start to smile. Let that joy overcome you. You are in a spiritual place, and it is supposed to engulf you.

SOLVING PROBLEMS WITH SPIRIT

The solutions to most of our challenges are right in front of us. From health to finances to relationships, the solution is always located in the challenge. When we can't see the solution, it's often because we're seeing the challenge only as something that is impeding our progress rather than as something we can step into to develop skills or learn more about ourselves. When we approach challenges by seeing them as stepping stones to stronger spiritual muscles, we breathe new life and energy into our challenges. They're no longer problems, they're opportunities. They're openings to new levels of awareness.

I had to take a large dose of this medicine recently when someone I attempted to support truly challenged me to decipher whether I was responding based on ego or Spirit. This woman was an artist who needed help getting her work placed. She asked me to give her feedback on it since I'd gone through a similar process myself. I was happy to help her and even provided a prototype of the product for her to use as a template. I told her that the model I was providing to her was what someone had provided to me and several other entrepreneurs, all of whom had great success.

I encouraged her not to reinvent the wheel but to instead "follow the program." She seemed receptive to those suggestions. I also told her that I was working on a book at the time and that my time was limited, but that I'd be happy to give her one round of feedback on her project. She agreed and off we went. I put her in touch with some of my professional colleagues who offered to help her bring her product to market because of my referral. I reiterated to her that my time was very tight and that I could review her product only one time and provide extensive notes. I wouldn't have time to do more than that. She understood and seemed up to the challenge.

Weeks later, she sent me her project with a long note about what she "wanted me to do on this next round of notes." Not only had she not followed the model that would have almost ensured her success at completing the project, but she also told me that she thought she'd have a better shot at success if she did it "her way," a way, incidentally, that included leaving out critical elements that a potential buyer would look for.

I went through the project and gave her the notes I promised her, telling her that she had a great start and that hundreds of people had done a project similar to hers, including me, and that if she wanted to sell the product, she should consider including the specs from the original model. She thanked me for the notes, and I thought that was the end of that.

A few days later, though, she sent me her second round of product developments, even though I'd made it abundantly clear that I was not available for more consultations given my commitment to the research and writing of my book. "As I shared a month ago," I wrote, "My current commitments do not allow me time to look at what you've sent." I never looked at her next round of changes.

That day I was sharing the story with a friend of mine, telling her how amazed I was that this artist who barely had a roof over her head would venture off to "do her own thing," when her success as we'd laid it out for her was all but guaranteed. I was shocked, actually. I would have loved for someone to lay out a plan for me, step by step. It's like being an apprentice to someone who's a master level expert. My friend and I talked briefly about being able to help only people who want to be helped. Then she asked, "Was there any part of your ego that enjoyed telling her that you couldn't assist her?"

I thought for a second. "No." It was an honest response. I was amused by this artist's audacity, but I laughed about that and spoke from my heart.

Sometimes we confuse human generosity with spiritual obligation. We are never obligated to help people beyond what we can do. I was on a deadline, and more important, I'd given this woman a prescription—and a free $5,000 consultation—for getting what she wanted, which she chose to ignore. That's not my problem. So, my work was done, as far as I was concerned. I had no emotional attachment to her decision not to follow the wisdom of those who'd gone before her, and I had no remorse about not being able to help her after she failed to follow instructions the first time. There's a beautiful Chinese proverb that says, "To know the road ahead, ask those coming back." This artist clearly thought she'd fare better by ignoring the advice of not one, but several artists, who'd successfully walked down the path she was about to get on. That decision was certainly her prerogative. Sometimes we think that blunt honesty is ego talking. It's not. Unless we attempt to make it personal or hurt someone with our words, being straightforward is not an Ego-centered behavior. It's as close to the heart as we can get.

HEALING YOUR FAMILY WITH LOVE

Your family can mean many different things, so don't limit what I'm about to say to your blood relatives. Rather, extend your love to our whole human family. This story happens to be about my brother, but it illustrates the power of love and kindness for all.

This year, my brother Larry turned fifty years old. We decided to throw him a birthday bash. We invited our extended family, of course, as well as some of his high school and college buddies. There was never any doubt in our minds that we were going to honor him on this milestone day, but for Larry, the day meant more than cake and candles. The gesture was confirmation that he was in our hearts.

You see, Larry has always been a rebel. He was the kid in the family that if Mom told him to be home by 11:00, he'd roll in at 11:15. He was an incredible basketball player whose artistry on the court made him one of the top talents in the country during his high school days. He was amazing to watch—flashy, unpredictable, and instinctive.

After he dropped out of college, we rarely saw him. And when Mom died, he became even more elusive. Over the past decade, though, he's been much more present in our lives. We always see him at the family reunions or other family gatherings. And occasionally he'll call out of the blue. Like I said, he's unpredictable.

My parents used to have regular barbecues at our house for him and his high school teammates. But this celebration was different. We were simply honoring him because we love him. It was a genuine show of our appreciation for who he is today. As he moved through the crowd, talking to people at the party, I could tell that this was more than a party. He was moved beyond words. In his birthday speech he said, "I never knew ya'll loved me to this degree."

We did, and we do. And ain't love grand?

So who can you love today? Call someone, write somebody, smile at a complete stranger, tell someone you appreciate them even when it's not their special day or their funeral. Just send love into the universe for no reason other than because it heals and restores.

So, when you get ready to blast pain, indifference, fear, or hate into the world, change your order. Think for a second and then send love instead.

Healing the World with Spirit

The Native Americans honored the land. They revered the Earth. They became one with their physical surroundings. This was sacred territory for them. To make the world a better place for us now, as well as for those who will follow us, we must have more respect for it. We must also allow our natural gifts to spring forth. We must work joyfully in our occupations, not because we're seeking a prize, but because we genuinely love what we do. And if you don't genuinely love what you do then find a job that you do genuinely love; or better yet, create an empire based on your passion and interests. When we ourselves are healed we are in a better position to do our part to heal the world and make a difference in our communities.

There aren't enough of us who believe we can make a difference in today's world. We become lethargic when it's time to elect public officials, saying that our vote doesn't matter. We won't picket City Hall because we believe the government is corrupt, and our voices won't be heard. We lock our doors, set our alarms, and check to make sure our gun is in the nightstand because the media has told us what a bad world we live in. We can't taste Spirit's sweet elixir of love and peace in our own homes because we've been seduced by negative images and rhetoric. Our world will not become a better place unless spiritual athletes get into the game. Too many of us are standing on the sidelines complaining and criticizing those who are engaged. The world we want to live in and the world we want our kids to inherit needs us to get involved.

This involvement starts within each of our own hearts. What you will become is already inside of you. We're all full of multiple seeds. If you plant a petunia seed, a lily is not going to grow. If you plant a tomato seed, a peach will not mysteriously appear. We must know that there are seeds of greatness in each of us. Our intention is the fertilizer that turns those seeds into what they already are.

The people we perceive as powerful men and women have the same seeds planted in them that we all have. The great athletes of our times have the same seeds in them that everyone else has. None of us is special, and all of us are special. The most provocative thinkers in history had the same seeds in them that you and I have. What makes a seed grow is that which nurtures it: water, sunlight, and air. Things that are in natural abundance. What nurtures greatness in the world is also in abundant supply.

Nothing magical heals us or the world we live in. What will make us more of who we are is the same thing that will make the world more of the place we want it to be—love.

Embracing your Spirit means many things. It means seeing the God (goodness) in all things. It means approaching every circumstance and situation with a desire to see not only what's good for you but also what's good in you. It means singing your song, telling your story, doing what makes your heart sing no matter what the world says or thinks. When you encounter fear or doubt or judgment, you can look it square in the eyes and say, "I am real, you are not."

Embracing Spirit means igniting your passion and not allowing anything to stamp out that fire that burns deep within all of us. That fire can set the world on fire with love and compassion. The spirit of that fire can turn our world from one of darkness to one of love and light.

One of the most tragic things to witness is a life without passion—a person whose light has grown dim by the winds of apathy, fear, or scarcity, an individual who's allowed his or her spirit to be broken by despair or mistrust. You were put here to do amazing work. With Spirit as your compass, there is nothing you can't be or claim as your own.

Don't leave this Earth with your song unsung. Don't leave with your story untold. Your life is a canvas and you are the masterpiece in progress.

REAL QUESTIONS, REAL ANSWERS

I am a college student, and I have so many dreams and things I want to achieve, but my family doesn't feel that I should pursue those things because they don't think I can't make a decent living at the things I want to do. I feel like my spirit is being crushed, and I find myself rejecting anything that has to do with spirituality. How can I reconnect with Spirit?

First, you are already connected to Spirit. We are both human and spiritual beings. Second, it is difficult to strike a balance between what we want for ourselves and what those around us want to impose on us. Your spiritual path cannot be traveled by someone else, even if that someone else happens to be your parent. You must have the courage to stand tall in your spiritual convictions no matter who is unhappy with you. Once you are able to separate from your parents' desires for your life and your own spiritual self-exploration, you'll feel revitalized and spiritually rejuvenated. And once your spirit is energized, you'll stand taller in the things you want for your life. Let your passion, not the promise of income, lead you toward your purpose.

I don't get the whole Spirit versus God thing. I don't even like the two words, but I do acknowledge that there is a force in the world that's greater than all of us. How do I talk to that energy or force? Where do I find people who don't need to call something God to be spiritual? Am I making any sense?

Absolutely! Most of us have had similar experiences, though few of us would readily admit it! There is no central location for all things spiritual. I can't point you to a website that answers questions of this nature because things of this nature require individual exploration and reflection.

Every single shred of religious or spiritual discourse came to be as a result of questions and dialogue. So, there are no right or wrong answers to your questions. My recommendation is to get quiet and to travel deeply into your own heart and you will gain clarity about what spirituality looks and sounds like for you. As for finding people who see things the way you do, they are out there. As you connect with your own Source, you will be aligning your intention to attract those individuals.

I am having a very difficult time approaching things from a spiritual perspective because everybody in my life keeps pushing my buttons! When I clear one hurdle, someone pushes another button. Help!

Ahhhh, the wonderful world of growing! Buttons are nothing more than areas that we need to heal or strengthen. Take a look at the archetypes in the Introduction, and I guarantee you'll be able to see what each of these people represents in your life, as well as which lessons your "buttons" signify. Although it's hard to believe sometimes, people are not trying to trigger us. They are growing just as we are. Sometimes they don't even know that what they're doing is "setting off our sensors." Our challenge as spiritual beings is to not be afraid to peel back the layers, to get beneath the surface and look at those patches of our being that require our attention. Rather than being upset at the person—the teacher, who is attempting to help you heal your wounds—try thanking him or her on the spot for their role in facilitating the next level of your spiritual growth. I've done this and it works like a charm!

*A*ccept Your Greatness

The jump is so frightening between where I am
and where I want to be . . . because of all I may become,
I will close my eyes and leap.

—*Anonymous*

*T*hose of you who are familiar with Dave Chappelle's work may be surprised to see his name in a book about spirituality, but don't be so quick to judge.

In the fall of 2005, comedian Dave Chappelle threw us all for a loop. Prior to the interview with Anderson Cooper I never paid much attention to the comedian. I'd seen him in a couple of movies and my brothers, Willie and Charles, had made me sit through one of his shows on Comedy Central, vowing that it would be the funniest thing I'd seen in a long time. It was funny but not the funniest thing I'd seen in a long time, guys. Anyway, the July 2006 interview focused on Chappelle's disappearance after Comedy Central offered him a $50 million contract for his show, *Chappelle's Show,* a sketch variety type show that featured mostly Chappelle. The unorthodox comic who started out as most comedians do, doing stand-up in his neighborhood, explained to Anderson Cooper why this time around, he couldn't be bought. By the age of fourteen, he was working professionally, and by the age of seventeen, he was on the entertainment scene with agents and representatives. He was going to be a star, they told him.

They were right. In 2005, after being on countless specials and achieving enviable success as a stand-up comic, Comedy Central gave Chappelle a $50 million contract. His critically acclaimed show had become a bona fide hit, and the check was in the mail. But something strange happened. Soon after the deal was announced, Chappelle disappeared. Vanished. No one knew where he was and, more important, why and how he could leave at what appeared to be the peak of his career. Would you abandon 50 million bucks? Many speculated as to why Dave would fly the coop at this particular moment, but no one really knew and no one could find Dave to ask him. A year later, Chappelle explained in a television interview, "I had to change my measure of success." According to Chappelle, the price of becoming Comedy Central's highest-paid comic was too high of a spiritual price. "What I was being asked to do and become . . . it wasn't worth it." I sat speechless as I saw a side of Chappelle I had never seen. He was introspective and thoughtful—and believable. He had really turned down $50 million. But why?

Had Dave Chappelle had a spiritual awakening? Some would say yes. My question is was he great for landing the deal or for walking away from it?

Dave didn't allow his ego to run his life, and for that I certainly salute him. I'd like to believe that I could walk away from 50 million smackeroos. Heck, I'd love to have that dilemma, wouldn't you?

Chappelle gives us a great example of leading with his heart and spirit rather than his ego. He gives us all something to think about as it relates to greatness and our definition of success. What Chappelle did was feed his highest self, and as a result, he was able to clear all of the clutter that often accompanies fame and external success and go deep into his heart to figure out what was right for him.

What Is Greatness?

When you saw the title of this chapter, what was your first thought? That I was going to talk to you about becoming the best engineer you could be? Or becoming a Broadway singer? There's nothing wrong with having those aspirations or goals. The world has influenced us to think of the word "greatness" as a term that emanates from the ego. It does not. Greatness is not something that comes from outside of us, although the word greatness has been used to feed the egos of those who have achieved a certain level of notoriety.

Greatness, as I see it, refers to an illumination of "good (God) ness." This flavor of greatness is less about accepting that you will be "seen as great" in the eyes of men and is more about embracing the fact that God-ness—greatness—is in all of us. Accepting your greatness means to accept that you were born with talents and gifts unique to only you and that when you nurture those gifts, you are accepting them. Fame, acclaim, and fortune may or may not come as a result of accepting your greatness, yet the "real" you doesn't step into greatness to get exterior validation.

Greatness is the embodiment of your stepping into your "divine assignment" with your whole heart and soul. Your divine assignment is what you were born to do. Teach, coach, innovate, lead, build, whatever makes your soul dance and your heart sing.

Accepting your greatness is about receptivity of your brilliance and genius.

The ABC of Greatness

To actualize into the full being you were created to be, we must first embrace three key concepts: Always be accountable, Bless those who seek to harm us, and Communicate openly.

Always Be Accountable

To be one with Spirit is to have integrity with yourself. That's what accountability is all about. Owning your stuff. Owning your behavior with yourself and owning your behavior with others.

Owning who we are—this is nothing more than accepting that you were created in love, even when your behavior isn't consistent with that creation. In other words, there's some good stuff in there and there's some other stuff in there.

The main reason we don't own our behavior is that we're afraid of judgment. We're afraid of what people will think if we admit that we made a mistake that costs the company a client. We're not accountable because we think that by admitting our shortcomings we will lose power in our relationships—parents do this a lot with their children. In relationships we lack accountability when we find that we're attracted to someone else even though we're already in a relationship. We fear consequences. That's why we aren't more accountable and honest in all of our dealings. Something bad will happen, we think, if we come clean. Why do we think this? Because our direct and indirect experiences teach us that this is true. Whenever someone tells the truth, they get punished, right? We want to avoid this pain at all costs. We don't see, then, that by not being accountable, we chip away at our spiritual integrity.

Bless Those Who Seek to Do You Harm

If we hadn't been conditioned in the "eye for an eye" school of thought, we would be able to do this one much easier. Our first reaction when we are harmed emotionally or otherwise is to do unto them as they did unto us! If she sabotages me this time, I'll get her next time. If he elbows me during the hockey game, he's going to be eating a knuckle sandwich later. If he brings up my faults in this argument, I'm going to tell him exactly what I think of his mother. This is what we do. This isn't the path to the real you. To stay on a true spiritual path, we must challenge ourselves to bless those who have intentionally and unintentionally sought to hurt us. Whether you realize it or not, your blessing actually neutralizes their ill will, yet we don't believe this. As much as we preach about the power of love, many of us believe that dark forces rule the world. That's why we often meet ugliness with ugliness. We don't truly know the power of love. If we knew the power of love, and I mean knew it, we'd meet every situation with love. Instead we are tricked by the ego into thinking that we must meet indifference with stronger indifference, that we must meet evil with weapons of mass destruction. Love is the key and, without question, our most powerful ammunition!

Communicate Openly

Ask five different people what it means to communicate openly, and you'll undoubtedly get five different answers. Some people will say that "giving people a piece of your mind" is communicating openly. Others will say that speaking from your heart, no matter how harmful your words are, is open communication. I believe open communication combines compassionate truth with a willingness to create a dialogue that moves you closer to spirit, therefore, to love.

My sense is that we can all be more honest and direct without bowling people over with our ego. Strive to share from your heart, making what you have to say less about what someone has done to you and more about moving to a place of love and harmony. Most arguments could end in less than five minutes if people spoke more from their hearts than their ego.

A few months ago, my sister Debra was visiting me from Fort Lauderdale. She wanted to know what I thought about an outfit she was going to wear. My response apparently came out rather terse, as she explained to me. "It was harsh," she said.

"Harsh?" I replied. "Come on. Harsh?"

"That's how it sounded to me," she added.

For a split second I wanted to get into a conversation about what is harsh and what is not, but as you know, that was my ego begging to come out to play. Instead, I went to my sister and hugged her. "I'm sorry. I can see how that must have come out; I didn't mean it that way."

"The jump between where I am and where I want to be is so frightening, I will close my eyes and jump anyway."
—*Anonymous*

In less than five minutes, we had returned to love and were on our way to dinner at one of our favorite restaurants. Open communication starts with open hearts and a willingness to let go of being right.

Whomever you decide to become rests squarely on your shoulders. Every great person in our society, past or present, chose to be great. They stepped into their light. The gulf between where you are today and where you want to be is much smaller than you think. It truly is.

Our constant challenge is in remembering who we are. Whenever I see someone who is not embodying love and respect for themselves or others, I say, "They've forgotten!" They've forgotten who they are.

Unchained Greatness

About six years ago I was asked to speak at a women's correctional facility just outside of Austin. They wanted me to spend some one-on-one time with a few of the women, sharing my story and encouraging them to lead more productive lives after they were released. I'll never forget the looks on the faces of these women—some of them mothers, some of them barely old enough to vote—as I started my presentation with a poem I'd written called, "Just Because You Forgot."

It was a quick poem about remembering who we are: God's most precious creation. *"Just because you forgot that you are significant, doesn't mean that you don't matter."* Some of them cried as they listened to the remaining words in the poem. Most of them felt that they'd been cast aside like an old coat that had seen its better days. Others felt that society had surely written them off, labeling them misfits and derelicts for life.

I wasn't about to dismiss the greatness, the God-ness in these women. I could easily have been one of those women. So could you. Because all it takes is one time to forget at your core who you are for you to make a decision that could change the course of your life forever. That's why we must always remind ourselves of who we are: children of God. This means that no matter what you've done, you are always in the loving arms of God. Yet unless you are accustomed to knowing what that feels like, you won't believe it. And if you don't believe it, you'll forget this fundamental truth. And if you forget this truth, you'll forget who you are. And if you forget who you are, you won't remember that love is the answer to any of your questions.

The Flight of Greatness

In the movie *The Contender*, starring Jeff Bridges and Joan Allen, there's a scene where on the eve of a major character attack campaign, one of the male characters says, "We are going to obliterate a life." It's a powerful scene about how easily the media can distort the truth and sway public opinion. For the next thirty minutes of the film, this man and those in his camp proceed to assassinate the character of the vice presidential candidate, Lane, the character played superbly by Joan Allen. Yet in the midst of accusations and filibustering, Lane never forgot who she was. She never responded to the lies and innuendos. She never lashed back at those who sought to crucify her and squash her greatness.

We must face opposition in the same way. Our greatness is too important to allow it to be stamped out by the illusions of others. We must appreciate the cheers of those who support our ascent into our God-ness, and silence the jeers of those who seem to be saying, "How dare you fly?" We must also fight the temptation to villainize those seeking to keep us from taking flight, recognizing that the ego abhors the exuberance of love, passion, and life. Remember, there's a bundle of blessings and lessons in everything we experience on this spiritual journey.

It is only our judgment about the things that happen to us that keeps us from seeing both the blessings and the lessons in them. We don't mind the blessings, but do we really have to embrace the lessons? Absolutely. When we see them both as equally important, we can be in full in-joyment of all that life brings our way.

Reach One, Teach One

When I step into my greatness it inspires others to do the same. When you have a breakthrough, it opens the door for others to have similar experiences. As we become more of who we really are, we fulfill a sacred covenant that is critical to the actualization of the world. That's why we must not only unleash our own greatness, but also encourage others to do the same. If we are all on the path to greater actualization, then earth has no choice but to become a more loving, spiritual, and harmonious planet. Each one of us must teach the next one and the next one and the next one.

And this doesn't have to be a grand announcement. There are many tiny gestures that show our support of others—a quick congratulatory note, an e-mail acknowledging a good deed, a friendly nod to the stranger on the street, a genuine hug when your child comes home from school, a high five when a coworker solves a problem. Furthermore, you can simply send love with your energy. No one has to know. Love doesn't need recognition to heal any situation.

You Are What You Repeatedly Are

One summer, my college coach required us to shoot 100 free throws a week. If you know anything about basketball, you know that free throws are not the most exciting things to do for long periods of time. They are essential, but they're not thrilling. I understood the need to become a great free-throw shooter, but this didn't make me any more motivated to go to the gym during the summer and shoot 100 free throws. But by the quarter-mark point of the season I found myself shooting a blistering 90 percent from the free-throw line, and I owed it all to the mandated free-throw practice.

It's the same with our spiritual fitness. We are what we practice. Practice generosity, and you take on a spirit of generosity. Practice mercy, and you become merciful. I always say we must give what we want to show up in our lives. If you want abundance to show up in your life, practice abundance.

Today can be changed so that you get what you really want. No one's set in his ways who doesn't want to be set in his ways. If you want some-

WILL THE REAL YOU PLEASE STAND UP?

thing different, do something different and be something different.

My father is in his early seventies, and he has made some major behavioral changes in the past five years—changes that have not come easily, given that he's done certain things all of his life; changes that his children have played a part in igniting, but the changes themselves were all him. We challenged him to look at how he's reacted to certain things and relationships, and to our loving amazement, he responded. I know so many adult children who refuse to challenge their parents to move closer to their real selves. They say things like, "That's just Mom, she's never gonna change" or "Dad's been doing it that way for thirty years." And while it's not our job to attempt to "make" people change, I believe we are here to gently remind each other of who we really are.

The Greatest Lies Ever Told

To accept this "God-ness" en route to becoming the real you, you must rid yourself of the lies on which your story—your life—is built. So, right now, let's get it all out in the open. What lies have you been told that are keeping you from becoming all of you—the real you? Some parents tell their kids that they'll never amount to anything. Teachers have been known to tell students that unless they go to college, they have no shot at securing a financial future. Clergy tell parishioners that if they don't pay the church's bills they won't receive a full measure of God's grace or blessings. These are not truths. They are lies. Lies that people have accepted as truth. When we buy into lies about who we are and what we can become we severely limit our ability to manifest the riches we deserve. Not just financial riches but emotional riches as well. For many years women were told that they couldn't become doctors, lawyers, and businesswomen. Blacks were told they didn't have the right to vote. Today incarcerated individuals are told that they are less than human because they are in prison. These lies and others like them are all lies that millions of people buy into on a daily basis. Basically, there are two sets of lies that all of us operate under at some point in our lives: (1) the lies that others tell us, and (2) the lies we tell ourselves.

The Lies They've Told Us

You are the product of what you believe about yourself, plain and simple. And what you believe about yourself comes from many places—family, friends, and the media, as it were. It's not always easy to face how we truly see ourselves, especially when that truth isn't what we want to see. It is, nevertheless, the first step toward accepting your greatness. So, to get to who you're really supposed to be, we have to undo those lies. To undo them we must face them head on. So, let's think about the lies others tell us or have told us.

Parents

It may be hard for you to admit that your parents have told you lies and other untruths that didn't support you in becoming more of who you are, but in many cases it's true. So, do a quick sweep of your parents or whoever raised you, and I want you to list the lies they told you.

1.

2.

3.

Teachers

These can be folks from school or the community.

1.

2.

3.

Religious or Spiritual Leaders

1.

2.

3.

WILL THE REAL YOU PLEASE STAND UP?

Media

1.

2.

3.

Others

1.

2.

3.

If you need more space, write it in your journal.

Now, take a long look at those lies. No judgment. Just have a long look at them. You've been living your life, to some extent, based on those lies. Which ones will you stop believing in this moment? Why? Can you identify the ones that have kept you from the life, job, or relationships you desire?

The Lies We've Told Ourselves

I don't know which is worse. The lies others have told us or the ones we tell ourselves. Some of us tell lies by simply perpetuating the lies others have told us. Either way, it's time for some truth. But first, we've got to get out all of the lies you tell yourself. *I'm never going to get out of debt. I'm never going to finish this paper. People like me don't get advanced degrees. She's never going to go out with me. I'm not good enough. I'm not smart enough. I'm not pretty enough. I'm not enough.* These are all lies. What are the lies you tell yourself?

A little bit harder to admit? Probably. It's always easier to make someone else responsible for our circumstances, isn't it? It's a lot more difficult to stare in the mirror and know that we're responsible for who we are and what we've become. What are the lies you've told yourself and the lies you perpetuate based on what you've been told? Either way, the responsibility for today and the future lies with us. List the lies you tell yourself. You can use the five areas of the Wholeness Matrix as a basis from which to start. We can continue to believe and live the lies, or we can create new truths.

Lie #1:

Lie #2:

Lie #3:

Lie #4:

Lie #5:

CREATING NEW TRUTHS

Now, take one long look at both lists. These lies have robbed you of your greatness—your God-ness. They've stopped you from in-joying your life to the fullest. They've stolen your passion. They've stopped you from starting that business, going on that vacation, leaving an abusive relationship, managing your finances better, going back to school, or taking more time off from work.

Go ahead, take one last look at the list of lies above. It's time to create new truths. New images. New stories. New realities. For example, one of the lies I told myself was that I could create my billion-dollar media and television empire and not make a move to a larger market to build my brand. I loved living in Austin, Texas, but the truth is that if you want to be on Broadway, you go to New York. If you want to be a country singer you go to Nashville. So, while I wanted to believe that I could do every-

WILL THE REAL YOU PLEASE STAND UP?

thing I wanted without making any major moves, that just wasn't reality. I had to replace that lie with this new truth: I am destined for multimedia greatness, which means I had to be willing to invest in myself at a level I've never known and be open to relocation. I moved to Los Angeles and my new truth opened up a world of possibilities for me. I appeared on *The Tonight Show* with Jay Leno in January 2006. I've appeared on numerous national television shows and continue to build my brand as a host, author, speaker, and expert. All because I was willing to stop lying to myself and simultaneously create new truths. So, what about you? Let's write some truths to propel you forward. What new stories will you tell yourself that will allow you to be in your greatness? What new tales will you create that those around you can soak up and learn from?

If you're wondering how you can go from believing a lie to believing a new truth, it's simple. Just start believing the new truth. That's precisely how the lie became your truth for you all those years. You heard it, and you believed it. So you already know how to breathe something into existence. Your charge is to breathe something more positive, healthier, and more real into your life. Go ahead, breathe it in right now. Breathe in good health. Breathe in honesty. Breathe in power. Breathe in passion. Breathe in a new career path. Breathe in a $1 million payday. Breathe in quiet mornings by the ocean. Breathe it all in. It's yours. New truths. New realities. New you. A real you.

Your Anointment of Greatness

There are people who believe that greatness, riches, and success are reserved for a select few. There are poor people who believe that they "have" to be poor. There are people reading this book right now who believe that their biology determines the end of their biography. You've been anointed to do and be something great—something that no one else can do and be. That's your anointed appointment. Every single human on this earth has an anointed appointment. Some of us will not, cannot believe that our name and greatness belong in the same sentence, but it does. This anointment is extremely difficult for many people to accept, especially those who have been oppressed and disillusioned by their social, familial, or spiritual belief systems.

Still today, your road to becoming more of who you are starts with living an in-powered life—a life that is powered by God, powered by Spirit, and powered by greatness (God-ness). In-powerment is not an event or something outside of you or something someone gives to you. It's in you! You come here in-powered. You just need to get plugged in to the source that will allow you to go from running on batteries to high-voltage consciousness.

In-powerment can be accessed daily and on a moment-by-moment notice. It's not reserved for the rich and famous, engineers, scientists, and creative geniuses. In-powerment and greatness are your birthright. When you allow your in-powerment to lead you to your greatness, you'll see incredible and immediate rewards. You'll transcend your physical, spiritual, emotional, financial, and mental hurdles. Your consciousness will expand beyond your imagination. You'll break through those walls that stood in your way for years. You'll no longer feel the need to remain in unhealthy relationships. But my personal favorite for accepting your greatness is that you'll be so excited about the direction of your life that you'll go to sleep with a million thoughts and you'll wake up with a smile on your face—every day!

As you've moved from the ego to a more Spirit-centered life, your greatness will ooze out of you. You'll attract people and things you've been "working to attract" for a long time. They will mysteriously appear in your life. And not only will you start to be a magnet for all that is good and whole, you'll be in a better position to be a mentor to someone else on their path to the real them.

You'll never lie awake at night and say, "I wish I knew what I'm supposed to be doing here" or "What's my purpose?" You'll know.

THE ROAD TO GREATNESS

There's a line in the movie *Sister Act,* starring Whoopi Goldberg, that I'll paraphrase, where one of the nuns says to her, "Do you ever get the feeling that if you can't be yourself that you'll just burst?" She quickly retracts her statement, asking Whoopi's character if that sounds like "vanity." The road to who you really are is paved with God-ness. The enormity of that reality may feel like it's ego-driven. It's not. What's in store for you can't be contained. It's supposed to feel huge! Your contribution to the world is significant no matter how small it seems in your mind. Accept your contribution—your greatness—as necessary to moving the planet forward, and feel good about that contribution.

When I tell people in live seminars to "feel good and be proud" of their contributions and achievements, I always get a strange mixture of responses. Some people sink in their seats. Others applaud loudly. And some folks come up to me afterward to say that they felt embarrassed to stand tall in their greatness—that somehow they feel like they're boasting. I assure them that what they are giving the world is no small feat and that by playing small, they are not accepting their greatness. Many of us believe that we're being humble when we do things like tell audiences not to applaud for us or when we pretend not to enjoy adulation. This isn't humility, it's a shade of playing small. Some of these individuals are truly afraid of appearing arrogant, and some of them secretly believe that they'll be stripped of their blessings if they appear to be too excited by or too proud of their accomplishments. This is nothing more than the trickery of the ego.

Besides, if you ever want to know if what you're doing is ego-centered rather than heart- or Spirit-centered, ask yourself these two questions:

1) Would I do this if no one knew about it? In other words, if the newspapers weren't going to write about it and the television stations weren't going to cover it, would I still be as passionate about doing it?

2) Am I willing to remove my name from the project and allow the goodness to happen anonymously?

The road to greatness begins with three kinds of wholiness: sacred, physical, and emotional.

SACRED WHOLINESS

To accept your greatness means that you must also accept what I call "sacred wholiness," a deeply personal covenant you make with yourself to strive for wholeness in every area of your life.

Sacred Wholiness is achieved through the consistent communion with God, the Divine, whatever or whomever you identify with as the source of your spiritual connection. For me communion means prayer throughout my day. For you, it could and should be something that is uniquely you.

When I moved to Los Angeles two years ago nearly everyone said, "Wow, L.A.'s such a shallow place, how will you survive there?" or "People are so fake in Los Angeles, how will you deal with that?"

The truth is that the people in L.A. are no more shallow than the people I knew in Austin, Texas. All of those projections about Los Angeles were designed to perpetuate separation. They were designed to make me think I was different so that I could cocreate that energy once I got here. Instead, at the urging of one of my spiritual and financial coaches, I started to visualize Los Angeles as one big red carpet. I saw the city welcoming me into the fold. I didn't see it as a place that didn't want me here. I believe that's why I was able to manifest what I wanted so quickly once I arrived.

PHYSICAL WHOLINESS

Taking care of our bodies is one of the most holy and wholly things we can do.

Physical wholiness isn't some euphoric idea of obsession. Wholiness is a commitment, and commitments are to be taken seriously. I am committed to physical wholiness always, but my behavior isn't always consistent with that commitment. I strive for 100-percent compliance to my fitness and wellness goals. I achieve about a grade of 95 percent most of the time. And that other 5 percent of the time, I don't beat myself up for not going to the yoga studio or for not doing my ab work last night. Judgment is not necessary. As you look at your own physical and health goals, ask yourself how committed you are, and after you ask that question, remind yourself that taking care of your health is completely in your hands. God's given you a body for this journey. You're either a good steward of it or you're not. How whole are you physically?

EMOTIONAL WHOLINESS

Every relationship we have has an emotional component—our relationships with our friends and intimates, our relationships with our coworkers. We even have a relationship with our cars, houses, and money. We experience emotions with all of these things. If we focused on becoming whole in every relationship we have, we'd be able to see life a lot clearer. Unfortunately, we don't normally aspire to wholeness or wholiness in our relationships. We want to be in love or we want to be adored—both experiences that come from places outside of us. When we say that we're in love with someone that love is typically based on how we perceive the "other" person "makes" us feel. Therefore, the feeling comes from outside of us. Is it possible to feel that level of love without someone else being in the picture? Yes, it is, but most of us don't believe that. We've been programmed to believe that "being in love" is something that we can only feel if another person does something for us, to us, or toward us. If that is truth for you, you will never know the depth of your ability to love yourself. And more important, your joy in the world, your experience with love will always be dependent on something or someone else.

We can't truly achieve emotional wholiness until we heal the places within us that need healing, and that starts with knowing that we have a much deeper capacity to experience love without others. If you have children you may know what this feels like. Before you started heaping your expectations onto your kids, remember that overwhelming love you felt? They didn't have to do anything and you still felt that way, right? That kind of love needs no nurturing or promises of tomorrow. It's a pure, innocent love. You are "in" love deeply.

Achieving wholiness in the emotional area requires that we go deep. One night before moving to Los Angeles, I went to the grocery story to pick up a few things. One of the main reasons I'd gone to this particular store was they had a particular brand of ice cream that I was loving at that time in my life. When I got to the freezer section, there was a man looking for a particular flavor of ice cream.

"What kind are ya looking for?" I asked.

"Toffee crunch, but I don't think they have it," he said.

That was the same kind I was looking for. My smile turned upside down. I'd driven way across town for this ice cream, and I couldn't believe they didn't have it. This was not how I'd written the script!

"You sure? They always have it."

"I know," he said. "But I've been looking for the past five minutes with no luck. Nothing."

I got down on my knees so that I could see the bottom two shelves.

The man chuckled at my apparent desperation. "You're not going to find any, but good luck." And with that he walked away.

As he turned the corner, I reached all the way to the back of the freezer. I saw two pints sitting there all by their lonesome. I pulled them forward and became delighted by what I saw. Two pints of toffee crunch ice cream. "Yes!"

Moral of the story? Sometimes you have to get on your knees to get what you want. And most times you have to dig deeper to find what you're looking for. Most of us don't want to dig deeper. Like my friend in the grocery store, we accept most things as they appear to be on the surface. Few things are what they appear. Had the man in the ice cream section dug a little deeper and investigated a little while longer, he would have found what he was looking for.

What's beneath your surface? What do you need to address so that you can go to the next level of sacred wholiness? What do you need to get rid of so that you can experience the joys of emotional wholiness? How badly do you want your toffee crunch ice cream?

Commit to morning communion at least once a week. By doing so you invite your emotions, body, and mind into a space where wholeness and wholiness are a part of your day.

A New Approach to Prayer

It's a popular cliché yet still very true—we will get precisely what we put into anything. If we pray or meditate only when the "Spirit hits us," we'll perceive that God's presence isn't always there. If we approach prayer and communion with God as if we are standing in front of a large vending machine, waiting for our "goodies" to pop out, we'll only see periodic signs of God's greatness. Wholiness requires practice. It requires repetition. The longer we stay in God's gym, the stronger we become. The stronger we become, the more capable we are at facing life's many and diverse challenges.

A lot of people get hung up on "how to pray." Or I love it when I hear people say he's a "good pray-er." We're so ego-driven we even judge prayer! Don't be surprised if you see *Prayer For Dummies* on a bookshelf soon.

Your greatness and your realness depend on your ability to reflect God's love on a daily basis. You are already an image of God. Prayer, communion, and meditation bring that image more to the surface so that people can see their image of God reflected by you! So forget about all of your preconceived notions about "how" to commune or pray or meditate and just come as you are. Even if you feel that you are already a "master" level Ninja prayer warrior, each day gives us all a chance to grow in Spirit.

Let's take a quick break. I'd like for you to clear your mind, inhale what you want to see in your life, and exhale that which you want to fall away. Surrender to your highest good. Repeat this for as long as you are able to remain in a state of quiet. If that's five minutes, then five minutes it is. If it's thirty minutes, then thirty minutes it is. There are no judgments or prizes for those who can pray the longest. You will, however, build your spiritual muscles and endurance as you spend more time in the "gym." Try praying for qualities rather than "perks" this week.

In other words, instead of asking to close the account or to get the loan approved or to get a second date with the hot guy or girl in your biology class, ask for greater compassion, unconditional love, or serenity in a noisy world. Ask for clarity in difficult situations and strength to lift your voice when it's not the popular thing to do. See how differently you move through your week when your focus isn't on your worldly desires but on accepting your greatness and your divine assignment.

A New Twist on Atonement

We judge each other harshly daily. We revel in making people "pay" for what they do to us. We punish them with silence, withdrawal, passive aggressive behavior, sarcasm, and violence. We didn't learn this from God because God doesn't judge us! The Bible reads: "Judge not lest you be judged." Many people interpret this as "if we judge people then God's going to judge us." Consider an alternate interpretation: What we do to others, we do to ourselves. In other words, when we punish other people, we punish ourselves because what comes out of us is about us. When we seek to hurt our brothers and sisters, we hurt ourselves. When people say, "You think you're so much better than everyone else" what they're really saying is "I don't think I measure up. I don't think I'm good enough." When someone says, "You're never going to become a millionaire, folks like us don't get rich," what he's really saying is that he doesn't believe in the vast possibilities for his own life. It has nothing to do with you. What we do and say to others, we do to ourselves. We think we need to forgive people who do things that offend us, but we don't. What we need to do is not to judge them in the first place. If we looked upon the actions of others and didn't need to assign a value to what they did, we wouldn't be bound by their apology (or lack thereof) and we wouldn't continue the dialogue in our heads about "needing to forgive them." If you feel that you've been wronged, know that you can heal yourself. You can choose to be bound by what someone else did (to themselves not to you) or you can acknowledge that when they projected their fears onto you, that their actions had nothing to do with you.

Atonement, on the other hand, is a heart-centered spiritual practice that gives us the opportunity to take a nonjudgmental look at what we say, what we do, and how we treat our fellow warriors and to lay down a more loving, peaceful, or harmonious slate. If you say something that is unkind to someone, atonement is what you do to get back into balance— not to win points with that individual or God. Yet that's exactly how we've set up the forgiveness game. The offended feels like the offender "owes" him an apology. The offender, knowing that he's been unkind and that the offended expects an apology, hesitates or refuses to say, "I'm sorry." Why? Because the ego's convinced the offender that apologies are not the way to go. Forgiveness, then, is one of the ego's most elaborate ploys. I say, forget forgiveness. Atone, atone, atone!

Atonement returns us to that loving place. Atonement is not correction, it's a reminder of who we are—God's children. And why we're here—to love. That's why atonement is necessary. For those who are stuck in the chains of forgiveness, atonement is not possible. Right now, there are things you've said and done that you're not proud of, you're maybe even sorry that they are a part of your history. And even though they may be five, ten, or even twenty years removed, you can still atone for them. There are tons of ways to atone for past behavior. You can call the person and share from your heart but I don't recommend that you follow my example. Don't do what I did. . . .

A few years ago a friend did something that infuriated me. In this instance, she filled the Shape Shifter role in this scene of my movie. She made an insensitive comment during a time when I was very stressed about getting to an appointment on time, so I hung up on her in the middle of our phone conversation. Click! But before I hung up, I told her precisely why I'd hung up on her. "I don't need this right now!" Click!

I was immediately sorry for my behavior. I was running late for an appointment, and I told myself that I was going to call her as soon as I got out of my meeting. I hated that I'd hung up on her, even though my ego convinced me that she deserved it. By the time I got out of my meeting, my heart had crawled into the backseat of my car and my ego was in the driver's seat. So, you can probably guess what happened next. Right, I didn't call. Instead I gave my ego the keys to my car and let her run wild! A few days went by, and I decided I would call and apologize. She didn't answer my calls. I called her home, no answer. I called her cell, no answer, no returned phone call. I e-mailed her and told her that I wanted to meet with her face to face. She responded by saying that she'd prefer that I just write whatever I had to say.

Here we were, two people who had shared a very nice friendship, but suddenly we couldn't even sit in the same room and talk? This was not a total shock to me. I'd watched this friend deal with conflict with other people in her life. She'd rather not deal with it. She'd rather just pretend that it didn't happen and she certainly wasn't going to be vulnerable by having a face-to-face conversation with me. Getting in the same room with her was going to take an act of Congress. But since I'd vowed a few months earlier not to write e-mails on important matters, I did the next best thing to speaking with her. I recorded my thoughts and sent them as mp3 audio files via e-mail. The audio apology was going well until the end when I told her that essentially she deserved to get the dial tone that day. It was a classic, "I'm sorry, but you asked for it" apology—not a real apology.

So I never got to have that heart-to-heart I wanted, but guess what? I still got to atone for behaving in a way that wasn't in my highest good that afternoon. I went into my heart and said what I would've said to my friend. I spoke from my heart, and when it was over, it was over. I have never looked back. I no longer carried any negative feelings around that issue because I was no longer judging myself and I was no longer judging my friend. I couldn't do anything about wherever she was on the issue. For me it was done.

I'd made several attempts to atone in person. I'd acknowledged my part in our cocreation, and I was willing to do my part to rectify the situation. My conscience and heart were free. I even called her a few months later to wish her a happy birthday. It was truly over for me. That's what atonement will do. It releases you from that icky "What if he's cold toward me when I see him?" feeling, or "I wonder if she'll speak to me when we get to work on Monday." Atone and let it go. Your greatness depends heavily on your willingness to see the God in others. Your greatness also depends on your ability to rejoice in your own frailties because they are always overcome through God's love and mercy.

What are you carrying around with you that you need to atone for? You are hindering your spiritual growth by holding on to it. It is your ego that is convincing you that calling or writing that person isn't the best thing to do. The ego tells us the following:

If you call him, he'll think you're not over him.

If you contact her, she wins.

If you write him, he'll know he's got you over a barrel.

If you speak to her, she'll think you're weak.

Does any of that sound even faintly familiar? All of this is the handy work of the ego. But let's say that you decide not to make direct contact with the individual, you still must engage in a private atonement session so that you can clear the way for your greatness. Go for it!

Accessing Your Greatness

There are two kinds of greatness. The first is the most important greatness and that's your God-ness—the service you were born to carry out during your time here. Your divine assignment. I don't know what that is for you, but I suspect you do. We've all been given an assignment to help make the world a better, more loving place. Mine is to bring people into the full understanding that they are more powerful than they could ever imagine. Now, don't get all freaked out on me, you don't have to pack your gear and head to a Third World country on a mission—unless of course, that's your calling. For most of us, our service can be done right in our own communities. That's certainly a good place to start. We all have many causes that are near to our hearts, and I'm not talking about the things you "feel bad about." That's not necessarily your call to service. You can feel bad about the starving children in Ethiopia but not have a sincere desire to get in the trenches to do anything about it. Don't worry or judge yourself if that's not your call. Answer your call! How do you know what your call is? Ask. Get quiet and ask. The answer will be revealed to you.

The second type of greatness is spiritual greatness. If we strove to be an Olympic spiritual athlete, how much better would the world be? If we practiced everyday spiritual principles like honesty, integrity, keeping our word, being accountable, or judging less and loving more, we'd operate at a much higher spiritual frequency in our personal and professional lives. That's spiritual greatness. We won't win any awards for it. We won't be featured on *Oprah* or *Larry King Live,* but the impact of this greatness will be felt for generations to come.

❧ REAL QUESTIONS, REAL ANSWERS ❧

I'm married with three wonderful children. My husband is an executive in a large corporation. We have lots of money, I want for nothing, my kids are happy and healthy, but it's not enough. I know that sounds strange, and when I try to talk to my husband about it, he tells me that other women would love to have my life. I suppose they would, but that doesn't make me feel any better. I guess I don't want to wait until my kids go off to college to have the life I want for myself. I've always loved painting, writing, and the arts, but am I being selfish?

Yes, you are being selfish. Congratulations! It's been said that most of us use less than 10 percent of our capacity to create during our lifetimes. We are such powerful beings that it is in our very nature to want to express that power in ways that nurture and fulfill us. Your desire to be more of who you are is exactly what *Will the Real You Please Stand Up?* is all about! Step into that inner writer, painter, and artist, and don't allow your kids, your husband, or that active committee in your head to keep you from your God-ness or your great-ness! You *can* have it all!

I was taught not to think too much of myself—to defer to other people and to be content with what I have and be thankful that God's blessed me with it. So I feel ungrateful in wanting more from my life. Like, I think I could be really famous in my field, but there's something inside of me that won't let me go there. Any advice?

That something that won't let you go there is called ego. The ego would like nothing more than for you to play small. Because if you stifle your gifts, that's one less powerful warrior walking the Earth, and that makes the ego very happy. Being famous isn't something you can control, so stop trying to control your greatness and just be great! If you are fueled by passion to do whatever it is you do, do it. There's nothing honorable in not becoming all of who you are. There's nothing spiritual about struggling financially. You are not getting any heavenly brownie points by being a martyr. Accept your God-ness, and your light will urge others to do the same.

*L*et Go

We lay too much stress on stick-to-it-iveness.
I once had a professor who wisely hung this sign
over his desk: "Oh Lord, teach me when to let go."
—*W. G. Carleton*

*W*hen you have a moment, go to the sink in your home and turn on the faucet. Put your flat hand underneath the running water and catch as much water as you possibly can for ten seconds. Now turn the water off. How much water do you have left in your hand? A drop? Maybe two? That's how much control we have over most things in our lives. We can influence the world we live in, but we cannot control the behaviors of others.

THE ART OF LETTING GO

Letting go. It's one of the most challenging things we'll ever have to do. Athletes have to do it. Movie stars have to do it. Parents have to do it. Lovers have to do it. We all have to let go sometimes. Life demands that we do it in every area of our lives. Letting go is a major component of spiritual fitness and maturation. We can't move to new levels of enlightenment if we cling to what used to be or what we perceive to still be.

There are countless times during the course of our everyday lives that we'll have to let go. The receptionist at the doctor's office is in a mood. Let go. Your spouse left the top off the orange juice—again. Let go. Your boss doesn't acknowledge your part in a key project. Let go. Your name is misspelled in the company directory. Let go. An old friend spreads vicious gossip about you. Let go.

Easy to say? Yep. Hard to do? You bet. Things are only as difficult as we "frame" them to be. God gives us a magical tool: perception. If we look in the mirror and we don't like what we see, we have two choices: change what we see or change *how* we see it.

Through my personal trainer practice I've found that both are equally hard. I've certainly had to develop a discipline around my own perceptions of others and myself. I've learned that working out is extremely difficult for some people. That's why we're always looking for the next hot weight-loss fad. We want our change to be instant, and we want it pain- and effort-free. A good friend of mine is always complaining about her middle section. "It just won't go away," she says to me every few weeks. When I tell her that the fastest way to shed a few inches in the waist area is through the one-two-three-four punch of good nutrition, cardiovascular workout, core work, and abdominal exercises, I always get a moment of silence followed by, "Hmmmph." She doesn't want to hear it because she's only interested in achieving her goals through nonphysical exertion. She'd rather spend $29.99 on a bottle of pills that claim to "go right to the area in your stomach where the fat is and melt the fat away." We want to avoid pain so much that we'd believe things that are so far-fetched, they're funny! A pill that goes right to the fat area and sucks it out? C'mon! This is what I meant earlier when I said that we are motivated by the prospect of less pain. I used to design fitness plans for my friends and family members until I realized that most of them weren't interested in change from within. They wanted lean muscle mass, flat stomachs, perky bottoms, and buff arms, but they weren't willing to participate in a program that would ensure them lasting results. They had to let go of their fantasies for a better body, and I had to let go of my attachment to their commitment to the program. I found myself being frustrated with the same conversations. "I need to start working out, you got any suggestions?" I started answering no. And finally they stopped asking me for fitness and wellness advice. We both had to let go.

Surrendering—Waving the White Flag?

When we use the word "surrender" outside of spiritual circles it usually means to "give up," to acquiesce; therefore, "surrender" isn't one of the most desirable terms in a world where being on top means everything. For those who are committed to a spiritual walk, surrendering isn't the same as waving the white flag and walking out with your hands held high. Surrendering is the act of letting go of that which we can't control anyway. The frustration we experience as a result of holding on too tightly to so many things—our relationships, agendas, material possessions, loved ones who've transitioned from the physical world, and even our youth—comes because our spiritual nature knows that we have zero control over most things in our lives, yet our human

Your canvas can be filled with brilliant hues and textures, or it can remain dull, lifeless, even blank. The day you trade in your mask for a paintbrush is the day that you start the luminous journey toward the real you . . . and your masterpiece.

side wants to cling to these things. What we do have input on continues to be our choices, attitudes, beliefs, and behaviors. Everything else is beyond our control. When we are quiet and listening to the voice of God, we know this. We know that we cannot control most things. Yet it is the duality of our human/spiritual existence that keeps us wrestling with this basic truth. That's why we must be in constant communion with Spirit.

If we are in momentary alliance with our highest selves, we will be consistently reminded to "let go" and to "surrender."

Easy to say, harder to do. A few years ago, I had a consulting client who would constantly proclaim his commitment to a spiritual walk, yet he repeatedly engaged in behaviors that appeared to cultivate an environment of mistrust, betrayal, jealousy, sabotage, and dishonesty. I was shocked by these behaviors and quite disillusioned. I didn't understand how he could repeatedly tell people how "spiritual" he was and still engage in behaviors that were incongruent with the spiritual giant he proclaimed to be. When I pointed out these behaviors to him, he would either ignore the notes or engage in even more ego-centered behaviors. He began keeping me out of the loop on things that were essential to doing a good job for his business. He would withhold information until it was too late for me to do anything about it. He would tell me one thing and tell someone in his company another. It was some of the most bizarre behavior I'd ever witnessed in my ten years as a business consultant. It was clear that I needed to do three things. First, I needed to let go of my need to understand this behavior, which I must admit was very difficult. I was never going to understand this behavior. Second, I needed to discontinue my relationship with this client as soon as possible. And third, I needed to let go of the idea of the potential financial gain that would have resulted had I continued the relationship. Of the three things I needed to do, which do you think was the hardest? The money? Nope. That was the easiest. It was extremely difficult to let go of my need to understand how this client could behave the way he had. Had he not advertised such a spiritual approach to things, I would not have had such high expectations of our relationship being one that transcended traditional business dealings. So, it wasn't the client who needed to surrender. I needed to surrender in the area of expectations. Which leads me to my next topic.

No Expectations, No Disappointments

We don't realize how much we expect of and from people until they don't do what we expect (and want) them to do! Even those of us who claim to be Super Ninja Spiritual Beings have expectations of people. We expect the customer service rep from our credit card company to be courteous. We expect our kids to hug and kiss us before they leave the house for their week-long trip to Cancun. We expect our spiritual, civic, and political leaders to live by a certain code. We expect the driver in the next lane to signal before they make a move into our lane. Expectations will get you every time. They are the kiss of disappointment. But guess what? If you have no expectations, there could be no disappointments.

Our egos keep us engaged in expectations because it knows that disappointment is one of the main emotions that keep us from living lives full of love and Spirit. Disappointment has stopped many of us from "going for it." We're too afraid of the possibility of disappointment. What if it doesn't happen? What if she doesn't show up? What if he does exactly what he said he'd never do again? What if? What if? What if?

What if you could let go of your expectations in just one area of your life? How different do you think your life would be? What would you have to do to give up expecting people to behave the way you want them to behave? Let me tell you, it is the most freeing experience I've ever had.

I had to learn this the hard way. One of my very dear friends has a way of doing exactly what I wish she wouldn't do! She's kind, she's loving, she's compassionate, and she's sometimes forgetful. Not only is she forgetful, but she also appears to forget only the things I'd like for her to remember! Like calling me back to let me know if she has a resource that I needed yesterday. This is not something new. We've been friends for a decade, and it's always been this way. You'd think I'd have "let it go" sooner than I did.

Each time she forgets something, she says, "I'm so sorry. You know that I love you and it has nothing to do with you, I just spaced out." Is that beautiful or what? How can you be angry with someone who's so honest and accountable? And each time she'd say that, I'd vow not to expect her to remember the next time; but of course, I would. And we'd do the same dance a few months later. Finally, after one of our episodes, I hung up the phone and started to laugh. "When are you going to get it, girl?" I said to myself aloud. "No expectations. No disappointments."

So that's what I started to practice. And it changed the complexion of our friendship. I could no longer make her wrong for forgetting—which my ego hated—and I stopped expecting her to do anything she said she would do. Does it sound hard to do? It was. But I did it and so can you.

Think about the key people in your life. What are you expecting them to do? I warn you, this is not going to be an easy breezy exercise. Your ego does not want you to master this area of spiritual growth but I guarantee you, if you do this, you'll see an immediate transformation in your emotional, spiritual, mental, and even physical health.

Since most of our expectations are of people, let's use five relationships that most of us are in today. Write your expectations of these people. Don't hold anything back, and don't let your ego trick you into thinking that you don't need to do this exercise. You do. It's critical to getting to the next level of spiritual mastery no matter where you are today. We all have expectations of people that are unfair and unnecessary. What are yours?

Spouse/Mate

Kids

Parents

Friends

Employer/Client/Employee

Changing How We See What We See

It's true; if you change the lens through which you view anything or anyone, what you look at will change instantly. This is true for people, circumstances, and things. The reason we don't change how we see things is that we're too invested in how we see them. We get a payoff for seeing them that way. In relationships, if we don't want to see our friends and lovers as untrustworthy, all we have to do is see them as trustworthy. In my seminars, I always get men and women who say, "I want to trust him or her." My response is always the same: "So trust him."

"It's not that easy."

"Yes, it is. Trust her."

This is always met with puzzled looks. "I can't just turn my trust on and off like that."

"Yes, you can. Do you want to trust your wife?" I asked one newlywed.

"Desperately."

"Then trust her."

"I can't."

"Then leave her."

"What?"

"Leave. If you can't trust her, why are you with her?"

"Because I love her."

"Then trust her."

Do you see what's happening here? We say we want certain things, but we're not willing to do the things to give us what we want. Change what you see or change how you see them. Love 'em or leave 'em, those are the only options. Love or let go.

But we won't let go because we're too invested in the movie we're producing to let go. If we let go, we perceive that we lose the upper hand. If we let go, we perceive that we lose. If we let go, we think they'll think we're a marshmallow. If we let go, we think we're giving them permission to do it again. If we let go, what will we have "over" them? If we let go, what will we have to talk to our girlfriends about? If we let go, what will we talk about in Confession? This is why we won't let go. We're too invested in being right, being on top and being in charge. Which leads me to my next topic. . . .

LETTING GO OF ILLUSIONS

Recently, two of my nieces, Micha, sixteen, and Taylor, eleven, were sharing in great detail, as teenagers do, about their day. Some stupid boy had done something. They needed to go to the mall to find something to wear to a party. How were they going to do their hair? So many big decisions were facing them on this day.

As I listened to them talk about solving their problems, I got inspired to have their stories, their journeys, recorded. I remembered what it was like to hang out with my friends as a teenager and how everything was always so funny to us. The more I listened to them, the more fascinated I became by their journeys. Being a teenage girl in 2006 is probably a little different from when I was a teenager. I decided to pitch an idea to them.

"Yo, how'd you two like to write a book?" I asked, wondering if the "yo" would make them giggle even more. Whenever I use a term like "yo" or "whatup," they always laugh, like I'm a relic. And then I have to remind them that I'm not *that* old. So I was surprised that I got to slip the "yo" in without them laughing hysterically.

"About what?" Micha asked, as only a sixteen-year-old can.

"About your lives. About what you're going through as a girl in 2006. You know, what it means to be a girl, how you feel about your life, boys, dreams, that kind of stuff."

"I'm not really in the space to talk about that right now, Auntie Fran," Micha responded.

"What about you, Taylor?"

"Does this mean I'm gonna have to be famous?"

I started to laugh. "Maybe," I replied.

"I'll have to think about it, then," Taylor said. "That's something I gotta think about."

I was stunned. Not by the fact that Micha wasn't in the "space" to discuss a pending book deal. It was Taylor that had me dumbfounded. Her perception was that if she wrote a book that she'd be thrust into the public eye, and she wasn't sure if she was okay with that. Clearly there was a price to pay for being famous. That was her picture—her illusion. Where had this come from?

Micha and her brother Jon think that I'm famous. They are convinced that I spend my days hanging out at lavish parties with Hollywood stars. That's their illusion!

What illusions are you acting on that are keeping you from the real you—the loving you, the compassionate you, the ego-free you.

Remember, the movie you see isn't necessarily the real story. Sometimes the movie of our lives that we're producing is based on illusions that we "want" to see to keep telling our stories the same way.

What Is an Illusion?

An illusion can be an image, a picture that appears real but is not. An illusion can be a misrepresentation or a lie that we not only believe but may also act on. It only appears real because the lens through which we see or perceive it makes it real. Two people can walk out of their homes in the same neighborhood at precisely the same hour and see different things. One might see a gorgeous day filled with possibility. The other may not see the sun at all and perceive that the day is overcast. Each has his own illusion of what the day looks like. So, illusions are not bad unless we choose to see things in a way that does not support us positively. Let's say we walk down the halls of our office and a coworker appears to walk by without speaking. If your perception is that the coworker ignored you or is upset with you, and you decide to act on that and ignore him the next time, then you acted on an illusion. Especially since there's no way to ascertain that your perception is accurate. This is a simple example that carries powerful connotations if we take a moment to consider what we do each day of our lives. We create pictures and images of everything around us—people, places, things, concepts, ideas—based on our experiences and sometimes the opinions of others.

Not only do we create pictures, we take it a step further, and we behave as if those illusions are real. A few months ago I was working with a client who was hiring a few people for his organization. Part of my role was to forward interview information to potential candidates, and then the client and I would interview those candidates. On the day we were to interview one candidate he called the client's office to say that he had not received my e-mail containing the interview information. After receiving the call, the client promptly called my office. "We just got a call that the candidate never received the information you sent."

I informed the client that I had indeed sent the e-mail to the candidate, and I even forwarded the sent e-mail to the client. In the interim, the candidate proceeded to talk about how he hadn't gotten a chance to adequately prepare for the interview because "Fran never sent me the information."

Never mind that I'd given this candidate two phone numbers to call if he didn't receive the information within twenty-four hours. He never called. It wasn't until the morning of his interview that my client and I even heard from the guy. When we sat in front of the candidate that Monday morning, he proceeded to explain that the reason he wasn't prepared for the interview was because "you never sent me the information, young lady," he said in my favorite chauvinistic tone. "Well, actually, a more accurate account of what happened is that you never received the information."

"That's right, because you didn't send it."

On cue, I slid the e-mail confirmation across the table. As he read the e-mail and saw the successful transmission notes, he laughed nervously.

"I don't know why I didn't get this," he said, embarrassed.

"It's okay, it probably went into your junk mail box. Happens all the time," I replied.

Illusions. Pictures. We create them all the time. And we act on them most of the time. This candidate was certain that I had not sent him an e-mail. He was convinced that he was right and that I was wrong. His picture was clear based on the lens in his camera.

Emotional Illusions

We're spiritual beings having a human experience, as I said earlier; therefore, we are emotional by nature. We experience life on an emotional level because that's what humans do. We feel. We experience. This is neither good nor bad, yet it does create situations that result in undesirable outcomes—especially in the area of love. Love is arguably the most powerful human emotion, primarily because we seem to be under the impression that it's in short supply. It's such a powerful experience when we feel love that we immediately become afraid that it's going to disappear. This is why when we meet someone we like, we sometimes go nuts. "Omigod, what if he doesn't like me like I like him?" "What if she's dating someone?" "What if we start dating and he doesn't love me as much as I love him?" "What if she finds out about <fill in the blank>?" If we could just have the questions and leave it at that, we'd be fine, but, no, we have to take these illusive questions and cocreate an experience based on them. Some of the more common emotional illusions include "I'll never be loved the way I want to be loved" or my favorite, "No one's ever going to love me the way Person X loved me." This picture leads us to manufacture energy that creates the very thing we claim to want: real love. But real love can't be attracted to a heart that's closed. The person who operates under the illusion that "true love" was a one-time shot will have that precise experience. The person who believes that it's only possible to have one "love of your life" will have only one love of their life. Until that illusion disappears, this individual will continue to be a magnet for Love Impostors.

Physical Illusions

My mama was big. My auntie was big. My people are just big. I'm paraphrasing, but this is what I once heard Oprah Winfrey say as she discussed her challenges with her weight. Everything about our society says that we are driven by the outer—what we look like, the package. This widely held belief (notice I didn't say reality) creates myriad physical illusions. Magazine covers and Paris runways determine the standard for physical beauty. We value outer beauty first and always. There is no value for who we are on the inside. This is made clear to us as soon as we arrive, and it's perpetuated until we leave the nest. Go change your clothes, you look like a bum. If you wear that, people are going to think we're terrible parents. You're not going to wear that, are you? We're under some illusion that we are going to be severely punished if we don't look a certain way.

Social Illusions

We're taught to be socially acceptable or be banished from society. Teens want to be a part of the "in" crowd. Adults crave a place in the right country club. We think that somehow if we can gain acceptance into certain social circles that somehow we'll be significant. That's what we really want: to be significant or to be enough. This is both a social and psychological illusion. We search for these things outside of ourselves, and that's why some of us never feel valued or truly know what it means to be our real selves.

Our social illusions don't stop with our desires to be in the right circles. This need manifests itself in the neighborhoods we strive to live in, the cars we drive, and the schools we send our kids to.

I remember when I was deciding on a college. I was seventeen years old and excited about the next four years of my life. I was going to be playing basketball at a Division I university and that was thrilling for me. It had come down to the Final Three: the University of Texas (UT) at Austin, 187 miles from my hometown of Dallas, Texas, and one of the top colleges in the state; Southern Methodist University (SMU), about twenty minutes from my house—the only reason it was even in the running (SMU's women's basketball team was not in the same league as UT, even though they competed in the same conference); and then there was

Princeton. Need I say more? Princeton was on the list because as my high school coach put it: Very few people get to go to Princeton. You should consider them just because you can. As I continued to talk to people in my immediate circle about the decision, I heard all kinds of sentiments: *UT's a great school, but a degree from SMU carries more weight. A Princeton diploma on your wall will open doors for you that neither UT nor SMU can even crack open.* The message was clear: you are more significant if you attend certain schools. Maybe you won't win an NCAA championship, but people will see you as more important. It was all too confusing, but it came down to what felt right in my heart. I needed the best of both worlds. I loved school, and I loved hoops. I would have been miserable at SMU or Princeton because at the time, both schools had fledgling athletic departments. I decided to go to UT.

Financial Illusions

If God wanted me to be rich, I'd be rich. I've decided that the most I'm probably ever going to make is $50,000 a year. I'm just a $50,000 man. I can't seem to get out of debt. If I could just keep my head above water. Have you ever heard these statements? Ever made one of these statements? When we feed our subconscious cues about lack and scarcity, it listens. It takes heed, and it helps you to create precisely what you want. Most of us believe that our financial hands are the cards that are dealt to us. Nothing could be farther from the truth. If this were the case, only those born into wealth would be rich today. Instead, we live in a world where anyone can change their fortune instantly.

The financial illusions that plague us are the result of those lies we talked about earlier. Replacing financial lies with truths will increase your odds of manifesting that which you wish to see in your bank account.

The Christmas television advertisement from the over-priced jewelry retailer says, "Show her you love her with a diamond."

From Illusions to Love

Love seeks and finds the best for and in you. It is a noun more than it is a verb. It is the purest energy source that we can give to the world. But we've made love into a weapon in many cases. If you tell someone that you love them unconditionally, that is not an invitation for abuse. Unconditional means that you love without judgment, plain and simple. Staying in a relationship that does not serve your Highest Good is not unconditional love, it's spiritual insanity. You are never required to stay in a relationship—personal or professional—that is not of a healthy, loving nature. Ever.

The problem is that many of us are confused about what love is. We've gotten so many different messages throughout the course of our lives that we don't know if what we're giving or feeling is love. We believe that if someone loves us, they'd tell us more often or write it on a cute little note card and leave it beside the bed in the morning. Or they'd remember which kind of toast we like with our eggs. To many of us, this is love.

We also think love is about pain. We think love must hurt to be authentic. If it doesn't hurt, it's not real, we tell ourselves. We even feel bad for leaving a relationship where someone says, "How can you leave me when I'm trying to get clean?" or when a company executive says, "We need you to take a $20,000 pay cut for the good of the company."

We don't see that by dishonoring the earth with pollution we're missing out on an opportunity to love. We don't see that by silencing our own voices we're engaging in unloving behavior. We don't see that by telling our kids that we're going to finance their tuition only to the schools of "our" choice we're misusing love. We see nothing strange about remaining in relationships that have lost their luster. We stay, we say, because of love.

A few weeks ago I spoke at a wellness conference in Riverside, California. In my keynote, as in most of my presentations, I encouraged the audience to leave or reenergize lackluster relationships—not just relationships with other people, but relationships with themselves, as well as Spirit. I received thunderous support for saying those words. Afterward, a very handsome older gentleman, probably in his early seventies, came over to me in the cafeteria. He leaned in and whispered. "It ain't so easy to leave a relationship after you've been in it for thirty-seven years," he said. "Even when ya wanna leave." He howled in laughter.

"If you say so," I responded.

"Young lady, you got some good stuff to say, but you're gonna get me in a whole lotta trouble if I keep listening to you!" And with that he walked away.

We shared a nice moment, and I could see his sincerity. He loves his wife, but he said that he no longer wants to be married to her. For him, he is simply serving time—almost finishing out a sentence. He wasn't willing to let go, and it was sad.

Life is far too short a ride to "do time." Yet that's what most of us do—not just in romance but in life. We get on a train and we stay on that same train until we die. We never stop to get exposed to all of the wonderful sights and sounds along the way. We're too afraid of losing our seat on the train. We're afraid of what might happen if we take in the sights on another train. Strangely, we feel safer in our misery than in what potentially lies beyond the horizons of our lives. We'd rather continue to have the same experiences rather than let go of the sameness for the promise of something wonderful.

THE FOUR BIGGEST ILLUSIONS

It's safe to say that all of us operate under illusions sometimes in our lives. Whether it's thinking that the boss doesn't value our contributions to the company because we didn't get a raise. Or maybe it's that we don't think our lover is still in love with us because he or she forgot our anniversary date. We can't help it. There are going to be times when we think something is one way and discover later that it wasn't the way we thought after all. In those instances we must have the courage and spiritual discipline to admit that we were operating based on our illusions. On our journey to our real selves there are certain illusions that are certain to challenge us. Here are four of the more popular ones:

I'm Not Worthy

I once had a client who would be considered rich by most standards. He's building a very nice portfolio of assets and enjoying his rise to the real estate penthouse. Yet despite his outer achievements, this client was in a constant battle over the fact that he didn't finish his formal education. He has no high school diploma, no college degrees, no advanced certification. In his mind, all he has is "money." For some, this would be enough, but he's constantly concerned that people aren't taking him seriously because he's not educated in the traditional way. "They think I'm a joke," he likes to say. "What do I have to do to prove that I can play in this arena, Fran?"

"Nothing," I answered. "You have nothing to prove. It's all in your head."

"What?" he replied.

"It's all in your head," I repeated. "Who cares what 'they' think?"

My client spent the next twenty minutes providing examples of how people had disrespected him and ignored his advice and how they wouldn't have done those things if he had a degree.

"So get a degree."

He stopped his rant midstream. "What? I don't have time to get a degree. You know how busy my life is."

"Then let go of your illusions about your worth."

The telephone line went silent—an experience that is so rare when the two of us speak. I knew he was thinking about what I'd just said. I'd talk to him on numerous occasions, joking that his mind was like an elf factory, only his elves were busy building new illusions to keep him up at night.

Finally, he spoke. "Are you saying that I'm being paranoid and that these people aren't really thinking what I think they're thinking?"

"No. They could be thinking precisely what you think they're thinking, but more than likely your frustration comes from you not believing that you belong in the ring with them. This is not about them. It's about you and your feelings of self-worth."

"I don't like you," he laughed. "I'm not paying for this session because I don't like the news!"

"That's why I require advanced payment," I said. "Most people don't like the news in the 'Daily Fran.'"

I understood exactly what my client meant. When my coaches and mentors are helping me to grow and get out of my own ego zone, I don't want to hear it either.

Fortunately, this client began to work through his own feelings of how the world views education. Slowly he stopped projecting his own fears onto his potential business partners and, as a result, his business flourished.

Who I Am Inside Is Not Important

People cling to their youthful looks because they fear that they'll be discarded. We believe that who we are—whoever that is—is not important. We've created a collective illusion that looks are more important than anything. We go to great lengths to preserve our looks because we actually believe that people will pay more attention to us if we look a certain way. It's all a scary illusion—one that has young girls contemplating breast augmentation surgery; one that has men and women going under the knife for a little nip and tuck. As a society, we simply don't value the inner. We can change this. We have to change this within ourselves first, and then in the world. That's the way real changes happen. What we want to show up in the greater society, we have to work on in our own lives. If we want our world to be a place that values who we are inside, we have to value who we are inside.

I've never thought a whole lot about growing old, probably because I'm still young, but I have noticed that I am looking at my face more. I am noticing things that I didn't notice a few years ago. I don't like that I'm noticing them. I try not to be too hard on myself for noticing them, so I honor them aloud, and then I move on. This system works for me because it allows me to give a voice to my feelings. And while I don't have to fertilize these feelings, I've found that trying not to think about a thing has just the opposite effect. You actually think more about that thing.

One of the things that I believe has helped me not to feed society's notion of outer versus inner beauty is I don't have television. I have the "box," but I don't have cable and so can't receive any channels. What's funny is that this wasn't planned. I actually like television, but I had so much difficulty getting the cable people to install the service that I just decided not to get it. It's been more than two years, and I don't miss it at all until I want to see a big event like the NBA playoffs, the U.S. Open, or the Academy Awards. Then I go to my favorite sports bar!

I think there's something to the constant exposure—even overexposure—that we get about our outer selves. Commercials tell us that we must look a certain way, dress a certain way, and drive a certain car to be important in our world. None of us is exempt from these messages. They're everywhere! Billboards, newspaper, television, radio, and now, even our cell phones. It's difficult to escape them, yet that is precisely what we must do. And we must talk to our kids about these messages so that they don't lose sight of their real selves.

People Are Out to Get Me

A few weeks ago, I was speaking at an event in Los Angeles, and as she always does, Silvia, my former assistant, was assisting me with setup and breakdown. I felt as though she wasn't fully present during the event. This perception was based on several things. First, she had arrived late to the hotel. Then the photos she took of me during my presentation were taken from one side of the room rather than from different angles that would give her better pictures of me for the website. Then she needed to call and set up an appointment for me the following week but had left the phone number and contact with me rather than taking a copy for her records. Then I had to remind her to gather my display and presentation materials after I left the stage. All of these things were out of the ordinary for her because she's one of the most efficient people I know. But for some reason, this day was different. On top of the things I just mentioned, she left the event before I got a chance to do a face-to-face debriefing with her. Seven hours later, when my brain was fried from coaching and answering questions from conference attendees, I decided to touch bases with Silvia via e-mail. I didn't want to wake her because it was late at night. Yet my mind was still fluttering from the day, and I needed to get these notes to her while they were still on my mind. I wrote the first e-mail about how important it was for us to be on time. I hit send. Then I remembered another issue. She hadn't helped me breakdown the room. So I wrote another e-mail asking her to please remember this on our next engagement. Then I remembered the photos. That was another e-mail. Then I remembered the phone call. Yet another e-mail. Then I went to sleep.

The next day I got an e-mail from Silvia apologizing for a few of the things. She hates being late and made a promise to leave her house even earlier to ensure punctuality. Before she closed the e-mail, though, she reminded me of all the things she "does right," telling me that she doesn't feel appreciated for those things. Hmm, I thought. I can't address something that serious in an e-mail. We should talk.

So I responded with a short e-mail that read, "Thank you for your response, we should talk tomorrow." And even though I'd given her that Monday off, I felt it was important for us to talk in person, so I asked her to meet me for a few minutes. What happened in that conversation is a model for what I believe needs to happen more in personal and professional settings. We talked. I tried to not be her employer, even though I know it's difficult for an employee not to see her employer as an employer. I had to do the best I could to ensure her emotional safety during our conversation.

I was completely okay with her saying that she didn't feel appreciated for running my errands, although I didn't believe that she truly felt that way. But if she did, I needed to know. So I asked her if she truly felt unappreciated or if she'd simply gotten defensive because I pointed out a few things that we needed to dust up on. "I know you appreciate me," she said. "It's just that when I got four e-mails in a row from you, it felt like you'd only noticed the 'bad' things without taking into consideration the things I do well." Then she smiled, "I have a tendency to see only the 'bad.'"

Silvia understands accountability very well even though she's only twenty-three years old. She helps me to grow in this area, as well. I understood and then explained that it was late and that my sending serial e-mails was because I honestly couldn't think of anything else to say in each e-mail prior to sending it. "I can see how it must've felt like I was nit-picking from your perspective," I said. "Would you like to offer me any suggestions should something like this happen again?"

"Maybe just one long e-mail," she laughed. "Instead of four in a row like a machine gun."

Point well taken. A marathon e-mail it will be next time.

Silvia felt attacked. It doesn't matter that I wasn't actually attacking her, that's how it felt to her. That's the lens she looked through. I value who she is inside so it is in my best interest to see who she is inside rather than trying to make her wrong for seeing things the way she sees them. We have daily opportunities to honor each other without condemnation and judgment. We owe it to ourselves to let people know that we're not out to get them when we say things that are corrective. First, we have to stop trying to "get people" when we talk to them. Many of us have every intention to give people a piece of our minds. We have to also come from our hearts when correction is necessary, as it sometimes is. I was able to develop a deeper connection with Silvia because I didn't project my ego-based emotions onto her. And from what she's told me, she was very appreciative of the fact that I invited her to talk and that I actually listened to her.

How often do we think that people are out to get us? A lot of times, it's

WILL THE REAL YOU PLEASE STAND UP?

all in our minds. And if even if they are out to get us, we can diffuse the impact by changing how we receive their actions and behaviors.

I Can Control the Way People See Me

Deep down, we believe that if we're kind and considerate people will see us as kind and considerate. Not so. In fact, if we turn the cameras on you for one full day and sequestered a group of five people in a room to watch you on a closed-circuit television, those five people would differ in their opinions about who you are based on what they see. We all see things the way we see things! And the way we see things is based on our point of reference, our attitudes, our beliefs, and our experiences. That's why we have to let go of trying to control how people perceive us. Our perceptions are so powerful that sometimes we even see what's not there.

A few years ago, a woman who'd watched me play basketball during my four years at the University of Texas at Austin saw me in a grocery store. She walked over to me and said, "Did you ever get that ATM to work for ya?"

I had no idea what she was talking about. "What ATM?"

"The one in the airport last week."

"I wasn't at the airport last week."

"Fran Harris, I saw you kicking that ATM last Friday afternoon at the airport when it wouldn't spit out your money!"

What? I'd been conducting one of my seminars all day Friday, Saturday, and Sunday. It was not physically possible for me to be at the airport on Friday. "Must've been someone else," I said, thinking that she would agree. She didn't.

"You were cursing up a storm, girl."

Now I was really laughing at the sight of me kicking and cursing an ATM. Not that these behaviors were beyond me, but I certainly didn't exhibit them on the day in question. "Sorry, that wasn't me, but I hope whoever she was got her money." I started to walk away.

"I can't believe you won't admit that it was you," she continued. It was obvious that this woman not only believed that she'd seen me that day in the airport but based on her persistence also apparently had an investment in her story. "It can be our little secret," she added. I waved and continued walking. I had no desire to continue the conversation, but it did show me just how active our imaginations and perceptions can be. Remember, what we see is rarely what we see. And if it is, it's certainly not always the full story.

LET IT BE

When I announced that one of my long-term relationships was ending, my friends were shocked. You would have thought someone died. And I guess to my friends in many ways, something had died. For them we'd been the model couple. Very loving and affectionate. Highly communicative and affirming with one another in public and private. They thought our relationship would last forever. Many of them sent long notes of condolences when we finally announced that we'd be going our separate ways. They were even more stunned when they found out that there had been no indiscretions or any of the "normal" breakup drama. "We've walked as far as we can walk together as a couple," I told one friend. "We'll always love each other, and we'll always be there for each other."

"I don't get it," one friend blurted out. "You two were perfect for each other. If you love each other, why are you breaking up?"

"It's the end of our walk together," I repeated. "It's all good."

No one understood this. We've all been conditioned to think that all relationships end in forever, when most relationships run their course within the first few years. The difference is that most people stay in relationships because that's what people expect them to do, even when they're not fulfilled in those relationships. Letting go of relationships is one of the biggest challenges facing us as human beings. We don't know how not to project unrealistic and unfair expectations onto the people we get involved with.

"I don't know what I'll do if we break up."

"If she leaves me, I'll just die."

"I'll never find someone who makes me feel that way."

"I know this one's forever."

What pressure! No wonder we can't let go when it's time to let go. We've invested too much in the fantasy of what relationships are supposed to be. I know that's not popular to say, but it's still true. We bring all of our projections to our relationships. We care so much about what our family members and friends think about our mates that we project their fears and emotions onto the mate as well. This makes letting go that much harder. We can't divorce our mate because we'd have to endure the sneers and jeers of those who are also fantasizing about foreverness in relationships. This was brought home to me when my brother Alonzo shared that he thought one of my relationships was "forever."

"I would have thought that relationship would last forever," he said.

"What's wrong with *right now*?" I shot back. "Why does everything have to be forever? Every relationship's not forever."

Alonzo thought long and hard about those words all day. During our basketball game, he was thinking. As we did yard work, he was thinking. Later that night at dinner he asked and answered his own question. "So, we're just supposed to enjoy and love each other for whatever time we have together? Is that what you're suggesting?"

"Yes! Yes! Yes!" I responded enthusiastically. "What a concept for us to love in the moment and let forever take care of itself."

He took a bite of his enchiladas and chips. "I still want forever."

Most of us do.

There come times, in the context of romance, when we must let go and move on to new lessons, new experiences. This is difficult on so many different levels—because we operate under the illusion that relationships are supposed to last a designated length of time; because we are worried what people are going to think and say about us when they hear the relationship has ended; and because we have come to attach our self-image and worth to our ability to "succeed" in relationships. For some of us, the realization that foreverness isn't a part of every relationship is a sobering reality. It is only devastating because we are invested in the illusion of foreverness. If we could appreciate the relationship for what it *was* rather than what we *wanted it to be,* we could let go of our dreams of foreverness and be thankful for what we had in those relationships. We walk away from every single relationship with valuable lessons about ourselves. We often devalue these gifts because we're too distracted by our illusions of how we wanted our movie to end. We saw the credits rolling with us sitting on the porch sipping tea and our children running around in the front yard.

Sometimes when a relationship ends people say, "It wasn't meant to be." Sure it was. Maybe it wasn't meant to be what you wanted it to be, but it happened, so it was meant to be. Every person we meet is meant to be. Every circumstance we find ourselves in was meant to be. The course of our destiny is determined by our responses to those events.

The film *Sliding Doors,* starring Oscar award–winning actress Gwyneth Paltrow, shows how her life turns out based on different choices that she makes—from the men she chooses to date to which train she takes in London. It's the same with our own lives. Each decision takes us on a unique path on this spiritual journey. There are no wrong or right turns, only those that give us the opportunity to become more of who we are.

If we could truly be grateful for those with whom we've shared our lives and accept them as gems on our journey, we'd have an easier time of letting go and wishing them well.

LETTING GO OF JEALOUSY

I've been jealous two times in my life. They were scary experiences. Thankfully, I learned very early in life what jealousy and envy are all about. Armed with this knowledge, I didn't have to waste time living in fear—because that's what jealousy is all about.

My mother was sitting at the table across from me and one of my cousins.

"What do you want? Girl or boy?" my cousin Donnie asked her.

"Doesn't matter to me," Mom answered.

My cousin turned to me and asked the same question, "What about you, Fran? What do you want?"

I looked straight at my mom and cried, "I don't want anything!"

I was ten years old, and my mother was about to deliver the love of my life—my baby brother, Chris. At the time, I thought of the baby to come as my "replacement"; that's what I feared. I'd been the baby of the family for ten years, and that kind of membership definitely has its privileges! I was not interested in someone coming along and dethroning me.

Later that day, when the tears had dried, I came to understand what jealousy is all about.

"You'll always be my baby," Mom said, hugging me tightly.

"Why'd you have to get pregnant?" I asked, and Mom laughed.

I'm sure she was wondering the same thing for reasons I wouldn't understand until much later in my life.

"This isn't just my baby," she explained. "This is your baby too."

That was a novel idea. Did Mom think I was actually going to love the Replacement? She must've been crazy! There was no way I was ever going to have anything but resentment for this child. I was already plotting ways to make its life miserable.

Of course when Chris arrived, it was quite a different story. We fell in love. And the fear I felt before he was born was replaced with a wonderful joy.

My second bout with jealousy came about eight years later when I was in college and another "new baby" showed up. My sophomore year promised many things for my basketball career. Our coach brought in one new scholarship player, Andrea, an All American from Idaho. She was one of the most heralded players in the country that year, and our coaching staff was thrilled that she'd chosen Texas. They made such a fuss about her that the other kids in the "family" started to feel less special. I felt the same way I had when I found out my mom was having a new baby: *This new kid's trouble.*

I remember thinking to myself, *I've felt this way before,* but I couldn't pinpoint what I was feeling. I liked Andrea, but she was still the "new baby"—potentially my replacement, so she was not to be fully embraced initially. Like my mom, our coach had to assure all of her baby Longhorns that the new bundle of joy was not going to spell extinction for them. *Whew! What a relief.*

WHEN LETTING GO FEELS WRONG

When my mother died, I'd have vivid dreams about her coming home from work or showing up at school to pick me up from basketball practice. These dreams were so real that they would plunge me into major bouts of crying and depression when I'd wake up and realize that she wasn't ever coming home from work again. It was very painful. These dreams continued for one full year. That's how much I wanted to hang on to my mother's physical presence on earth. I wouldn't let go. I couldn't let go. There was a part of me that believed that I was dreaming the whole thing—that she wasn't really dead, and one day I'd wake up and my life would be back on the right track. This never happened, of course, and my grieving continued. There was also a part of me that felt I would be dishonoring my mom if I let go. This was normal, I learned later in therapy. What I learned through prayer and meditation, however, was that the deep longing I was feeling for Mom was preventing me from being fully present in my life.

Some of us refuse to let go of a friend or loved one who has passed on. We can't bring ourselves to do it. It feels wrong, disrespectful even. So we wear our grief like a badge of honor, showing the world just how bad we feel about the death. I've read accounts where mothers who've lost children never resume their lives. They go into a shell, an emotional abyss, never to return. I understand the desire to want to retreat from the world. It feels safe. It feels less painful in some cases. Yet it also has an adverse affect on your spiritual health and growth. The depth of the pain of losing a loved one is so intense that our entire neurological and physical systems are compromised as we grieve. In other words, what shows up in the physical realm is created in the spiritual realm first. We don't realize that the extended periods of grief and sorrow actually stop our systems from operating at optimal levels.

I've never liked the phrase "get over it." It sounds harsh and insensitive. Thankfully, no one's ever uttered those words to me, but I have had friends who've implied those sentiments but were much too kind to actually say those exact words. I don't presume to be able to tell anyone how to grieve, but I will say that we should all be aware of how we allow experiences to take us away from living in the now. What we have right in front of us is the most precious gift—a gift that we'll never get back once it's gone. I honor my mother each day, but I no longer ache for her to be here physically. Instead, I rejoice in having known her and give thanks for the sixteen years that I got to spend with her. All I have is right now, and her spirit is ever present in my life.

Letting Go When We Don't Understand

The year I moved to Los Angeles was an exciting yet anxious time for me, primarily because I was frustrated that I didn't have the ability to see the future. This was a very frustrating time. I wanted to know exactly what was going to happen now that I'd taken the plunge and followed my dreams of hosting a nationally syndicated television show. I attempted to make the right connections, attend the right workshops, and network with the right people. Fortunately, I had a few friends "in the business" who were willing to help make some introductions. One of those introductions was to a man and woman who helped screenwriters workshop their script. We'd gather around in their living room, and actors would read the screenplay so that the writer could hear the dialogue and even work through some of the structural issues. It was a fantastic opportunity to drastically improve your writing. So I was thrilled when they agreed to have a reading for one of my scripts. I hired the actors, and the reading went very well.

I'd gotten one of my actor friends to participate, and he needed a ride to work immediately following the reading. So when the reading was over, I rushed out to get him to work on time. In my haste, I forgot to help the hosts put their room back in order. When I realized my oversight, I called to apologize. They wouldn't take my calls. I e-mailed them. I called again. No answer, no returned calls. I wrote them a handwritten letter, thanking them for the opportunity and apologizing profusely for being in such hurry that I left the room in disarray. Then I wrote another e-mail. Finally, I received a response.

"Thanks for your note. We've decided not to have any further professional affiliation with you."

That was it. No explanation. No reasons for the decision. Nothing. As I read this now, I'm laughing out loud because the experience was priceless. You can't pay for this kind of human interaction. Back then, though, I was devastated. I was literally sick about it. I wanted, needed to know "why." How could they just shut me out and not tell me? I didn't mind about being banished from the readings, but it seemed so unfair not to at least let me know why. So for a whole week I agonized over the situation. "I don't understand," I kept telling my closest friends. "I don't even know what happened."

After hearing me go on and on about "wanting to know what happened," my sister Debra said something to me that I'll never forget. "You may never know, and you just have to let it go. If these are people who don't value open communication, do you really want them in your life?"

The answer was no. And in that instant, I let it go. I couldn't control their decision to discontinue their relationship with me, and I certainly couldn't control their decision not to let me know why they'd made the decision. It was in my spiritual best interest to let it go and let it be. So, I did.

As you read this, I trust that you're thinking of a situation in your life that you're fixated on in the way I was with the screenwriter's group. It's time to let go and let it be. You can't control it no matter how smart you are, how spiritual you are, how many people you know, or how good you are at manipulation. You can't control it. Let it go. Today. This moment.

LETTING GO OF WHAT WAS

"I used to be so thin."

"I used to be so fast."

"I remember when it only took me five minutes to do that."

"My voice isn't what it used to be."

Not only do we mourn for the people we love, but we also mourn for the things that used to be. These things also keep us from maximizing the moment. They keep us from appreciating who we are today. They keep us from being in-joy every second of our lives. We mourn for our past because the past reminds us that the end is near, I suppose. When you're a teenager, death isn't usually at the top of your list to think about each day. As we get older, though, the topic sticks its head through the windows of our minds on occasion, forcing us to deal with our own mortality. We don't like that. So we quickly stop thinking about it. Yet we continue to long for better days, for younger days. This is the ego's way of stealing the show. In hoops, we call that "ball hogging." The ego is adept at grandstanding, and this is yet another one of its tricks: "*If I can convince him to think about what he was like twenty years ago, there's no way he's going to see how blessed he is at fifty-one. Look at him, he's healthy, virile, and energetic, but he doesn't believe it because he assigns those words to the thirty-year-old he wants to be again. This is awesome!*"

That's a trailer from the movie your ego's producing about your life. That's why we have to be ever-present. We have to patrol the grounds of our minds so that we are being good stewards of our lives spiritually, emotionally, mentally, and physically. We have to constantly remind the Ego that it's retired. It's not on the active roster any longer. This is a chore because the ego is akin to a washed-up athlete who refuses to join the seniors' league. It refuses to acknowledge that the game isn't what it used to be and that there's no use for it any longer.

The ego is strong-willed. Like us, it doesn't believe that its better days are behind it. Many of us want to continue seeing those in our lives as they once were. We won't accept that things have changed because we don't really like change even when the change is good for us. We still resist it.

This seems especially true for parents whose children are moving from adolescents to teenagers. I can remember when my younger brother was going from twelve to thirteen. While he appeared to be rebelling, what I know now is that he was simply attempting to make sense of all the things that were happening to him emotionally, physically, and psychologically—things only he could understand. The effect of having lost Mom was weighing on him heavily, and he felt very different. I could identify with that experience, yet I wasn't him. His experience was uniquely his, and I needed to respect his journey. Letting go of him at this stage was particularly hard because I was about to go to Italy to play professional basketball. It was excruciating to think of being thousands of miles away from him, not being able to talk to him on the phone every night before he went to sleep, the way we had when I was in college. I couldn't let go of "what was." Our relationship was evolving, but I refused to let go of the six-year-old who'd jumped into my arms the day after my Mom died and asked, "Do you know [that she'd died]?" That day is forever etched in my memory. They are so precious when they're that age. I wanted to hold on to that period in our lives. Living in Europe would signal that things were definitely going to change. Maybe he'd forget about me. Maybe he'd get involved in drugs or gangs if I wasn't going to be around to talk to him. Maybe, maybe, maybe. I had to let it go. So I did. And we both survived. As we always do.

WILL THE REAL YOU PLEASE STAND UP?

Our challenge as parents, lovers, friends, and family is to know that when we surrender, we free ourselves up to be available to live and love in the present. By holding on to and fretting about the things we can't control anyway, we miss out on the chance to create new magical moments with those we love. And isn't that what life's really about anyway?

There is a saying: Let go, let God. For most, if not all, of us, the letting go that we most need to do is a type of surrender. We need to surrender to life itself. This means that we need to let go of our illusion that we actually can control most aspects of our lives. In many cases, rather than to fight "what is," we need to learn to accept and to be at peace. . . . Too many of us are trying to keep a tight grip on things that are out of our control. This is like trying to grip the water flowing in a river. Put your hands into the river. If you try to trap the water by grabbing it and clenching your fists, it goes right out of your hands. If you relax and open, gently cupping your hands, the water flows into your palms. By relaxing, opening, and trusting, we can hold on to more of what is precious to us. By letting go, we actually allow more of the mystery of life to come in for us.

✒ REAL QUESTIONS, REAL ANSWERS ✒

I'm a college student who recently broke up with this girl I've dated since I was in the ninth grade. We tried to continue our relationship, but she's attending a college on the East Coast, and I'm on the West Coast. The problem is that I'm having a hard time letting go of her because we were together for so long. It's not even that I love her, really. I guess I'm just used to her. She says she feels the same way.

What you're going through is very natural. We all create bonds with the people we've grown up with or spent any significant amount of time with. I think the fact that you're able to talk about it will help. It might help to make the effort to meet new people so that you can start to make new connections.

Journaling is also a great way to get our feelings out and into the universe. While this may sound like a simple prescription for "letting go," it is only the beginning of what you need to do. You've acknowledged that you don't really love her, so how about trying to figure out what exactly it is that you're hanging on to. Sometimes it's not the person we're attached to—it's the feelings we remember having with them or the nostalgia of all the things we shared with them. In this case, letting go is less about letting go of the person and more about letting go of the illusion that you will not or cannot have those experiences again. In other words, we mourn relationships sometimes because we truly believe that what we share with one person cannot be duplicated ever again. This is a huge illusion. There is never just one person who's a good fit for us. Next, I recommend journaling because sometimes a journal gives us someone that we can be 100 percent honest with. Sometimes we share more openly with a pen and paper than we do in therapy. You have to decide the depth of your grief for this relationship. If you need to talk to someone, don't be afraid to seek professional help. Finally, I do think it's important to attempt to make new connections. New connections don't have to mean romantic involvement, they can simply entail meeting new people who offer you new opportunities to create new memories so that you're less focused on your past.

I've been in the same job for the past five years, and I have hated every year of it. I took the job because it pays well and it keeps me and my family in a lifestyle that we've grown accustomed to. Any time I try to broach the subject with my wife of maybe starting my own business, I get cold feet because we've had a rough time and we're finally starting to get out from under some of our debt. I guess I'd feel like I don't have the right to put my family through that again.

Sounds like you already know what's going to happen! Letting go of perceived security is much tougher than it seems. But staying in a job that you "hate" carries with it an even stricter penalty: your spiritual, emotional, and physical health. People always underestimate the damage that's done by working in jobs that they detest. My recommendation is to

WILL THE REAL YOU PLEASE STAND UP?

first have a "real" conversation with your wife, and second, start developing your exit strategy. This can include months or years of saving and researching to start your own business. Either way, you are doing yourself and your family a greater disservice by staying in a job simply because it's keeping you in a certain lifestyle.

Yearn for Righteousness

The world we want to live in, we must help create.
Emmy Award–winning Actress Beah Richards
(from the documentary Beah: A Black Woman Speaks)

here once was a new king who lived in a very big house. He was surrounded by servants and handlers who spent most of their days telling him how amazing he was. One day this young king met a queen. Like the king, she, too, was surrounded by servants, assistants, and handlers. The two became acquainted and started a wonderful friendship.

The king recognized that the queen could teach him many things, and he asked her to help him complete several of his projects. The queen gladly obliged and offered her expertise free of charge. It was more important to her to help the young king find his way. As their friendship grew, the king and queen learned many things about each other. The king learned that the queen was allergic to grass, and the queen learned that the king couldn't read. She started teaching him to read and training his servants how to write his correspondence.

Months later, when one of his projects was completed, the king invited the queen to the unveiling of his masterpiece. He publicly thanked her for her contributions and told the royal subjects that his project could not have been completed without the generosity of the queen.

Later that evening the queen and the king chatted privately in his library. As the queen was about to leave the king's palace, she overheard him conducting an interview with a reporter. "This project has been a labor of love and passion," he said. The reporter asked him to elaborate on the queen's contribution, and he replied, "The queen was merely my muse. I am responsible for this masterpiece."

The queen walked away from the library in a state of confusion. She had spent almost a year of her life helping the king churn out his masterpiece. She'd forsaken other projects to be available for him, and he didn't even acknowledge, let alone appreciate, her contributions. As she gathered her belongings and headed for the door, the king rushed over to her. "Why are you leaving? We haven't had our celebratory feast."

The queen looked sadly into the eyes of the king. "I do not eat at the table with paupers." And with those words, she disappeared out the door.

The king was baffled. Pauper? He was the richest man in the land. How could she say such a thing to him? Weeks passed, and he tried many times to reach the queen. Each time he would call, her assistant would say that she was unavailable. Finally the queen took the call.

"Why are you avoiding me?" he asked. "What have I done to deserve such treatment?"

The queen shut her door and looked out onto the starry night. "Do you remember the night of your party?"

"I do," the king replied.

"I overheard your interview with the reporter. I heard you say that you had no help in completing your masterpiece," she continued.

The king contemplated lying, but instead he stuck out his chest and said, "That's right. I did. You were great company, but I drove the distance. There is nothing you can say to convince me otherwise. I am right. I am always right."

The queen smiled into the phone. "But are you righteous?"

And with those words, the line went dead. The king stared into the

WILL THE REAL YOU PLEASE STAND UP?

phone, not sure of what just happened. He dialed the number again, but this time he got a recording from the telephone company. The number was invalid. He dialed and dialed and dialed a hundred more times. The line could not have been disconnected that quickly. He had his driver take him to the queen's estate. It was gone. That night, the king lay in his royal bed, a servant rubbing his feet, the words of the queen still ringing in his ear: "But are you righteous?"

Sometimes in our efforts to be right we forget to be righteous. It is possible that the king actually did most of the work for his masterpiece, yet his comments to the reporter, while "right" in his mind, were hardly righteous. They did not honor the role that the queen played in the completion of his masterpiece. How often do we want the credit for things we have not done or the spotlight for the things we have done? How often are we afraid that by acknowledging the efforts of those around us somehow our brilliance will be dimmed?

WHAT WOULD GOD DO?

The problem with asking this question is that we all know what God would do, but we don't want to do what God would do because we're too invested in being right. God would choose righteousness over rightness in every situation. But rightness has a big premium in the human dimension. We perceive that we have too much at stake to give up "being right."

Righteousness is what most of us only pretend to seek on our spiritual paths. It's much more gratifying for us to be right. Righteousness is for wimps, we believe. If I do the righteous thing, I'm going to be perceived as weak, soft, and unauthoritative, and I can't have that. No, I'd rather be right.

I want to be right with my kids, with my spouse, with my friends, with the cashier at the department store, with the customer service rep on line two, with the UPS guy, with my banker, with my lawyer, and everybody in between! I want to be right. I feel better when I'm right. Does this sound like anybody you know?

WHAT IS RIGHTEOUSNESS?

Righteousness is that which seeks to achieve the highest good. That highest good is God. If we seek to see and experience God in every person we meet, we are yearning for righteousness and that which is good (God). If you looked up "God" in the dictionary, you'd find that part of its definition is goodness. Not good as in "average" but good as in God. Have I totally confused you? Our highest self is God. We are images of God. Images of good. We were created in God's image. Therefore, what is righteous in all situations is that which achieves the highest good.

One of my life-coaching clients asked me a great question. "Whose highest good takes precedence when you're in a relationship?" The highest good for the situation isn't about the people involved in the situation. This client couldn't conceive of a "highest good" that didn't result in somebody winning. Yearning for righteousness in relationships means relinquishing your "position" on the subject and seeking the best solution for the situation. For example, you and your friend are traveling on a cross-country road trip and one of you wants to drive all the way through to save time and to miss traffic. But you are tired and don't feel comfortable sleeping while your friend drives through ghost towns at three or four o'clock in the morning. What is the righteous thing to do? In this case, what is righteous is safety. You and your friend have to be able to agree on a few things including (1) driving through towns without potential places to gas up isn't a smart idea and (2) unless two people can be awake, driving at night may not be the optimal situation. This is not about who's right but rather "what's" right.

Few of us can let go of what we want—what our egos want—to achieve what honors the circumstance at hand. If you're in a conversation about how to discipline your son who came in an hour past his curfew, the highest good isn't based on your fear of what he's doing during the hour. The highest good isn't based on what you know you were doing when you came home late at that age. The highest good isn't about your perception that your husband is too lenient; therefore, it's your chance to point out that your son came in late because of his leniency. The highest good isn't about your projection that your wife always comes to his rescue when he's in trouble. The righteous thing to do in this instant is to come to a consensus about how to create an environment where house rules are respected and there's buy-in from your children.

In relationships, we tend to be in constant battle over preserving power. So it's easy to lose sight of what's truly best (highest good) when both people are so invested in winning. Nobody wins when somebody feels unheard, misunderstood, or undervalued in the relationship.

WHY WE CRAVE RIGHTNESS

We kill for it. We steal for it. We even die for it. Being right carries a hefty premium in the human dimension. Ever heard someone say, "I was right"? or "I told you I was right!"? Ever said anything that sounds remotely like one of those two sentences? Most of us have. We take such pride in being able to say those words. We go to great lengths to be able to say those words. We'll do hours of research on the Internet and conduct informal polls just to be able to call someone and say, "See, I told you I was right." When what we're really saying is, "See, I told you I'm insecure."

We crave rightness because we're afraid that we won't be significant if we don't triumph in all situations. That's real. We want to win. Not only that, but we want you to lose. It's not enough that we get to hold up the trophy at the end of the debate, we also want to taunt you because we enjoy watching you lose. Part of winning and being right means we get the chance to enjoy the other person's experience of defeat. It's a fringe benefit of being right.

Some of you are reading this and you're cringing. You had a physical reaction to reading those words, didn't you? But you also know that they are true. If you've ever looked across at someone and said the words, "I'm right," then you know what I'm talking about. In those moments, if you could bring yourself to do it, you'd probably stand on a tabletop and exclaim, with King Kong chest-beating vigor, "I'm riiiiiiiiiiight! I'm right! I'm right! I'm right!" Okay, so you were right. Now what? What's next?

The human psyche is very fragile, and we must accept and understand this to understand our need for rightness. We are weakened by our egos. We seek to feel important every day of our lives. If someone doesn't say "thank you," we go bananas. If someone doesn't acknowledge a job well done, we lose it. If someone doesn't say "I love you" with just the right voice inflection, we blow a fuse. My friend Rebecca forgot my birthday one year (she was off by one day), and you would have thought I was three years old! It was pathetic! I pouted and sulked for about an hour. Okay, two. And you know what? There's nothing she could have said to make me feel better. Why? Because I didn't want to feel better. I wanted to be right. That's how we humans operate.

Being right is only fun if we get the extra bonus of punishing you, too. We believe that if we can look mad enough and be silent for long enough, you'll feel the sting and we would have achieved the ultimate: hurting you. Checkmate. Next.

You see, being right isn't just about winning an argument. It's not just about being correct. It's about conquest. Dominance. We want to feel important. We want the whole world to take notice of how significant we are. That's why when we're right, we tell everybody we know. We pull out our Rolodexes and Blackberries and start dialing for applause.

"Hey, remember when I told you about Chad and how he said that I didn't turn in my report on time? Well, I forwarded the original e-mail back to him and he had to eat his words. I told you I was right."

Sound familiar? No?

Next call. "Hey, Mom? Oh, me, not much. Work? It's okay. Oh! Did I tell you that I made my boss eat crow? I didn't? Well, if you've got a second...."

Now is it sounding familiar? Of course it is. You've done it, and you know you've done it! We've all done this. It's all a part of our campaign to feel important. Yet, we're already significant because we're children of God.

This issue with wanting to feel important is that we have been conditioned to seek this feeling from outside of ourselves. We rely on the world to validate our very existence. Writers know this very well—especially writers who have publishing deals. Authors are often judged by their sales, not the content of their work. The question isn't "Did the work transform lives?" The question is "How many lives did the work transform?"

There's no judgment in any of that, it's simply important to know that just because you live in the world doesn't mean you have to be "of" the world. You don't have to subscribe to the rules and ideologies that don't feed the real you.

Once we realize that there is no honor in triumph over another human being, we'll let go of our insatiable need to be right.

That's why the story from earlier about the man who got the tour of heaven was so poignant.

HUMAN OR GOD?

To find righteousness, we have to let go of our need to make God, Allah, the Divine, the Creator human. God is Spirit. Research any religious dogma and this one thing is consistent. This is the one thing Christians, Jews, Mormons, Hindus, and Muslims actually agree on—that higher power is Spirit. Yet we have related to God as human since the beginning of time, which explains why there's so much judgment and condemnation in the world today. Humans operate on an approval-seeking reward/punishment paradigm, which encourages us to relate to God in the same way. The cycle goes like this:

Do things to please God. (Seek approval.)

Get rewarded for pleasing God. (Get the elixir.)

Get punished for disappointing God. (Avoid the poison.)

That sums up our relationship with God and our relationship with everything in the world. It's how we raise our children. It's how we interact with our coworkers. It's how we set up our intimate relationships. It's how we seek friends. We seek first to gain approval. Do you really love me? Once approval is secured, we set up a system of rewards and punishment. *If you love me, you wouldn't do that to me.* If people behave as we want and expect them to, they escape our poison—our silence, anger, rejection, and resentment.

If they don't behave as we'd like, we heap our judgment, condemnation, and punishment on them, and the cycle starts all over again—seeking approval to get back in our good graces, getting rewarded once approval is granted, punishment or retribution the next time we screw up. This is the world we've created. Sadly, this is also how we believe God deals with us.

Recently, a friend of mine who's forty-plus years old decided to do something different on Sunday rather than going to church. He went sailing. He'd had a hard week full of deadlines. He needed a break in a big way. When he got home, he called me sounding like a new person. "You've gotta go with me sometimes," he said. "I can literally feel the power of God when I'm out there." He had gotten recharged, I could tell.

When his father found out that he'd chosen to go sailing instead of going to church, the father lit into him about his priorities. My friend desperately needed some alone time. The ocean where he lives is fairly desolate early on Sunday mornings. It seemed like the best time to go, and he didn't see anything wrong with his decision until later that evening when his father called to "check to see if he'd made it to church." After speaking with his father, though, he felt guilty for not going to church. His father admonished him, "God has blessed you with that boat; the least you can do is thank him by showing up at his house on Sunday morning."

My friend now felt like he had to seek God's forgiveness and approval because if Dad were right and he'd indeed screwed up by not attending church service, then surely God was in a mood, which meant that he'd have to win back God's approval or face the wrath of the Almighty, right? How many times have you felt like this in any relationship?

My friend's father was projecting his own interpretation of God onto him. Just because the Dad experiences God as a tyrannical, gavel-toting God didn't mean that my friend had to have the same interpretation or experience. My friend yearned for righteousness for his own life. Sailing the magnificent Pacific Ocean was righteous for him. For his father, though, my friend's actions were not right.

My Godmom, Jean, and I do a dance almost every Sunday. She calls me and asks me two questions. First, "How's my girl?" When she is sure that I am safe and well she moves to question two: Did you make it to church today, baby? My answer is almost always the same. "Yes, ma'am, I did." This answer always leads to a third question, "Was the service held in your living room or did you actually venture out to a building where other people were present?" We laugh. Well, I laugh mostly but she's also entertained. It's our thing. You see, I met my Godmom at church, when we were both there seven days a week and three times on Sunday. She's a gifted pianist and singer who I'm sure attends enough services for the both of us so I don't worry about missing one or two. Attending church is what she does and it's a part of her Sundays and even some weekdays. I love hearing about her Sundays and the sermons but I don't feel the need to go to church every Sunday. Sometimes I will go to the ocean to commune with God, praying for hours because that's what feels righteous for me. This may be on a Sunday morning or it may be on a Tuesday afternoon or a Friday night. I move when the Spirit moves me and that's not always on a Sunday morning even though I've been programmed to go on that day. Every day is the Lord's day.

We have to know what is righteous for our own lives. We must know that what is righteous for our own spiritual nourishment may not be righteous for the next person, even if that person is someone we love dearly. How many times have you scrambled around after offending someone? How many times have you jumped through hoops to get back on someone's "good side"? The real you doesn't have to do that. The real you is always in God's good graces because God only has good graces! If you have chosen to experience Spirit in a way that is similar to how we treat one another, I invite you to have a different experience. Yearn for your own righteousness, and that which is not the real you will slip away. Every time.

I invite you to have a different experience with God. Imagine God as Spirit who begins and ends with only one thing: love. There's no judgment. No condemnation. No betrayal. No fire and brimstone. Nothing but love. If it's hard for you to accept this new view of God, know that it is only because you are invested in the old system of approval seeking and rewards/punishment. It's all you know. It doesn't matter which school of spiritual or religious thought you graduated from, it's probably steeped in that dogma. *Seek my approval. Get a dog biscuit if I like your tricks. Get a swat on the butt if I don't.* That's been God for most of us. That's why many of us have not discovered the path to our real selves, our highest being.

NEW LANGUAGE

I discovered the power of language many years ago. When it came to God, I prayed "Our Father" like every other Baptist. I referred to God as "He" because that's what I heard every Sunday in my church. I accepted God as male because that was the unspoken understanding among most religions. As a six-year-old I remember looking at a picture of a man I later learned was supposed to be Jesus Christ. He was hanging on a cross, blood gushing from his hand, a crown on his head. More blood streaming down his face. What a terrifying picture for a six-year-old to see. I remember thinking to myself, "Why is there a scary picture of a white man on our wall?" It was very curious to me. So, in true form I asked one of the adults in our church what was, for me, an obvious question. "Who's he?"

"That's the Son of God."

So God was white? That didn't seem fair. The white people get to claim God as their father. Why was I praying to the white people's father? These were questions that weren't welcomed in my house or my church. Not because curiosity wasn't encouraged. It was—but not on these matters. The teachers at church were busy helping me to remember the books of the Bible, they didn't have time to deal with my questions about God!

It took me twenty years to understand that these questions had been met with vagueness not because they didn't think a six-year-old would understand, but because *they* didn't understand! They, too, were somewhat shaky on the details of what they taught each Sunday.

I didn't ask many more questions, but the questions still remained in my mind. I had tons of questions. Why were there only men sitting in the special area called the pulpit? Why were the people who showed us to our seats usually women, but the people who carried our money to the back of the church were predominantly men? Why did my Mom and all of my friends' moms wear pants every day except to church on Sunday? Were pants bad? And if so, weren't they bad on Tuesday, too?

As I got older, I started to understand that the church like every other organization had its share of politics. This explained a lot to me. It explained why men, in general, believed they deserved higher status in the church and in God's eyes. Since the pictures of Jesus were of a "white" man, it explained to some degree why many white people believe that they're the superior race. If all of the important people looked like me, I'd think I was pretty special, too! This was all the handy work of the ego. I don't blame racists, sexists, lookists, or any other "ists" for what they personify and perpetuate. They are mere hostages of their egos.

This explains why many women believe God has sentenced them to be second-class citizens—less status, fewer votes, slim to no rights. The ego is the reason women didn't have the same rights as men until the twentieth century. The ego explains why some men have an inflated sense of entitlement and why some women are afraid to become the powerful souls God created.

The real eye-opener came during one of my afternoon chats with my goddaughter ten years later. Whenever I'd pick her up from school, I'd have a question of the day for her, and then we'd take a walk around the park discussing it.

"What do you think God looks like?" I asked. And without hesitation she answered. "I think he's white and big."

"White and big, huh?" I repeated.

She nodded. "Yep. And maybe he has a beard."

This, from a seven-year-old white girl. She thought God was a big, bearded white man.

That was all I needed to hear, even though the truth is that most of us see God this way. Most religions reinforce the maleness and/or whiteness of God. That's not my opinion, that's based on empirical data. We accept that all of the Apostles were cool, white guys in sandals. We accept that there were only a few great women in religious history because if there were more, wouldn't there have been more records of their work? If you study history, you'll find that women had a significant role in the development of spirituality, as well as what became the modern-day church. Their exclusion from published works is the result of ego and politics, not the absence of their contributions.

To move toward our real selves, all of us must know that we "can" become all that we can become. It's impossible to actualize as a spiritual being if you believe that the God you pray to discriminates against your group. How can the real you stand up under these circumstances?

God embodies both masculine and feminine energy. There is no "man upstairs." These are stories that have subtly subjugated women for centuries. I didn't write this book to refute everything that's been written or recorded in our spiritual or religious annals. You've got to answer your own questions. I did, however, write this book to encourage you to question everything you've believed up to this point in your life so that you can move closer to the real you—the you God intended you to be. God welcomes questions. You can access God without going through a middle man or middle woman. You've got a direct line to Spirit. The real you depends on your ability to know that God is an equal employer Spirit. If you do not know this, you will never become all of you because you will always feel that you have limits placed upon you by God.

What We Really Yearn For

We all want to live in a righteous world. A world where people are kind, compassionate, generous, and loving. We do live in that world. Sometimes we simply don't see it as such. We also live in a world that is constantly trying to find its own identity because the people in it are on an ever-changing trek to find their real selves, as well. We want a real world. To have the kind of world we want to live in, we have to participate in the creation of that world.

I believe that's what Beah Richards meant when she said in the documentary about her life, "The world we want to live in, we must help create. It needs our input." In other words, we can't simply sit around and hope for a better day, we have to get involved. Our first line of involvement is in becoming the person we're supposed to become. Becoming the real you. Once we begin to get our own houses in order, then we can venture out into our families, communities, and the rest of the world. But it starts at home in our own hearts. Most of us are comfortable reaching out to help others. It gives us a distraction from what's really happening at home. It's easy to project onto the world what we fear will happen if "we aren't careful," but that's the extent to which most of us get involved. Spiritual enlightenment is an everyday, 24/7 journey, yet most of us approach our spiritual fitness in the same manner that we approach our New Year's wellness goals—when it fits in our schedule. And I'm not talking about going to mass or Sunday morning worship service, I'm talking about walking with God, with Spirit, every day of our lives. I'm talking about yearning for our greatness and for righteousness on a consistent basis.

In a recent conversation with Debra, I exclaimed in some exasperation,

"It's hard being enlightened." We both laughed. "It's sooooo hard to be on a path of spiritual enlightenment."

I once saw a card that read: "Sisters are a blessing." But that's not necessarily true. A friend who happens to be your sister, I feel, is a true blessing. My sister Debra is one of my closest friends. We share a real connection that isn't devoid of hills, mountains, and valleys, yet we truly have an abiding affection and love for each other, and we enjoy each other. We speak by telephone many times during the day, and she's often the first person I call when something good or challenging happens to me.

Our relationship has gone from big sister/little sister to confidante, spiritual advisor, life coach, business strategist, and friend. What we have is quite special because we build our relationship on righteousness rather than on rightness. We fight and disagree like any two people with varying perspectives, yet what unites us is our commitment to righteousness. We've built our relationship on this one principle. We've agreed that basing a friendship on genetics isn't always ideal. Instead, we've opted to get to know each other and support each other in an honest, loving fashion. One of the things I appreciate most about my sisterfriend is that we talk about righteousness when we're sharing challenges in our professional or personal lives, and that keeps us both yearning for the very thing we want to create in our lives.

As I state in my book *The Intentional Millionaire*, people who think it's easy to always be in a state of awareness and aliveness are not aware and alive. Because if they were, they'd know the minute-by-minute challenges that come your way when you're on a spiritual path. Spiritual enlightenment is challenging because we can't deny that we're part human. We're spiritual, yes, but we're also human. The human part of us is about preservation, dominance, and ego. The human part of us is supremely invested in being right, not righteous. In knowing this, we must constantly silence the voice of the ego and listen to the voice of God, which, again, always wants not only what's good for us, but also what's good in us.

How Righteousness Grows

Conflict is our greatest opportunity to learn about righteousness. A professor friend of mine shared a story about a situation at his college. He had a student who believed she deserved a higher grade. Rather than come directly to my friend, the student started a campaign to sully his name. Those efforts made the inevitable showdown between my friend and this student even more volatile. By the time they sat in front of each other, each had built up mounds of resentment. Having a civil conversation was virtually impossible. As the student sat in front of this professor, the negative energy was so palpable, it could be cut with an ax. The professor started the conversation by saying that he stood by the grade he'd given. The student blurted out, "You don't like me!" Nothing could have been farther from the truth. The professor actually had a great deal of admiration for the student. She was bold, bright, and outgoing. But she had not been diligent in her assignments, which is why she was receiving a C in the class. "This is not personal," the professor replied.

"Just admit it. You don't like me."

The professor was having a difficult time hearing these words, knowing what the student had said about him to other students and even faculty.

"Let's stick with the facts," the professor said.

"The fact is you don't like me, and you're intimidated because I'm smart."

The professor had had enough. His efforts to be mature and professional were being challenged by what he perceived to be adolescent rants. "Your problem is that you think you know more than I do."

The argument escalated from there until the professor paused for a moment and heard the noise in the room. He sat back in his chair and listened as the student cried about feeling like she had to prove her intelligence in the professor's class. From that moment on, the dynamics in the room changed. The professor wasn't just listening at this point, he heard the student. "I feel like I have to prove myself in your class." This wasn't about class. This was about a student who, for whatever reason, felt she had to prove herself. She brought that baggage to class and by receiving a C, she had once again "failed to prove how smart she really is." As I listened to this story, my sense was that the student's fear of "not making the cut" had actually immobilized her, and that's why she could never seem to turn in her assignments on a consistent basis. This behavior led to C-level grades, which in turn, rendered results she didn't want but had actually created.

How often do we create the exact results we claim not to want? All the time. I have several traits that if I'm honest, I must say they bug the hell out of me. I'm working to be less judgmental of people who aren't direct and honest, but I have to admit it's a challenge.

RIGHTEOUSNESS VERSUS SELF-RIGHTEOUSNESS

When I talk about righteousness, I'm not talking about self-righteousness, I'm speaking of righteousness. Seeking the highest good in all situations.

As I think back on this story, it was clear that the professor chose righteousness over rightness. If we come from Egoland, the professor was "right" and could have stayed in a tug-of-war for rightness with this student until the next midterm, but because he chose righteousness over rightness, he was able to hear this student's heart and ignore what his ego was selling.

How many times have you been in an argument and decided that you needed "to make your point"? Or how about those moments that you'd planned your attack for the next time you and your husband get into a fight? You're going to get him! You line up all of your artillery. You're gonna pull out the AK-You-Never-Say-Thank-You bullets. You'll whip out the You-Don't-Appreciate-How-Hard-I-Work card. You'll wait for the right moment to fire and then you'll let him have it! And it's not enough for you to want to be right, you also want—need—the other person to be wrong, right?

It's the ego that needs to triumph over another soul. As I thought about the situation with the professor and the student, it made me think about all of the opportunities we have to yearn for righteousness. Throughout the day, we have countless chances to choose kindness over indifference, to choose acceptance over judgment, but something in us wants to be victorious in all situations.

I was driving down the 405 in Los Angeles the other day, and I needed to get into the right lane to exit, but no one would let me over. The road was packed like a can of sardines, and I knew that I had to rely on the kindness of strangers to be on time for my appointment. Cars continued to zoom by. "Come on!" I yelled as I laughed about the insanity of Los Angeles traffic. "Gimme a break!" Finally, I think this guy must've dropped his cell phone or something because a space opened up for me to get over into the middle lane. Just one more lane and I'd be on the home stretch. I just needed one more angel to let me over. His generosity opened the door for more kindness, and pretty soon I was exiting on Wilshire Boulevard, only a few blocks from my 1:30 meeting. As I entered the busy ramp heading toward UCLA, I accelerated to get through a changing light. As my car glided through the "orange" light, the female driver of the car who pulled onto the street from the adjacent street pointed her fingers at me as if to say, "That's a no-no." I smiled and kept driving. She must not have seen the orange light.

A few moments later I pulled up to a busy intersection where this same female driver was cursing out the driver next to her. She was very angry because apparently the guy in the next car had cut her off in traffic. "You coulda killed somebody!" she said.

"Take it easy!" the guy in the car next to her screamed.

The woman in the car continued to curse. She wouldn't let it go. She wanted to be right. I didn't understand. What did the guy in the car next to her need to do so that she felt justified in what she was doing? Did he need to acknowledge his wrongdoing? Apologize? What?

The world is full of people who want to be right. People who live to be right. Do you know anyone who must at all costs be right? It's truly a sad sight. I once had a friend who could not let a sentence go by without correcting the person speaking. If I said it was 101 degrees outside, she'd say, "Actually, it's 105." If I said a television show comes on at either 6 or 6:30, she'd say, "I think it's 7:30." If I said a dog had a hair ball, she'd say, "Actually, cats get hair balls." Are you frustrated yet? The only reason you might not be frustrated reading this is perhaps you're the Great Corrector!

Where did this come from? When we're born, we're born with no sense of what's right or what's wrong. We're simply in the land of "being." Around the age of one year old, we can interpret our parents' "correction" as rejection of who we are rather than of what we're doing. We interpret it this way because of two things: the way they say it and their body energy—not body language. By allowing this kind of righteousness to be your compass, it is difficult to harm, hurt, or offend the world or the people in it.

The real you has no need to triumph over someone else or to make someone else wrong. The real you operates on a frequency of righteousness rather than rightness.

THE SEVEN THINGS WE MUST DO TO EMBODY RIGHTEOUSNESS

Once we move from a place of needing to correct, judge, or make everyone else wrong so that we can be right, we will experience a new level of security within ourselves. A security that's not predicated on how little we can attempt to make others feel or how important we think our "rightness" makes us appear in the eyes of others. Once we feel the sheer elation that righteousness affords us, we'll lose our appetite for "rightness." Here are seven other things we can do to embrace the power of righteousness and move toward becoming our real selves:

Rid Ourselves of All Judgment

There are two kinds of judgment. The first type has to do with your *assessment* of a situation. We make thousands of these "judgment calls" each day. Take the freeway or the back streets? Go to the grocery store near the house or the one across town? Accept a job offer or start your own business? Go to college in your hometown or the college across country? These are all "calls" we have to make to advance our lives. The second kind of judgment that stops us from actualizing has to do with value statements that we assign to people or things.

We may judge people because of their gender, ethnicity, social class, eye color, height, education, or even the clothes they wear. These judgments do not nurture the real you. They feed your ego—that part of your personality that needs to feel important. More important than the next person. To be who you really are, you must rid yourself of all judgments. You think it's impossible, don't you? Okay, I'll respect that, but let me share something with you, and then I want to challenge you to do something powerful.

I mentioned one of the automatic signatures on my e-mails that went something like this: "Imagine one day without judgment." More than twenty-five people responded just to that signature. This kind of response was second only to my "namaste" signature. For some reason, the thought of a day without judgment resonated with people. So, guess what many of those twenty-five folks did? They tried it—one day without judgment. No judging themselves and no judging other people. That meant no "I'm so stupid," "I should've known better," "My coworker's a real [fill in the blank with your favorite expletive]." No judgment for one twenty-four-hour period. The results were astonishing. People wrote to me saying that it was like going cold turkey from alcohol after drinking for thirty years. Others said they never realized how much they judged themselves. And still others shared that they discovered that 75 percent of their thoughts and actions were judgmental in nature. 75 percent! That's a lot of judgment.

Why do we judge? Because we haven't retired our egos. It's still running our lives. Our hearts have no use for judgment, only our personality. Our ego believes it knows what's best for us and those around us. That's why we judge. Only when we turn down the volume on our ego-centered thoughts and rid ourselves of judgment can acceptance grow and love exist at the center of our every breath.

Have No Expectations

I covered this briefly earlier, but if I asked you to make a list of all of your expectations, I bet you'd have at least two lists: one for your expectations of yourself and another for the expectations of other people. But what if you let go of the second list and had no expectations of people. How different do you think your life would be?

What if you had no expectation that your friends would remember your birthday? (Ouch.) What if you had no expectation that your kids would be grateful that you clothe and feed them. What if you had no expectation that your company would give you a plaque for giving it twenty years of service. How would it feel to let go of all of these expectations and just accept whatever happens? Scary? Unrealistic?

We are programmed to have expectations, so it's not in our natural rhythm to let go of them. It is, however, possible to do. Like everything else, it requires spiritual discipline and a conscious awareness. Think about the expectations you have of your spouse or lover, children, parents, and friends. What do your expectations create for you? Expectations create anxiety. When we expect people to do things, we bring into existence a currency of spiritual discourse. For example, as your wedding anniversary nears, what thoughts do you start to have? I wonder if she'll remember that I need a new set of golf clubs? It would be nice if he does something different than the flowers and candy. If you're a parent, you probably wonder if your kids will cruise the mall on the Saturday before Mother's Day or Father's Day. What happens when our expectations aren't met? You guessed it. We induct the disappointer into the Hall of Disappointment, where he or she shall remain until they do something worthy of clemency.

Let Go of Disappointment

In the smash hit *The Devil Wears Prada,* Meryl Streep's character repeatedly says to her assistants, "You disappoint me." It's one of the funniest and most tragic lines in the movie because it illuminates the pleasure we gain from being disappointed. We enjoy it. I once got into a heated debate with a friend of mine for saying that he "enjoyed disappointment."

"I do not," he said.

"You love it!"

"That's absurd. Who loves being disappointed?"

"You do," I repeated. "You love it because you get to keep telling the same story of how all the women you date disappoint you."

He was furious. "You're not my therapist."

"'No, I'm your friend, and I'm simply doing what we said we'd do with each other—tell the truth as we see it.'"

"Well, your truth is your perception," he shot back. "And I reject it."

We both cracked up. "You reject it?" I laughed.

Ultimately, my friend, who is definitely a spiritual warrior, came to the realization through his own soul-searching that he did indeed create the disappointment he constantly complained about. He created it by consistently choosing to date women who were unavailable: women who were married, on the rebound, self-proclaimed serial daters, or otherwise unavailable. The results were always the same—disappointment. When we understand that we play a role in our disappointment we can make more righteous choices in our personal or professional lives. Choices that clearly nurture our spiritual growth and development. When we make righteous choices we relieve the other person of having to do something to meet our expectations because we've already made a choice that serves our highest good.

Turn in Your Victim Card

This one's hard for a lot of people. We enjoy the "Martyr's Club." We get to talk about how hurt we've been; how people have done us wrong;

how all of our lives we've had to suffer; how we can't love again because we've been hurt so many times. Are you serious?

What if I get hurt? What if I let you in and you break my heart? What if I allow you to see the real me, will you leave me? What all of this means is that we're victims. We want to feel sorry for ourselves and we want other people to feel sorry for us, too. When you play the victim card you are not yearning for righteousness because you are instead choosing the opposite of your highest good. Victims believe that others must create their happiness. Victims believe that their well-being is not in their control. By yearning for righteousness we open up a space to create and attract healthier interactions with other people because we're not constantly projecting our fears onto them and we're not making them responsible for any part of our lives.

Stop Vilifying

Over the next week, I want you to pay attention to how many times you send negative energy to someone. Notice how many times you shoot back obscenities when someone does something you don't like or don't agree with. This is a form of villainization. In yearning for what is righteous for the world, we must create a spiritual landscape that is without judgment and condemnation. Every relationship we enter—regardless of the length—presents us with prime opportunities to become more of who we are. Challenge yourself to see greatness, God-ness, in everyone you meet. Do this for one week and you'll notice a shift in your consciousness, your mental outlook, and your spiritual health.

Go Simple

Keeping your life free of clutter and contamination is not always easy. Look around at your circumstances. There's a good chance that there's a closet in some area of your life that could stand to be cleaned out. Do you need a spiritual "Roto-Rooter" session? Do you need to keep drama-filled friends at bay? Do you need to let go of your need to complicate your life with people, things, substances, and places that always lead you away from your highest self and the real you? Make a decision to keep it simple. By keeping it simple, you'll automatically be keeping it real. So how does going simple help us in the righteousness category? That which seeks our highest good is not complicated. What complicates our decisions is our ego and its incessant need to make us think that righteousness is for wusses. By yearning for the simple things, we are not likely to miss the many opportunities to create a more righteous and peaceful world on so many levels.

Be Childish

Last Sunday I went to return a sweater to the outdoor mall area known as the Third Street Promenade in Santa Monica, California. In addition to the retail stores and restaurants, there are always artists who line the streets to display their talents. Sometimes there's a clown named Bango making balloons for kids. Sometimes there are mimes. Sometimes there are dancers, painters, or installation artists. On this day, there was some kind of petting zoo, and as I walked to my car, I decided to stop to see the animals. Suddenly, though, I was struck by the kids who were standing around watching the show. They were transfixed by the animals. Their faces were filled with such amazement as they watched the miniature horses. They smiled and giggled at the slightest movement by these animals. They were in-joy!

We never lose the capacity to be childlike. We shut off this part of our selves because we're afraid of what people will say if we laugh too loud, get too excited, or squeal with glee when something good happens to us. Sometimes I call friends and family members who are so busy being adults that they don't know how to have fun anymore. This is one of our greatest miracles as human beings. The ability to laugh is a true gift that many of us ration like there's a famine. We don't want to use up our laughter on any ol' thing because something may happen later that we truly want to laugh about. Get real; you'll never run out of laughs.

One of my favorite memories of my mother is her laughter. Especially when she was on the phone with her baby sister, Margaret. She would laugh so loud, we could hear her at the other end of our house. I learned as a child that laughter was good. Now, I laugh loudly, and I don't care what anyone thinks!

Another cue we should take from children is honesty without ego. When a child is honest, he is not attempting to be mean. He's simply telling it like it is. If you're fat, a child will tell you that she thinks you're fat. If you're nice, they'll tell you that you're nice. When I was playing basketball in Italy, another American shared a beautiful story about a five-year-old Italian boy who had been staring at her in a restaurant. She waved to him and smiled, but the boy just stared at her. When he and his parents were about to leave, they walked by her table, where my friend said, "Ciao," to the little boy. He continued to stare. The boy's mother urged him to stop staring, but he wouldn't. Finally he looked at my friend and said, *"Perchè è la vostra faccia il colore di cioccolato?"* which means *Why is your face the color of chocolate?* The mom looked mortified as she grabbed the boy's arm, but my friend laughed heartily. She thought it was priceless. Throughout dinner, this had been what was on this boy's mind. Why was his face one color and my friend's another? So he did what was normal and natural for a five-year-old child—he asked.

How easy was that? How often do we wonder about something but fail to ask because we're afraid of what might happen if we're honest? This is our enduring projection: if we're honest, bad things happen. If we ask questions, people will not like us. Children teach us that there is a way to be honest without being rude. They teach us that honesty without ego is the way to go! If we yearn for honesty—and embody it as well—we will attract honesty on all levels. The Bible says, "Blessed are those who hunger and thirst for righteousness, for they will be filled." [Matthew 5:6]. What we yearn for, we get. We will become magnets for that which is just and righteous.

As we move through the final steps of the REAL YOU system, do you feel yourself peeling back the layers to your authentic self? Are you ready to retire your ego, embrace your spirit, accept your greatness, let go of all the things that keep your from becoming all of you, and yearn for more righteousness? Then let's continue to go deeper.

⤚ REAL QUESTIONS, REAL ANSWERS ⤙

My wife and I love each other, but when we fight, it's like World War III. We've gone to counseling and nothing seems to help. She complains that I don't appreciate her, and I complain that she doesn't acknowledge all the things I do to make her life easy. She thinks she's right, and I think I'm right. We've run out of ideas. We've even tried taking time-outs!

There could be many things going on with you and your wife, but what I hear in what you described is a classic case of miscommunication and a fear of not being heard. People need to be right only when they don't think they're going to be heard or understood. Next. If your wife doesn't feel appreciated, try asking her what appreciation "looks like" to her. You see, if you're doing all the things that you think show her that you appreciate her, but she doesn't see those things as signs of appreciation, you're spinning your wheels for nothing! So ask.

You're doing things that you perceive are making her life easy, but just because that's your perception doesn't make it her reality. It's not your job to make your wife's life easy. That's a responsibility that rests squarely on her shoulders. Sounds like you and your wife should try communicating with each other and asking a lot of open-ended questions. You should probably set some team rules: no assumptions, no name-calling, and no judgment.

I see the same qualities in my nine-year-old son that I'm trying to move away from. He's very competitive, and when he plays with his friends, the games will sometimes be interrupted because he wants to prove that he was right about something. I know he's like this because he's heard me say a hundred times to his father, "You don't want to admit it, but you know I'm right." How can we break this unhealthy habit with him now?

The first thing you can do is to model the behavior you want your son to copy. Your son needs to see you and your husband engaging in healthy disagreements. He needs to understand that conflict is necessary for growth, but that being right isn't the most important thing. Your family should also discuss the concept of rightness versus righteousness. Kids have the ability to understand matters of the heart. Open communication coupled with healthy visual imprinting will have the greatest impact on him.

Overcome Fear with Faith

Faith is the only known cure for fear.
—*Lena K. Sadler*

I can still hear the doctor's voice. "That lump is a problem." I turned to my friend Rebecca, who turned to her mom, Dinah, with a look of sheer terror. The oncologist proceeded to share the full diagnosis. My thirty-something friend had breast cancer, and according to this guy, it needed immediate attention. What happened in the next few days amazed me. I watched Rebecca balance her anxiety over this diagnosis and the fear-inducing news she got at every turn with a dogged determination to approach this condition with incredible positivity and spiritual vigor. She wasn't comfortable with the first doctor. He'd been too negative. So she sought a second opinion, but he was no better. He spewed more fear and more negativity. Finally, she found a doctor whose approach was more positive and more closely aligned with her spiritual beliefs. Rebecca did not come from a particularly religious background. In fact, at the time of her diagnosis, she was still finding her way on a spiritual path that felt right for her. Despite that, she was sure of one thing: no one was going to be on her Healing Dream Team who didn't believe that she could transcend breast cancer.

I was blown away by her courage and glad that she was my friend. She sought out alternative health care, including Chinese medicine. Although the first two doctors had encouraged her to undergo chemotherapy treatments, she said, "No, thank you." The final doctor, a soothing oncologist at M.D. Anderson, didn't think chemotherapy was necessary but did recommend radiation. Rebecca could handle that, especially since she was getting an A-plus protocol from her alternative doctors.

The preradiation treatments included tons of herbs, prayers, and special foods. And Rebecca jumped into the deep end of the pool. She had the discipline of an Olympic athlete as she followed her practitioners' protocol to the letter. Herbs and plants were all over her house. She was going to do everything in her power to participate in the healing of her body and spirit. She overcame her fear with faith, and, as a result, nearly five years later, she's cancer free and healthier than she was before the diagnosis. Even more miraculously, however, Rebecca's now a gifted healer whose work is helping others to heal their emotional, physical, psychological, and spiritual scars.

Some of our greatest lessons about fear are brought out in our professional lives. When I was toiling away in corporate America that last year, I discovered the degree to which fear pervades the halls of companies all over the country. I'd just gotten a new regional manager, and he had a reputation for being "unfeeling." His reputation with minorities and women wasn't the best. I had not experienced his "reputation" firsthand, but I had heard that he wasn't the poster child for embracing multiculturalism.

This is what I was told the day before I was to meet him for a review. I was already dealing with my own issues of wanting to leave the company to start my own company, so I was not in an optimal emotional state. Anyway, I met with this manager, and he made a comment about my commitment to the job because I wasn't willing to relocate. I started crying. I couldn't help it, and something inside of me didn't want to help it. By this time I was ready to leave the company anyway and his question brought up

WILL THE REAL YOU PLEASE STAND UP?

all of my insecurities about leaving what many saw as a "dream job." When I told my first-line manager about the meeting, the first thing she said was, "You didn't cry in front of him, did you?" Her disappointment and her own self-condemnation were all over her face. "I wish you hadn't cried in front of him." I could see the anguish in her face. She feared that my career would be stalled because I'd cried. Crying apparently connoted some kind of vulnerability that would have an adverse effect on my ascension up the corporate ladder and eventual collision with the glass ceiling. She didn't realize that I was out of there before the fountain overflowed.

My manager expressed the fear that many of us experience. Never let 'em see you sweat. Never let 'em see you with your boxers around your ankles. Never let 'em catch you with your guard down.

My tears were necessary regardless of what the new suit sitting across from me thought. If this company was going to let a little water get in the way of a brilliant sales career, then this wasn't the place for me anyway! So, if you've been trying not to appear human, you're falling into a dangerous and unproductive pattern. I challenge you to be more human in your dealings with people. Don't be afraid to let people see your frailty and humanity. That which we hold inside ultimately kills our dreams as well as our bodies.

Our fear of not being able to take care of ourselves is so intense that we create unnecessary stress for ourselves. One of my business coaching clients recently had a concern. I could tell it was bearing down on her. "How's the business planning coming?" I asked. "Good, I guess," she said, trying to sound optimistic. Optimism is a big part of what I teach. Be grateful for what is. Believe that all things are possible. So this client was doing her best to put on an optimistic face. Each week my Millionaire coaching clients have very specific exercises and tasks that they have to accomplish to have one-on-one coaching sessions with me. This client had done everything she was supposed to have done. "I have a problem— I mean, challenge," she said. (We don't have problems in my coaching world.) "Congratulations!" I said. (Yes, we celebrate challenges in my world.) "Right," she said. "Well, as I was completing the exercise where we have to talk about our business enterprise with people we know and don't know, something strange was happening," she said. There was a long pause on the phone. "Nobody knows what my prospective business is."

"Wow!"

"I know. That's why I'm feeling kinda down."

"No, that 'wow' is a great 'wow,' not 'whoa,' as in doom," I said.

"Oh," she said. My clients never know what I'm going to say.

"That's great! That's awesome."

"Did you hear what I said?" she repeated it. "People are saying, 'What is life coaching? Is that like therapy?'"

"Don't you see?" I said excitedly. "If they don't know what life coaching is, that means that they haven't been bombarded with life-coaching proposals—do you see the opportunity staring you in the face?"

Silence. It hadn't hit her yet. So, rather than run off at the mouth, I simply waited for the light to come on.

"Ohhhhhhhhh!" she screamed.

We laughed.

"Yes!"

She was excited. "So, I get to introduce them to a new business that can help them achieve their goals and realize their dreams . . ."

I was nodding. "And become the preferred life coach if you play your cards right," I replied.

I could hear her mind racing. She'd gotten on the phone feeling discouraged. After all, she's stepping out on her own to start a new business. Her target market is women who have been in abusive relationships. She's even taking on the church for not playing a more active role in the healing of relationships that have been destroyed by all kinds of abuse—sexual, physical, and spiritual.

Fear can show itself in so many different ways and on so many levels. When I work with people, I encourage them to get to the heart of their fears because if we can get to the root of what's causing us anxiety, we create more space for the real us to surface.

WILL THE REAL YOU PLEASE STAND UP?

My client was afraid that she would not have any potential customers. She thought she was offering a service that nobody wanted or needed. She was afraid of launching a business that had no market. That was her first line of fear, but underneath that was the fear that she would not be able to take care of herself and her three children. That was the heart level fear. But there's a place that's even deeper than the heart—our soul. My client did not want to have the experience of feeling that she had failed. That was the real issue that challenged her. Here's how I work through fears with myself and those I teach. First, we need to recognize what fears are and what they're not. They are not False Expectations Appearing Real. Instead of giving fear power over our lives we must turn our insecurities into declarations. Instead of focusing on what we don't want to happen, I'd like to offer a new approach to FEAR. One that encourages us to be more authentic and transparent.

Focus Every Action on Being Real

When we focus our energies on being transparent in our approaches to life's challenges, our relationships, and our business dealings, the anxiety that often accompanies wondering what could happen disappears. By sharing our truth—with ourselves and others—the power of a fear is greatly diminished. Ever had something that was bothering you, and then you talked about it with a friend and suddenly it didn't feel as big? The healing that comes from communicating in a real fashion minimizes the pictures we sometimes create in our minds about what might happen to us.

When I was a senior in college I noticed a slight discoloration on my skin. It looked like the beginnings of a skin disorder called vitiligo, which results in the gradual loss of pigmentation. I called my boyfriend and told him to meet me, I needed to talk. I showed him the "splash" of white patch on my right hand. "Look at this," I said.

"What?" he answered.

"What? Do you know what this means? You know that disorder where you lose all of your pigmentation?" I couldn't finish my sentence before I burst into tears.

"Fran, Fran, that doesn't mean anything!"

"Yeah, but it could! It could!"

He laughed. I had mapped out how the rest of my skin was going to be affected by this white patch of discoloration that was (and still is) about the size of the head of a stickpin.

I made an appointment with a dermatologist who came up with a bunch of dire prognoses that I didn't want or need to hear. Over the course of a few days I figured the best thing to do was to stop looking at my hand every other second, which was difficult, but eventually I was able to put it all out of my mind until six years later. I noticed another spot on another part of my body, so I called another dermatologist to schedule an appointment. This doctor must've been a cousin to the first doctor because he fed me some of the same fear-based medicine that the first doctor had tried to give me when I was in college. No one was providing any answers that made any sense to me. No one knew the cause. No one knew how to contain it. No one apparently knew anything about this condition! Eventually, I forgot about it again and moved on with my life—until seven years later.

I was working on this book and happened to look down at my left arm. I noticed these tiny splashes of depigmentation. I rose from my desk and went to my bathroom where I then saw maybe fifty little splashes all over my body. My fears and illusions were being confirmed. I was going to totally depigmentate! Is that even a word? At any rate, according to the doctors, this process is called depigmentation.

By this time, though, I'd developed a golden Rolodex of healthcare professionals from both the traditional and alternative medical fields. I'd also learned a lot about our ability to heal our bodies by simply changing our thoughts. So I wasn't nearly as freaked out as I had been in college. This time around I was more startled than I was fearful.

I called several alternative doctors and asked what they knew about this condition, since I'd heard from plenty of traditional doctors. Many of the alternative doctors and practitioners confirmed what I'd heard fifteen years earlier. Nobody really knows what causes it or what cures it. And isn't that the case with most conditions? So what determines or at least influences whether we heal certain conditions in our bodies and minds? I believe it's faith. At a cellular and soul level, I believe it's faith. I believe we have the power to change our realities instantaneously.

After speaking with another practitioner who hadn't spoken very confidently about vitiligo, I remembered my acupuncturist and traditional Chinese medicine doctor, John. The moment I remembered to call him, I felt better. It wasn't that I thought John would be able to allay my fears, it's that I knew that John had faith. He believes in the body's ability to heal and renew, and I needed that kind of consciousness on my team.

I called John, and he shared that the medical profession was as baffled by this condition as those who have it but that he'd had some success with treating patients with a combination of herbs and acupuncture. He also reiterated the importance of my role in the healing process. I needed to rid my life of any known stressors so that my systems could be fully optimized throughout my protocol.

This experience forced me to address my fears about having vitiligo. The first level of fear came from the ego. Ego said to me, "You know that if you have vitiligo you'll look different." I didn't want to look different. There had to be more. The ego's fear is never real. So I had to dig deeper (as if I were looking for toffee crunch ice cream) to acknowledge my heart's fear, which was that I wouldn't be able to make a living in television if I looked too different. It was tough to dig through to find that level of honesty. Finally I had to get to the core of what was really troubling me—my soul-level fear. And that was that I would not be accepted. I would be so different that people would look at me differently. I wouldn't be able to have a "normal" life.

On the next page is a simple diagram that explains the different levels of fear.

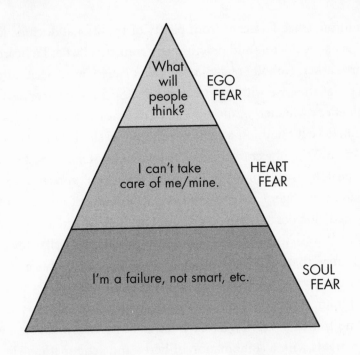

FACING FEAR HEAD ON

We live in times that encourage us to remain in our ego, to be fearful. There's an enduring sense of uneasiness in the world today, a massive amount of groupthink anxiety that nobody really discusses. If we discuss it, we have to acknowledge that it exists. If we acknowledge it, we might have to address it. If we address it, we might have to participate in the healing of it, and we don't want that. We don't want to heal because we enjoy the pain. And as long as we enjoy the pain as individuals, we'll never be able to heal the world.

"Fear knocked at the door. Faith answered. And lo, no one was there."
—*Anonymous*

Whenever I say the words "We enjoy the pain" people always come charging at me. "That's ludicrous! Nobody enjoys pain!"

WILL THE REAL YOU PLEASE STAND UP?

And I usually come right back with, "Actually, everybody enjoys pain."

My brother Alonzo recently injured himself in a pickup basketball game. He was in such pain that he asked me to type an e-mail for him because he couldn't put any pressure onto the right side of his body. I suggested that he visit an acupuncturist. He responded by saying that he was just going to ice it, put some heat on it, and maybe get in the whirlpool at his house. From what he described, his "treatment" was not going to make a substantial dent in his healing process, so I asked him a direct question. "Why won't you go see a practitioner or a doctor?"

"I'm feeling a little better," he said. "I'm gonna probably ice it tonight, maybe stretch it out."

"You have a strained muscle!" I laughed into the phone. "Stretching it twenty-four hours after the injury is the absolute worst thing you can do. Are you nuts?"

"Well," he said, chuckling, "I'm gonna see how it feels when I get out of the whirlpool tonight."

"So, basically what you're saying is that you don't want to feel better?"

"Not today," he answered, laughing.

We both laughed for a good three minutes at that moment. This is what I mean by us "wanting to be in pain."

Even when we have at our disposal the very thing that will make us feel better, we choose something else. We choose fear. We choose doubt. Why? Because we love the pain.

Pain doesn't always have to be the kind of pain you feel when you have a car accident or the way you feel when you stub your toe on a piece of furniture. Physical pain is only one kind of pain. There's also emotional and spiritual pain. The drama associated with a relationship that's going nowhere—that's pain. The pain of losing a contract. Both of these can cause us emotional, mental, or spiritual distress that tempts us to walk toward fear and away from love.

We always have a choice in whether we experience pain. And we most certainly play a part in how we respond to potentially painful situations, evidenced by Alonzo's story above.

So, what does any of this have to do with fear? It is our fear that keeps us in a constant cycle of pain. Pain in the spiritual sense means "away from love." Love in this instance represents our Highest selves—the real you. When we allow the possibility of pain (fear) to immobilize us, it's impossible for us to fully actualize as human or spiritual beings. For most of us, these illusions come in the form of several fears.

Fear of the Dark

The darkness I speak of here isn't what happens when we turn the lights off and the room goes black. I'm talking about spiritual and emotional darkness—our fear that we are not good people; our fear that evil or deadly forces will overtake us; our fear that our greatness pales in comparison to the dark forces we see on the ten o'clock news.

Fear of the darkness is real for many people, primarily those who don't know the power of their own light.

"Fear makes the wolf better than he is."
—Saint Thomas Aquinas

That's why becoming the real you is crucial. Only when we become aware of our ability to illuminate can we readily put the darkness into perspective. When we see how bright the light of love and peace shines, we know that darkness—in any form—is no match for us. The problem is that there aren't enough of us who believe in our own light. There are too many 100-watt beings playing life at a 60-watt voltage!

Fear of Failure

Like my client from earlier, we've somehow concocted a whole industry around the fear of failure. Self-help books reinforce the fear by saying, "Buy this book and you won't fail." Institute my twenty-one steps and you won't look like a fool. Some marketers even go as far as saying things like, "The other guys don't know what they're talking about. Listen to me and you won't fall flat on your face." I'm actually laughing out loud right now as I type this sentence because I've got more self-help books on my shelf than you could shake a stick at. Why? Because I've been under the same spell that most of you have been under! I used to buy self-help books so that I wouldn't fail. That's when I believed in failure many, many years ago. So you're probably saying, well, what's the difference between all of the other self-help books and *Will the* Real *You Please Stand Up?* This isn't a book about success, it's about what happens in our lives when we stop pretending to be what the world says we should be and we leap into who we really are. Big difference.

Through the process of becoming more authentic we will attract all of the things we desire—friends, love, abundance, and maybe even fame. As for success, there is really no such thing as success—although I do still use the word sometimes. There are only desirable and undesirable outcomes. That's it. Things either go the way you want them to or they don't. You either get what you were seeking or you don't. You either get the brass ring, or you get the plastic one. If you get the brass ring, you didn't succeed. You got what you wanted. By the same token, if you get the plastic ring, you didn't fail, you just didn't get the ring you wanted. There's still the next moment. And in the next moment, there's still a chance you could get the brass ring: the outcome you wanted!

I stopped believing in failure more than eleven years ago. I just didn't like the sound of the word. I didn't like how people felt energetically when they talked about being a failure. I'd never felt like I failed at anything. I felt that people were "trying" to project the feelings of failure onto me whenever I fell short of my targets. Ever notice that the world expects us to act a certain way when we "lose" a game or come in second in a contest? Ever notice that? We even punish the people who don't act "sad enough" when the team loses! There's a culture surrounding failure and I don't buy it. I felt so strongly about the topic that I even had T-shirts printed up that read: "Failure's Not an Option." I wanted to change the dialogue about success and failure. There needs to be a shift in our consciousness around what it means to succeed. To make my point about failure I printed some T-shirts prior to going to Florida to do a basketball camp for adolescent girls and boys. The impact was profound, which wasn't intentional, I must admit. There are times when I can pretty much predict the response of something I'm planning to say or do, but with these T-shirts, I had no idea. I was simply acting on spiritual intuition. I was speaking to a group of kids who were growing up in a financially disadvantaged neighborhood. Yet like most kids, they were smart, industrious, and curious about life. Their home addresses had not killed their spirits. In one of the opening sessions I asked someone to tell me what the T-shirt meant to them. This bright-eyed young lady said, "We can't fail."

"Why?"

"Because failure exists only in our minds."

"Whoa!" I was blown away. She'd hit the proverbial nail on the head. "Go on," I said.

"That's it. All we can do is give our best and whatever happens happens."

I ran over and gave her a big high-five. The other thirty or so kids applauded. This bright-eyed girl was the sunshine of the camp. She was the first one in the gym every morning. She encouraged the other kids. She listened to my coaching as if her life depended on it. And I'm convinced she was an angel in high-tops. She had a remarkable essence and spirit. One day after lunch, she came over to me and asked me if I thought she could make it in the WNBA. "What grade are you in?" I asked. "Ninth," she responded. I looked into her turtle brown eyes and saw the determination. She stood all of five feet, three inches—not very tall by most standards, yet her heart was the size of Texas. "Are you kidding me?" I said. "Just put me on your player's pass list so I can have a front-row seat in ten years. And don't act like you don't know me when I hold up my sign!"

She blushed as she happily dribbled the ball toward the other end of the court. I was looking forward to what I believed was going to be an outstanding basketball career. So when my sister called me later that year and told me that she had been murdered, my heart truly grieved. She was only fifteen. The angel in high-tops never got to fulfill her dream of playing in the WNBA, but she didn't fail. It wasn't possible.

Fear of Death

When I was a teenager I had some interesting thoughts and experiences around death, probably because my mother died when I was sixteen. For this reason I believe the topic was never far from my heart and mind. Although Mom hadn't died from it, the year she died I started to hear more about breast cancer so I started doing breast exams. At sixteen! Since I didn't have any literature on the topic I didn't know that sixteen was a little young to be doing breast exams and I didn't know what to look for or feel for. One day I thought I felt a lump and I freaked out. A few days later I had a dream about my own funeral and decided my life was almost over. I told my sister about the dream and explained to her that I was afraid of dying. She hugged me and said something that helped me more than she probably realized. She said, "You won't know it. It's like falling asleep."

That put it all in perspective for me. Living takes work, dying appears to be effortless. The dead don't mourn, I suppose. Therefore, death is scary only for those who know how it feels as a human to watch the march to death—the anguish on the family's face; the torture of watching someone succumb to a disease; the slow deterioration of our bodies. That's a form of death and what I believe many people fear. None of the living can say for sure what happens after they take that final breath, so I focus on the millions of breaths I get to inhale before the last one. It allays any fears I have about what may be on the other side. My faith teaches me that death is not to be feared. When we focus on living our best lives and experience God as a loving God rather than a God that can't wait for us to die so we can be judged, death loses its sting.

Fear of Destitution

Most of us work hard not necessarily because we love what we do but because we are afraid of what will happen if we don't. Living in that kind of fear keeps us from our real selves—free and peaceful. There can't be real peace if we're afraid we're going to be on the street if we make our boss mad. The heart cannot pump properly if it's constricted by the illusions of humanity. All of the messages we get from the outside world tell us that we should be afraid. If you don't stop using your credit cards, you're going to drown in debt. If you don't pay your taxes on time, the IRS is going to audit you. If you don't get your oil changed every 3,000 miles, your car's going to go ka-plunk. Fear, fear, and more fear. We can walk through this fear and any fear by focusing our attention on what is real. What is real is not what "could happen" or even what "has" happened, but rather what is. Faith allows us to know that we can always make an informed and positive choice to make our current situation better. The problem is that most people attempt to get rid of their fears rather than walk through them. Walking through the fear of destitution requires that you face where this fear started. Sometimes a fear of destitution comes from having been poor or some other kind of money trauma early in our lives. To walk through this fear I recommend going though the Lies exercise we did earlier. Fears are based on lies, so write down the lies you believe about this fear and then create some new truths that you practice each day and affirm as much as possible. Remember, if you're fearful of what "was" or what has happened in the past, that's an illusion. It's an image that you believe is real, and it's not. If it's not happening right now, in this moment, it's not real. Period.

Fear of Abandonment

Many of us enter relationships with one fear: *What if she leaves me?* We enter relationships with one expectation: *This is not going to work out.* That's the tone that we start most relationships off on. And they don't have to be intimate relationships, either. They can be professional relationships.

"I really want this job" really means, "I'm afraid I'm not going to get this job" or "I'm going to lose this job." Our fear of abandonment comes from the imprinting put on us by the world that *all good things come to end* or *if it sounds too good to be true, it must be too good to be true.* The real you isn't concerned about losing anything but is in gratitude for what he has. The real you isn't expecting the bottom to fall out of every life experience but instead maximizes the moments. Again, to walk through this fear you must understand the origins of this fear for you. Fear is based on a progression of lies. Write down the lies associated with this fear and then create new truths based on what your intention is for your life. For example, one fear might be that you're never going to be able to attract a mate that supports your ambition as a woman. This fear might be based on the fact that every guy you've attracted has bolted as you transitioned into more job responsibility or a promotion. On some level you may even hold yourself back to avoid the expected abandonment. To stop the cycle of attracting the very thing you fear, you must stop creating the energy that attracts abandonment. Remember, everything that manifests as a physical reality starts in the invisible reality.

Fear of Humiliation

Sports give us wonderful opportunities to push our bodies beyond their physical limits. It's also an arena that has come to be known as the ultimate arena for humiliation. Our fear of being embarrassed and humiliated is so acute that we go to great lengths not to experience either. The whole world watches as we miss the free throw. The entire stadium boos when we miss a wide-open fifteen-yard punt. The crowd throws tomatoes when we swing at a low ball. The announcer makes a snide remark when we miss a "gimme" shot on the green. Our friends rag us for tripping out of the blocks on the most important race of our lives.

We'd rather chew nails than be embarrassed. But we don't realize that embarrassment is not what others do to us, it's what we do to ourselves. We've been conditioned to think that the experience comes from outside of us, but it's really a condemnation of ourselves that creates this unpleasant experience. We hate ourselves for missing the free throw. The crowd just joins in with our condemnation. We beat ourselves up for blowing the punt; the stadium fans only reinforce what we're already doing to ourselves. When we turn the mirror toward us instead of projecting our fears onto those who are merely laughing, we lay the foundation for a higher level of spiritual accountability and integrity.

Ever been laughed at? Made fun of? It probably wasn't the most enjoyable experience. Most of us have had the unfortunate experience of being on both sides of this coin. And if we're honest, neither is truly fun. There's nothing honorable in attempting to make someone feel uncomfortable. And there's nothing particularly soothing about having someone point out something about you and laughing at or mocking it. I don't know anyone who says, "I had a great weekend," followed by, "Oh, it was great. On Friday, my friends and I got together, and they teased me unmercifully. Let's see, and then on Saturday morning, we had breakfast, and they chided me for two solid hours about one of my legs being longer than the other one. Oh, and then on Sunday we all went to church, and afterward, they laughed for a good thirty minutes about the note I missed as I was singing my solo."

We love going to comedy clubs where professional jokesmiths make fun of anything they want. That's okay to us because it's all in "good fun" but when the comedy is directed at us, we become painfully self-conscious. What's at the soul level of the fear of being humiliated or embarrassed? What is it that we feel when we're the butt of a joke? It's not like people aren't laughing at us behind our backs. They are. They're making fun of us. They're talking about our hair, our teeth, our voices, our bodies, our presentations, everything. Is it, then, that we're okay with what people say about us behind closed doors as long as nobody else hears? Here's what's at the soul level of the fear of humiliation. It's that we fear we will be alone in the world. It is one of the greatest fears we have. If everyone is laughing at me, then I am alone. The only way to move past the fear of humiliation is to face the lies, but with this fear you must also know that humiliation is about approval. You have to address your need for approval. When we do not seek the approval of others we aren't crushed by the rejection of others.

Fear of Ridicule

Humiliation, embarrassment, and ridicule are so close in nature that it's sometimes hard to distinguish the three fears. Ridicule, though, is a more active effort that puts someone at the center of harsh words, gossip, or malicious energy. Most of us want to avoid ridicule at all cost. Last spring I threw myself a huge birthday party in Dallas. I was excited to know that my cousins, some high school classmates, and even a few teachers were planning to be there. It was going to be a great night. I'd hired a wonderful DJ friend of mine, and the food was going to be out of this world because it was potluck, and my family members can really cook!

That morning when I woke up, Alonzo asked if I wanted to go for a run or a bike ride on the lake. "Sounds good," I told him.

The lake near his house spans four miles in circumference, so it was going to be a solid workout. We got dressed, strapped the bikes to his truck and headed for Bachman Lake. We rode for about twenty minutes, and just as we were about forty yards from finishing the ride, I felt my cell phone falling out of my pocket. And instead of allowing it to tumble to the ground, I reached into my pocket to secure it.

That's when I hit an uneven stretch of payment and flew off of my bicycle. Before I knew it, I'd fallen head first—no helmet—onto the pavement. Bam! Suddenly I was writhing in pain, praying that I was not going to die on my birthday!

I lay there for another fifteen minutes until the pain subsided, and then Alonzo helped me to my feet, and we headed home. I spent the rest of the afternoon icing my head to get the swelling to go down. By the start of the party at 7:00 that night, I had a nice egg-sized reminder to wear my helmet the next time I went for a ride.

No one even noticed the bump on my head. And it wasn't until a few days later, when the massive black eye showed up, that anyone noticed or at least said anything to me.

On Monday I started a consulting gig with an advertising company. As I pulled into the parking structure, I got a load of my shiner in my rearview mirror and laughed. When I walked into the company's office, though, you would have thought I had six ears or something. The sales manager walked over to me with a look of concern. "Honey, what happened to you?" she asked as she inspected my black eye.

I laughed and told her the whole story about us going riding around Bachman Lake. "Crazy, huh?" I said.

That's when I noticed that she wasn't finding my story as funny as I was. "Wow," she said. And then she walked back to her desk.

A few minutes later she came back over to my desk. "Are you sure you're okay? I mean, you fell off your *bike?*"

That's when it hit me. She didn't believe me. She wasn't buying the bike story one bit. This woman thought I'd been beaten! I started laughing again. Not because domestic violence is a joke but because I understood how people felt who don't want to be exposed. I understood the fear of ridicule.

That afternoon, the energy in the office was suddenly full of suspicion and worry. I had to decide if I were going to make an announcement over the intercom that "everything was okay" or just let it go. I was expecting someone to slide me a pamphlet for a domestic violence hotline. After lunch people started being nicer to me. It was hilarious.

I decided not to say anything. Ego defends. And the truth is that I didn't really care what the client thought about my black eye. They never asked me about it. And I never offered another explanation.

Shortly after this incident, a seminar attendee said to me, "Okay, so how do I get past my fear of ridicule?" The answer is simple. Listen closely. Divest in the opinions of others. Divest, I say! Stop seeking the approval of others. Stop wondering whether your parents approve of your latest move. Stop fretting about whether your boyfriend likes the dress you're wearing. Stop obsessing over whether the guys at the office noticed your eight pack! When we can stop seeking and desiring the approval of others, we will be oblivious to their ridicule.

Fear of Rejection

This fear is merely the shadow to wanting to be loved. So it's not rejection that we fear, it's the possibility that we won't be loved—a fear that is created by the notion that we are not enough. We're told this by academic counselors when we don't score high enough to get into Yale. We hear "You're not enough." When our kids don't make the varsity team, they feel like they're not enough. When someone breaks up with us, we believe we're not enough. If we were enough we would have "gotten in," "made the team," and "stayed in the relationship" we think. All of these experiences feed the fear that most of us have about being loved. The challenge is not to squash this fear but to turn inward for feelings of love. Rejection is also tied to approval, as I mentioned with the fear of ridicule, but that's only level one. Beyond our need for acceptance is our need to feel love—not loved. And because we've been programmed to seek love outside of ourselves, moving through the fear of rejection is difficult for this group of people. If you can't steal a moment in your day and feel intense, abiding love without involving someone else, you're going to struggle finding everlasting peace and self-assurance. So your work on extinguishing this fear starts with rereading the section in this book that talks about love.

Fear of Criticism

This is the first cousin of Fear of Rejection. It feeds our issues of "enoughness." We aren't programmed to breed abundance, but rather scarcity. So we receive any messages that appear to attack our virtues as criticism, as a commentary on our worthiness or enoughness. When we stand strong in our faith, we are unshaken by "feedback." We realize that criticism is only someone's story about who you are or what you've done.

It doesn't mean it's true. Who they think you are is an illusion, just as who you think you are is an illusion. Most of us have no idea who we really are because who we think we are has been informed by people and things in a world that's designed to make you who they want you to be. None of us is immune to those messages. That's why the work we're doing in this book is so critical. We need a plan for minimizing the impact of external messages that don't seek to serve our Highest good.

When I was in high school, I remember the football guys sitting in the cafeteria reading the newspaper a few days after a big game. They'd look at their statistics to see how great they'd been on Friday night. They seemed to be able to relive the entire game just by looking at their individual stats and team numbers. It was always fun to hear them go through every play as if it were happening in that moment. It was a rite of passage, I thought, that all athletes experienced. One day before basketball practice, my teammates and I were sitting around reading the recap after a holiday tournament when my coach walked in and saw us doing what he called "reading our own press." He immediately made us put the paper down and do what every athlete hates—"run lines." That meant that we'd done something wrong. Only we didn't know what it was. "On the line," he said. We all jumped up and headed for the baseline of the gym. The clock started, and just as we were about to take off, he said, "If you believe what they write about you, you'll believe what they write about you." Huh? We all looked at one another and shook our heads. Coach Stevenson was always saying stuff that made no sense to us in the moment. Off we went to the other end in less than four seconds. The whistle continued to blow and the clock continued to run. What was he so mad about? We continued to sprint. Then, after running about ten of those four-second sprints, we all panted along the baseline the way new military recruits do on the first day of boot camp, waiting on our next command. "Harris, what did the paper say?"

I didn't say anything. Sounded like a setup to me. "That's not a rhetorical question, Fran Harris. What did the paper say?"

"It said that, uh . . . " I knew exactly what it had said, but I didn't want to say. "It said we won and that, uh, we'd held them to 22 percent shooting . . . "

This wasn't what he wanted to hear, and I knew it.

"Fran Harris, you've got three seconds to tell me what the *Dallas Morning News* said about the game that had all of you so intrigued, or do you want to run about thirty more of those down-and-backs?"

I looked around at my teammates, who pleaded with me to answer correctly. I lowered my voice a little. "It said that I had twenty-eight points and that I shot twelve of nineteen from the field."

"And what else?"

"It said that Vicki had ten assists and that she was one of the top point guards in the country."

He walked in front of each of us, eyeballing us with that knowing stare. "Uh huh. Did you like reading that, Harris?"

"Sir?"

"You heard me. Did you like reading about how good you are?"

"Uh . . . "

"I think you did. I think all of you did. What do you think about what I said, Harris?"

"I think it was good." My teammates snickered. Coach Stevenson tried his level best not to laugh.

"I'm not looking for strokes, Harris," he said, clearing his throat. "Tell your teammates what it means."

"Well, I think it . . . "

"I don't wanna know what you think. Tell your teammates what it means when I say 'If you believe what they write about you, you'll believe what they write about you.'"

I honestly didn't know what it meant until he said it a second time and I actually "heard" the words again. "It means that if you believe the good stuff that you'll believe the bad stuff."

He stopped right in front of me. Our eyes locked on one another. "Get a drink."

We all walked slowly off the line to the water cooler. Years would pass before I realized the spiritual wisdom in my coach's words. If we believe what people say about us, we'll be tempted to believe what they say about us. Our fears about what people will say about us is so severe that we don't follow our hearts or pursue our dreams. We stand still in our tracks. We become paralyzed by the stares and comments of others. Fear is an excuse for not moving forward. If we can rest in the arms of fear we never have to push ourselves or test our mental, emotional, physical, spiritual, or financial boundaries. We can just say "I'm afraid" and move backward—not stay where we are. We are never stuck. We either move forward, or we move backward. We're either growing, or we're regressing. There's no such thing as "I'm in the same place as I was last year." You're one year older chronologically, which means that the world is moving; it's turning. You are never static either. You're moving ahead, or you're traveling backward. Our fear of rejection is the reason most of us don't move ahead in love or life.

A few days after the newspaper incident, Coach Stevenson gave me another gift. He challenged me to move past my fear of falling short, or as some of you refer to it, failing. I was one of the captains of my high school team, and it seemed that he loved making an example of me. It was his way of helping me to accept my greatness, but sometimes it got on my nerves. One day during a practice, I started to shoot with my left hand, although I'm right-handed. He'd pushed all of us to become adept at handling the ball with both hands, so I thought I'd take it a step further and *shoot* left-handed, as well. Practice was going fine. I shot a six-footer and made the basket. I caught a glimpse of my coach out of the corner of my eye, who tried not to look impressed. As I ran to the other end of the court, he said, "You think that's cute, Harris?" This was a rhetorical question, I was sure, so I didn't answer. "Since you're such an All-American, why don't you shoot left-handed for the rest of the practice?" This, too, was not a rhetorical question.

"Okay," I said cockily.

WILL THE REAL YOU PLEASE STAND UP?

"Every shot has to be taken with the left hand. Inside, outside, wherever," he said.

"Fine."

"And I don't want to see you all going away from her in the offense. If she wants to be a hot dog, ya'll are going to run for it. If she misses, she's going to stand on the sidelines, and you guys are gonna run."

How's that for pressure? The practice continued for another hour, and I continued to shoot left-handed. It seemed like my teammates were actually giving me the ball more than they normally did! That was probably my projection, but that's the way it felt.

Finally, practice was over, and I hadn't missed one shot. Not one left hander. . . .

Coach Stevenson fumed. He hated (and loved) that I had taken him up on his challenge and that I wasn't afraid to "miss" for fear of what would happen. That day I made huge strides in what some people call the fear of failure. What about you? Have you turned down a recent promotion because you fear the responsibility the spotlight being on you? Have you decided to live in a studio apartment because you're afraid to take on $200 more in living expenses? Are you in and out of relationships because you're afraid that if you make a serious commitment that it might not last? What's your fear around "missing the mark"? Remember, only what "is" is real. Our projections about what "could" or what was in the past often immobilize us. It is without a doubt the stop that prevents people from starting. Maybe you're afraid that it will work out, which leads us to another popular fear: success.

Fear of Success

What if I do this well this one time, will I have to keep succeeding at this? The pressure to succeed in our society is immense. Some people are unfazed by the expectations of others, while others crumble at the thought of not living up to those expectations, previous records, or last year's numbers. This fear is diametrically positioned from the real you. The person you are supposed to be—the real you—is fully optimized, which means that worldly success, while not your focus, is an inevitable byproduct of becoming the real you. Yet this fear is so acute in some people that they would endure the pain of mediocrity to escape the elixir of love—becoming their authentic selves. Is it possible to overcome the fear of success? And are people really afraid of succeeding? Absolutely; the answer to both of those questions is yes. First, how do we overcome our fear of success? I'm a good person to ask because I used to attempt to stall my success. I didn't mind succeeding, I just didn't want anybody to notice me succeeding. Then I heard something that changed my perspective: you can't be outstanding if you're not willing to stand out. I have known since I was three or four years old that I was going to be on an international stage one day. The more I learned about dealing with fame and celebrity, the less I wanted to accept my divine assignment. See, sometimes we think that we have to accept our calling. We don't. You have the choice to step into your greatness or live out a life of nothing really special. It's up to you. Overcoming the fear of doing well is a journey that starts with you embracing the fact that you do indeed have a divine assignment. It's not an assignment to fail, so that's the good news. It's an assignment to soar. You don't need anybody's permission to live your dreams. If you leave this earth with your song still inside of you, it's nobody's fault but your own. Here are some quick steps to get you on your way. Step one to overcoming the fear of success? Repeat after me. I was born to do great things. Step two. I am engineered to succeed. Step three. I am not invested in what others think about my success. Step four: I will rejoice in accepting and completing my divine assignments.

FAITH IN ACTION

Like love, faith isn't something you do, it's what you are. You're faithful. Full of faith. There's no better way to know where you stand on faith than when you're faced with fear.

Claire, a photographer friend of mine, called me two nights before our photo shoot to tell me that she'd found an even better place to capture the true essence of what I was looking for "It's a lovely spot about thirty minutes from here." She added, "Absolutely gorgeous."

I was excited. As we started to drive near Palos Verdes, California, it dawned on me as we got out of the car that I was going to be put in a position that I wasn't exactly comfortable with. I might have to climb up or down a mountain. As we walked to the edge of one mountain and looked out onto the ocean, I was humbled. Claire was right. This place was unbelievable. Beyond breathtaking.

"Why don't you stand right there, Fran," she requested, pointing to a ledge that was a bit too close to the drop-off for my taste.

"Okay," I said, walking over to the spot and looking down into the brush. I took a deep breath. I could already feel my pulse quickening. Claire and Duffy, my maniac spin-yoga friend, got the equipment ready as I started to do some deep-breathing exercises to calm me down. "A little closer to the edge," Claire requested. I scooted over a bit more, as she started to snap the pictures.

Claire grabbed her things and started heading down the mountain. "Good," I thought. "We're going down instead of up." This I thought before I realized that I was wearing soccer sandals with virtually no tracking on the soles. Great. I'm gonna break my neck on the photo shoot for my book cover. That's beautiful.

Eventually all three of us made it down to the next level, which gave us an even more incredible view of the Pacific Ocean, the sunset, and an amazing backdrop of mountains. Immediately, Duffy (a friend I met at my spinning class and Claire's photography assistant for the day) and Claire began talking about where the best pictures were going to be taken, and ironically all of them had me on the edge of a cliff! We were losing sunlight, and I knew that Claire was sold on this vista for the photos. I didn't have time to be scared. So I started to do more breathing exercises.

"Let's have you stand on top of that big rock there," Claire asked. Up and over I went. "Perfect."

Yeah, for you, you're standing over there!

Pretty soon we were in the swing of things. Claire was getting the shots my publisher wanted, and we were feeling good about the shoot. That's when the cute little dog showed up. Did I mention that I'm not 100 percent comfortable around dogs? I'm not. So there I was, standing on top of a cliff looking down over a forty-foot drop into the Pacific Ocean when an unleashed dog and his owners come through on a hike. It was the perfect time to test my faith. I kicked my breathing exercises into to full gear and pretty soon, the dog was gone and my heart rate went back to normal.

What area of your life is like that forty-foot mountain I just mentioned? Take a look at your Wholeness Matrix and target one area that you'd like to become more intentional and faithful. Maybe you're contemplating leaving corporate America. Maybe you'd like to start a new musical group. Maybe you'd like to learn how to become an eBay millionaire. Maybe you want to go back to school after twenty years. Whatever you want to change or optimize in your life requires faith since no one can predict the future. Faith is our most calming tool. I believe when we align ourselves with our highest good and follow this up with intentional effort that we become magnets for our dreams.

Faith requires belief outside of what we know and what we can see. That's what makes faith such a powerful mechanism for change and manifestation. Like faith, fear is also invisible but instead it's (fear) based on what we anticipate will happen if we attempt to become our real selves. The real you has no need to "know" what tomorrow brings. There is a serenity when you are in your purpose that lets tomorrow take care of tomorrow. Today is still a mystery. This moment, however, is all yours.

✎ REAL QUESTIONS, REAL ANSWERS ✎

Sometimes when I want something to happen in my life, and it doesn't, my friend says I don't have faith. When I tell her that I do have faith, she then tells me that my prayers must not be sincere. I am sincere, and I do have faith, but I wonder if I'm praying hard enough.

Hard prayer isn't the answer. My guess is that you're very sincere in what you're "asking" for, which is where I'd like to offer a suggestion. Rather than approaching prayer as something you have to do to get something you want, start giving love in the direction of the things you want. If you want more money, love your money. Literally shower your money with love and affection. If you want more time to spend on the things you enjoy doing, start loving the things you enjoy doing. If you want less drama in your life, try praying for peace.

I have always been afraid of speaking in front of crowds, yet I want to be a professional speaker one day. I'm afraid my fear will stop me from pursuing what I believe is my life's work.

First, I'd suggest that perhaps your fear isn't so much about speaking in front of crowds as it is about lifting your voice. Could it be that you believe you don't have anything to say? Is it possible that you're wondering if anyone will actually listen to you? Are you asking yourself, "Who am I to stand before people and talk?" I'd say, who are you not to?! Your apprehension isn't uncommon among people who want to be in communication fields. My recommendation is to start by sharing your story to the most important audience you know: yourself. Record different stories for thirty days. Each day listen to your story. Marvel at how incredible your life is. Love the fact that you are lifting your voice, and pretty soon, it will be easy for you to share your story, and your voice, with the rest of the world.

Unleash Your Genius

A little girl was doodling in class one day while the teacher was
teaching English. The teacher noticed that she was distracted, so she
walked over to her desk. "What are you doing, Sherry?"
"Drawing," the little girl answered gleefully.
"I can see that. What are you drawing?" the teacher said
as she leaned in to look at the tablet.
"God," Sherry answered.
The teacher found this amusing. "Sherry, that's silly.
No one knows what God looks like."
Sherry turned to the teacher with smiling eyes and said,
"They will when I'm finished."

*W*hat are you drawing today? What's on your canvas? Are there
brilliant hues of color and textures reflecting your zest for life
and passion for living? Or is it full of the drabness of compla-
cency, negativity, and lack? We come to the planet as empty canvases with no
limits on our creativity and no boundaries on what we can become. We are a
mere lump of clay that can be molded into a magnificent piece of art—or we
can remain a lump of clay. It's our choice, it's not about favor from God. It's not
about which family you were born into. It's not about which schools you
enrolled in or which neighborhood you grew up in. There are no restrictions
on how high you can fly or which seas you can sail. Yet many of us leave here
with only a few splashes of paint on our canvases. You have so many different
rays of genius in you. You really do.

Two Christmases ago I was visiting with my Godbrother, Willie, and I
asked him this question: "Are you living your passion and purpose?" You
guys have heard me ask that question before, right? What I love about

Willie is that he not only hears but also listens. You see, it is one thing to actually hear what someone is saying but to listen requires a different level of awareness. Willie didn't answer my question that night, although I could tell he was thinking about it. Instead of responding to me in December, within a few months, he left one of his jobs in pursuit of a career that was more closely aligned with his skills and passion.

He teases me occasionally saying, "Before you came back on the scene, I had two jobs! My life was just fine. Then you got me thinking about purpose, passion, genius, and being an intentional millionaire. Do me a favor, okay? Don't ask me any more questions, and don't write any more books!"

Of course he's joking (I think). He knows there's no way I can't ask him to unleash his genius, because I know the rewards are unlimited. I know that he's all about being open to God's generosity. So, he's on the genius train too. In fact, he's now in a new role in a new company and seems to be doing great things. Now I'm nagging him with yet another question: Have you unleashed your genius?

No word yet, but I keep asking.

Spinning On Genius

Walk by the garage on the corner of Westminster and Abbot Kinney in Venice, California, on Saturdays and Sundays at 11:15 AM, and here's what you'll see. First, you hear beats that will make your heart pump and your body sway. You'll see about thirty-two stationery bicycles lined symmetrically in two rows in a narrow garage with brick walls and overhead ventilation. You'll see twenty to thirty fitness enthusiasts who are about to take the ride of their lives. And then, at the front of the room, usually dressed in all black, you'll see a genius at work. This is my YAS (pronounced yazz) class. It's the first thirty minutes of what I now affectionately call my hour of "Spoga" power. Thirty minutes of spinning, followed by thirty minutes of yoga with none other than the genius herself, our instructor, Julie Simon.

Spinning, for those of you who have not had the privilege, is a cycling class on a special bike called a spin cycle or a spinner. For a designated time period—usually forty-five to sixty minutes—you, along with a class full of other individuals, go through a workout at different speeds—sprinting, running, and climbing on the bike—to music. The music is what makes the class bearable and can range from reggae to rock to rap. What makes it enjoyable (or not) is the instructor. And that's why Julie's a genius.

If the class I just described sounds like a real slice of torture, it is on some days. It's a tough workout, but it's also a lot of fun (or so I tell myself every morning as I crawl out of bed). So you can probably imagine that the teacher plays a key role in your ability to endure the workout. That's why Julie's key. She makes you forget that you're working. She makes it fun. She makes it challenging. She makes it rewarding. You forget that you are climbing the incline of your life. It takes talent and know-how to inspire people, especially when they're working hard, but mostly it takes genius.

Now, to be clear, Julie's spin and yoga skills are probably on par with all of the top instructors at the YAS studio. So, her genius has less to do with technique and more to do with how she transforms a hot, humid, and sweaty brick garage into a haven where you want to "go to the top." The top being wherever you want to go in your life.

You see, spinning with Julie is not about the bike. Her yoga classes are not just about warrior ones and pigeon poses. It's about exploring the limits of your mind, spirit, and body. It's about finding balance in your life and enjoying the ride. Julie has a way of making each student feel like their journey is special. She is amazingly present as she instructs us to turn up our resistance in spinning or melt into our Warrior Twos in yoga class. She's there. She's not going through the motions, and she's not pretending to care whether or not you're in perfect alignment. She actually cares, and you know it. You feel it. She's right there with you. When I started practicing yoga many years ago I couldn't touch my toes while seated on my buns with my legs fully extended in front of me. I could only get to my ankles. Within weeks of actually going to yoga on a regular basis I finally got there. I still remember the day. There were about twenty five of us in Julie's class and we were about to head into our hamstring work. "I want you to take a deep breath and reach as far as you can," she said as she walked around the room. I leaned forward having no idea how far my hands would actually go. That's when it happened. When I touched my toes I almost squealed in delight. I didn't know that I'd become that flexible in such a short time. I'd only been doing yoga on a regular basis for about three weeks. Julie looked at me and said out loud, "You're touching your toes!" She looked as shocked and pleased as I'm sure I did. But what stuck with me is that she noticed. More than two hundred students come through the YAS studio in a day and she noticed that I was touching my toes. That's what I mean about being present. Genius.

We've been conditioned to think of genius as a word that's reserved for scientists and neurologists. Math wizards are called geniuses. High school students who enter college at age fourteen are tabbed geniuses. We're quick to call musical artists geniuses. Yet I think it's a pity that we've limited the use of this word to only a few vocations and gifts. We all arrive here with a wide array of genius, in many different areas. But because we've been programmed to see only certain people as geniuses, some of us never discover our own brilliance!

When I was growing up my mother would call me "her little genius." I had no idea what a genius was, but I do remember the light that shined in her eyes when she said it. A genius was a good thing to be, I gathered from looking at Mom's smile. My mother was planting the seed for my genius to grow. The older I got, the more I understood how important it was to be all that I could be. A genius is a person with distinguished prowess. This prowess can be intellectually, musically, artistically, vocally, you name it!

Maybe the thought of you being a genius has never crossed your mind. Maybe you wouldn't dare consider yourself a genius, but you are. We all are. This truth startles so many people because we generally assign the status of "genius" to people who have high, triple-digit IQs. Isn't that funny?

We value intellectual prowess but not creative prowess. We think doctors are better than painters, don't we? We think engineers are better than writers? Some engineers even think they're better (more valuable) than writers, don't they? Some of you are wincing as you're reading this because you know it's true, you hate to hear it and you don't want to hear it. This isn't about engineers, per se; this is about one "idea" of what constitutes a genius. It's the ego that avoids the truth. The truth liberates, it doesn't imprison. It's okay. Society has conditioned us to think this way about our genius, so on some level we all have biases and prejudices when it comes to what we accept as greatness or true genius. We don't like to admit that, but it's nevertheless true.

So, instead of saying you're not something you don't want to be, try being who and what you want to be. Imagine that. If we'd stop trying to convince the world that we're not one thing, we could free up our energies to become more of who we really are. You could actually become the real you. The only way to become the real you is to be truthful about the ideals you hold and the images you've created. You have the power to transform your ideals and images instantly. Yes, you can be sexist in one moment and not in the next. And if you don't believe that, it's because you don't know the power within you. Period. If every child were greeted with the words "you are a loving genius," the world would be a better place. Use the Wholeness Matrix as a barometer for your success. Measure your level of spiritual fitness in each area of the Matrix. Unleashing your genius is unapologetically about walking in your brilliance. It's about knowing who you are and living your life with passion.

I grew up listening to a very uplifting song entitled, "This Little Light of Mine." The next line, "I'm gonna let it shine," is the important one. I always liked the arrangement of this song. People smiled and clapped as they sang it. It was a happy song. Yet I didn't realize the profound power in the words until later. We all have a light—a genius—that we can "choose" to let shine, or we can hide. Most of us hide it. We're afraid of what people will say if we beam too much. People might not like us. Like

Akeelah in the movie I mentioned earlier, *Akeelah and the Bee,* we don't want to draw attention to our brilliance because we've seen what happens when our light shines. People tell you not to shine your light. They tell you, "You're not smarter than the rest of us." They tell us that we're just like everybody else and that we shouldn't "try to be more than we are." Ever heard sentiments like these?

Most of us have endured these comments more than we care to remember. Few of us have the courage to shine our lights despite the world's reaction to that light. We'd rather not hear those comments. How powerful is it that we'd hide our talents and gifts just so that we didn't have to hear the sarcastic and unsupportive comments from the world? We refuse to nurture our genius because it's too painful. But genius doesn't vanish because it's not nurtured. It may wither like a raisin in the sun, but it's still a raisin. It's still genius. It's still in there.

In one of Michael Jordan's most memorable commercials, he talks about success and failure. His script included how many times he's been trusted to take the game-winning shot—how many times the ball's been in his hand, and his team was counting on him. He concludes the commercial by saying, "I've failed many times . . . and that is why I succeed." Jordan is not simply speaking of the shots he missed, but also of the risks he was willing to take.

Jordan's genius wasn't his basketball game. His genius was taking a sport that a lot of people play "well" and making it an art. That's genius. His love for the game was genius. Basketball became the canvas that Michael Jordan painted on. He did things on the basketball court that other people have done, but his genius was in doing those things consistently. He painted a different picture every night on the court. He took the game to another level with his passion and focus. We loved watching him because we never knew whether he was going to paint with watercolors or oil, we just knew that when it was over it was going to be a masterpiece. Jordan was Da Vinci. He poured his whole heart into the game—not his occupation. The love that he obviously had for his craft made us love it too. That's the difference between artistry and genius.

THE GENIUS OF SUPERMAN

It's hard to say no to Superman. When Chris, my younger brother, was five years old, he wanted to enter a thirty-yard dash at "Fun Day" at a City of Dallas summer youth program. It was a project that was designed to give kids alternatives to just hanging out on street corners during the summer vacation. Chris, who at the time insisted that everyone in our family call him "Superman," had always been fascinated by running, jumping, and, yes, flying.

When it was time for dinner, Mom would say, "Chris, time for dinner, sweetie." But he wouldn't come. Mom would repeat herself. "Chri-iiiis, come and eat, baby." Still no Chris. Finally, I told her that if she wanted Chris to appear she'd simply have to call him by his name—Superman. "I'm not calling him Superman. I'm his mother, he'll come," Mom said, looking very serious. "Don't let me call you again, little boy!" Still no Chris. Finally, Mom caved in. "Supermaaaaaan!" And faster than a speeding bullet, Chris would appear, wearing the "S" cape that Cora, a friend of the family, had made him for his birthday. But he wouldn't just walk into the room like everyone else. Superman made an entrance. He'd make "ssssswoooop" sounds as if he were jumping from one building to the next and then he'd plop down into his seat. If Mom cooked vegetables that he didn't want to eat, he'd pretend that they were kryptonite. This never worked, but it was always fun to watch because he was so energetic and persuasive.

And that's exactly what I remember most about him as he prepared for the thirty-yard dash that day at the park—his energy and his gift for persuasion. His desire to express his running genius.

Each week that we went to the park, he would stand on the sidelines hypnotized as he watched the older kids run in races. And although he didn't really understand the concept of running a race (so I thought), he somehow knew that the atmosphere of competing and doing your best provided one of the greatest feelings in the world.

For three weeks, he'd run over to me, panting and out of breath with the same question, "Can I run today, Fran?" For three weeks my answer had remained the same, "We'll see," that worn-out phrase my parents used on me whenever they didn't know exactly how to say no with good reason. But on this one day, I finally saw the sparkle in Chris's eyes. He wanted—no, he needed—to run in that race, so I agreed to give him his shot.

As one event finished and they geared up for the next one, I found out from a parent that the other two kids in Chris's race were seven and nine years old. They were much bigger and more developed than my gangly five-year-old shrimp of a brother who'd just lost one of his front teeth. Oh, no, I thought. He's gonna get creamed. He'll hate me for letting him sign up!

I jogged over to the starting point, thinking that maybe I should pull Mighty Mouse from the race. Maybe encourage him to run with kids his own age. But something in Chris' spirit told me that age was nothing but a number in his mind.

The official called for the runners to take their marks, and I told Chris that I would be waiting for him at the finish line and that I'd be proud of him no matter what happened. I kissed him and sent him to the starting blocks, certain that I was making a big mistake.

A few seconds later the race began, and Chris took off as if he'd been shot from a cannon. And just as I'd imagined, the two older kids, one to his left, the other to his right, were leaving him in the dust. All of the spectators were going crazy, cheering for all three kids. I jumped up and down, waving my hands, wearing a smile as wide as Texas.

Chris kept his eyes on me and continued to run his little heart out. Finally, he crossed the finished line, leaping into my arms. "Way to go, Chris," I said, holding back a fountain of tears. "You were soooo good, baby! You ran so hard, I'm proud of you."

He hugged my neck so tight I was sure it would snap. With his sweaty face buried in my neck, he kissed me, pulled away and asked excitedly, "Did I win?"

Surely, he thought, he must have won as hard as I was smiling. I laughed but didn't even think twice about the answer to his question. I continued to flash my megawatt smile, took one look at the gleam in his eyes and the joy spilling out of his chest, and said, "You sure did, baby. You sure did." He hugged me again, this time tighter.

I now realize that the discomfort I had experienced prior to Chris's race had more to do with my own fifteen-year-old athletic ego. I had already been conditioned to believe that winning wasn't the only thing, it was *everything*. But at age five, Chris taught me that winning has many different faces. It's playing hard and having fun. It's giving it your absolute best every time you compete. These lessons helped me to land a spot on the Houston Comets' first WNBA championship team in 1997. These lessons continue to help me build a successful career in entertainment as a broadcaster, producer, and writer.

I can still see Chris on the sidelines on that blistery hot day. Stretching like he was Olympic gold medalist Michael Johnson. And there I was, sweating bullets because I thought that if he lost, he'd never run again; or worse, that I wouldn't be able to comfort him.

Chris's story is one that I share with athletes and parents all over the country. It's a prime example of the fact that it's not whether you win or lose, it truly is about how you run the race or how you play the game. That day he received a third-place ribbon for his efforts. In his mind, he'd won because he had enjoyed the race and given it his all. It didn't matter to him that he'd been the last one to cross the finish line. He ran like a winner.

Chris taught me that on some days, the opponent might simply perform or be better than you. That's the nature of sports, but hardly a reason to give up competing altogether. As a player in the game of life, my goal, thanks to my baby brother, is now very simple: to love what I do, give each day 100 percent, and know that these two things alone make me a winner—on or off the court. Unleashing your genius is about running like there is no finish line. It's about running like you have no competitors. It's about focusing on your race and completing your divine assignment.

When I think back on that scorcher of a day, I realize what Chris gave me was more than a life lesson or a sportsmanship jewel. He was teaching me about "being" rather than "doing." He was teaching me to be authentic, something that had apparently gotten lost in my short fifteen years of life. He showed me what genius in action looks like. It's letting go of the outcome. It's joyfully running your race.

I want you to put yourself in Chris's shoes for a second. I want you to think back to your childhood—to a time when you didn't have a Visa bill to pay; a time when you didn't have a boss breathing down your neck about a stupid report; a time when you laughed until your side hurt; a time when you could eat a vanilla ice cream cone without wondering if it had any trans fats in it. Remember that time?

What happened to that child? Somewhere along the way, that child was made to believe that he or she was not made in God's image—perfect. On that day, the child put on his mask and started the long journey of being someone else.

So just what does it mean to be made in God's image—to be a descendant of the Divine? It means that you are pure love. Pure genius. You may choose to behave in ways that don't reflect that genius, but that doesn't diminish the fact that you are still a bundle of genius. People forget this. And people question this undeniable truth. God is love, and if you are made in God's image, that means that you, too, are love.

You may ask, if we're all made in God's image, and if God's nothing but love through and through, then why is there so much suffering and pain in the world? The answer is simple: Because the world has forgotten— just as you have at times—that at the core, we are love. And when you forget something of this magnitude, you behave in ways that are diametrically opposed to what you are.

That day at the park, I forgot who Chris was. I forgot that he was pure love and that love knows and has no limits. I forgot that it wasn't my place to put a leash on his genius. He was creating his reality, and I came dangerously close to messing that up for him. Every day we exercise the power of creation. We have the opportunity to create a world that is based in love or one that is based in fear. We have the power to tame or unleash our genius. I was trying to create a reality for Chris that was steeped in fear and rejection, and, thank God, he didn't allow that to happen. I guess he really was Superman.

You Are Plenty

You are not enough. That's what the world and the media would have you believe, but it's simply not true. In fact, nothing can be farther from truth.

What is most amazing about Chris's race is that he had no concept of winning and losing, he was being real. He was enough, and in his heart, he knew this. By trying to discourage him not to run, I would have been sending him a clear message: You're not enough. You don't measure up to the other kids. It's not enough that you want to run, you must want to *win*. That's what my hesitation told him. What a crock! Fortunately, he was still young and innocent enough to ward off my ego-driven desires for his life. And when he lined up on the starting blocks, he knew. He knew.

He embodied God's magnificence through his desire to run in the race. He didn't know that the boy in the lane next to him was nine years old and that the girl on the other side was seven. He didn't care. He didn't really understand what it meant to be five! All he wanted was his chance to be real. He wanted the experience of running, of being. He was willing to accept whatever happened as a result of his participation in the race as long as he got to be, because to him, the experience *was* the running.

Kids respond to their adult stimuli. That's why at the conclusion of the race, Chris asked me, "Did I win?" He'd been around the block enough times to know that a happy face and loud cheers were commonplace when people were victorious. The same is true on the negative side of the coin. There's no better example than when a toddler is learning to walk and she falls en route to the parent on the other side of the room. The child will fall and think nothing of it until they read the expression and feel the vibration of the adult who says, "Ohhhh, no! She fell!" Then what happens? You guessed it, the toddler starts to cry.

The toddler intuits that she is not enough—not "enough" in the way that we've been raised to think of inadequacy but "enough" in the sense of being perfect. Not flawless but perfect. Does that make sense? A toddler who is trying to walk for the first time is perfect even if he or she takes half a step. That's why the expression on their face is of utter glee. They want the experience of putting one step in front of the other and seeing what happens. That's all they know.

So, why must we foil the experience by judging it? "Come on, one more step, you can do it." What is that? It's saying that what you're doing is not enough. We must stop this. We must learn that the greatest expression of love is acceptance. A toddler doesn't know that you're on the other side of the room; they're just giddy at the thought of those legs doing something different for a change. Let 'em have their moment in the sun. Let 'em enjoy just being without it having to "mean" something. This is being. This is perfection.

THE GENIUS OF FANTASY

It was September 1998, I'd just launched the nation's first national women's fantasy basketball camp series for women ages twenty-five to sixty. Imagine a group of women from all backgrounds, ethnic groups, skill levels, and disciplines in one gym for one purpose—to learn to play basketball. Some of these women had played ball many, many years ago. Many had participated on their high school teams long before the enactment of Title IX, the legislation that gave women the right to play sports in school. So this was the first chance for many of them to live out their hoop dreams. Some were scared—many of them apprehensive about being taught and perhaps of looking silly in front of other people. Some of them faked injuries to get out of being put on the spot. I understood.

Most of these women had watched me play in the WNBA. And I can understand why they have such respect for professional athletes. It is an honor and achievement to make it to the highest level of one's sport—but we are not gods and goddesses, and we are not infallible. But because I had heard so many "Wow" comments during registration, I knew I'd have to give them a reality check immediately. We all learn step-by-step. "Don't be afraid to be vulnerable out here," I told them. Nearly a hundred eyes focused on me and what I had to say. "I've been right where you are. I haven't always been able to dribble with my left hand, shoot a jump shot, or run for five minutes without passing out. There is hope," I assured them. "It's not that you can't," I said. "It's that you don't know how yet. You have to unleash your talent and see what happens. It's the only way to know what you can become."

Some of these women had never tested the limits of their basketball skills. They had genius that they weren't aware of because no one had ever put them in an environment to find it. Some of us are in touch with our genius, and we're living lives that reflect that knowing. But some of you reading this right now are not being all of who you are. You're hiding your genius. You're shoving it to the back burner to make other people feel good. You're ignoring it in favor of keeping your "good job." You're pretending not to have any genius so that you won't stand out.

When you become the real you, you access an enormous amount of time and energy that will lead you to new levels of peace, prosperity, and love. By implementing these final spiritual strategies of the REAL YOU system into your daily life you will begin to enjoy the life you truly want and deserve. And guess what? The world awaits your genius!

COMMIT TO SPIRIT

Having a clear purpose and commitment to a life that focuses on the spirituality in all things will keep you balanced when the ego tries to throw you a curveball or lure you with its bag of tricks. Align yourself with your commitment and intention to create a oneness with who you are and what you want to create in your life. Your commitment to living in-spirit opens up the channels for you to unleash more and more of your genius. Even if you're currently living in and on purpose, unpeeling the layers of ego and fear that suffocate your genius will reveal more of who you are on a momentary basis.

WAKE UP

No more spiritual sleepwalking. Become aware of the Spirit in all things. See the characters in your movie as people who can assist you in your journey and provide you with opportunities to grow into more of who you are. Your nemesis, the person or thing you have previously believed to be your "enemy," may actually be the your Teacher of the Year if you can stop vilifying him or her enough to see the profound lessons they are showing you. Become a nonjudgmental observer of life and a loving witness to your thoughts and behavior so that your level of spiritual alertness and awareness can soar. Genius is not only the full expression of your talents and physical gifts, it's also the full embodiment of your spiritual gifts.

LASER YOUR INTENTION

What we think about we ultimately become. If your days are filled with thoughts about how horrible your life is, your life will continue to be filled with people, places, and things that support that kind of thinking. If you fill your mind with spiritually uplifting thoughts, your life will reflect those thoughts. I want you to focus on your intention—that invisible force inside, waiting on us to channel it in the direction of our desires. It's the intention fertilizer that manifests thoughts into material reality. Devote screen time in your life movie only to those things you want to see on the screen and leave the rest on the cutting room floor! Remember, where there is no intention, there can be no manifestation.

Divest Now!

Opinions. We've all got 'em. Your ability to levitate above the minutia of fear-based ideologies will depend heavily on your ability to divest yourself of the opinions of others. Think of opinions as stock that's losing its market value. You wouldn't hold on to it, would you? Of course not, you'd sell it! Get rid of it! Divest today! You must do the same thing with well-intentioned people whose thoughts and opinions don't serve your highest good. By focusing on that which supports who you are on a real level, and simultaneously detaching from the opinions of those whose words don't support your journey, your genius has room to breathe and blossom.

Accept Your Assignment

Accept your many gifts and areas of genius. You came equipped with everything you need to create whatever you want. And even though some assembly is required, it's a journey that you are fully equipped to handle. Once you align your intention with what you want and accept who you are and your internal power, the voice of doubt, fear, and scarcity will no longer be a factor. Your genius will emerge and the roadways to completing your assignment will magically open up!

Power Up Your Beliefs

Beliefs are powerful, so brace yourself for this one: Many of the beliefs you hold are not your own. Ouch! It's true. Most of us adopt the attitudes and beliefs of those who raised us or influenced our lives—our parents, teachers, religious leaders, and even the media. That's why part of your spiritual-closet cleaning has to include an assessment of your belief system. Go back to the five areas of the Wholeness Matrix. That's a great place to start. What are your top five beliefs in those five categories? Are the beliefs you have about love, money, race, prestige, work, children, and spirituality your own, or are you leasing them from someone else? It's time to get your own belief system. Developing an inquisitive mind is healthy and normal. Be curious about how you came to be who you are. And then have the courage to change your belief systems so that you can unleash your genius.

OVERFLOW YOUR OWN CUP FIRST

Self-awareness brings you closer to self-love, which brings you closer to self-acceptance, which brings you closer to your genius. I believe we must always be going to the well to fill our own cups before we attempt to fill someone else's. Your nourishment of your own spirit and soul are non-negotiable in my mind. Many of us don't realize that we have plenty to give. We have plenty of energy to direct outside of ourselves. We are not being true to ourselves when we neglect and abuse ourselves just to be liked or to be seen as benevolent human beings. There is plenty of time to give what you have—once you have enough to give. You can cultivate your genius on a daily basis by filling your cup with thoughts and energy that move you closer to your purpose. If you know that you are here to be of service to single dads, nurture that genius by developing a list of topics that might be of interest to your target market. Once you have a nice representation of resources, topics, and tools for your audience, then it's time to take your message to the masses and pour a blessing into the cups of others. Many people attempt to give what they don't have. They attempt to love other people before they truly love themselves. Your genius will inspire others to unleash theirs, but remember, it must be unleashed first.

REFLECT AND RECALL

Every instance in life gives us the chance to reflect on who we are and what we've learned. Making self-reflection a part of your daily spiritual workout will bring more awareness and alertness to your path. A good time to reflect is when someone is telling you something about something you said or did. Rather than being defensive or reactive, try being reflective. Where's the wisdom in what they're sharing? Is there a morsel of a lesson that you can take from their words? When people give us feedback, we immediately feel a need to judge it or them. We either say, "That's not true" (judging it as true or not); or we say, "You're beating up on me, so I reject what you have to say." When we realize that we don't have to accept anything anyone says, we become free to reflect on the feedback people give us, and we become more open to the possibilities in what they are sharing. As you think about your areas of genius, reflect on how you can offer them to the world. Don't limit your offering only to your immediate world—your family or community—explore ways to expand the reach of your greatness.

ACTIVELY MEDITATE

We've been coerced into believing that all meditation has to put us in a hypnotic state. It doesn't. During active meditation you get to see what you want in your life as if it were happening in that moment—because it is! If you can see it, it's real. Many of us have such a difficult time seeing what we want to manifest that we don't realize that that's exactly why it hasn't shown up in the physical dimension. Practice active visualization and meditation every single day, and pretty soon, you'll see exactly what you see. By meditating on the impact of your genius, you subconsciously create a space for it to flourish and have a greater impact on the world.

LIVE CONGRUENCE

This is the purest alignment of your entire Self. When your spiritual, emotional, mental, and physical selves are in complete alignment, you are able to experience a miraculous flow of blessings with little or no effort. When you mix spiritual principles with powerful mental imagery, the results are often staggering. You no longer need to judge or appraise things or people. You become adept at maximizing the moments.

LOVE

Using my toffee crunch ice cream analogy from earlier in this discussion of love, I'd like to encourage you to go deep—to look beyond what's right in front of you today. Right now, fill yourself up with love. Just let yourself feel immense and intense love—love of God, love for yourself, love for service, love for family and friends, and love for your genius. Nothing but love for the next thirty seconds. I mean, really fill yourself up. Imagine that you're the size of a swimming pool. Fill your pool up with love. If you were able to feel the enormity of love just now, you have some idea of how powerful love is as an agent of change. With this new awareness, I urge you to wow the world with your love and your genius. Whatever you do, do it with more love. In your relationships, show more love. In your job or career, blanket it with love. When a problem shows up, love it!

FEEL THE CONNECTION

There's a connectedness that unifies us all. It's our spiritual nature. You can call it God, Allah, Creator, Spirit, the Universe, the Divine, the One, it doesn't matter. What is real is that this power is the ultimate expression of unencumbered, unconditional, and enduring love. And because we are images of this Intelligence and Power, we have the capacity to love in the same manner. All we need to do is access it through our intention. By being aware of our connectedness to God, we are able to align our thoughts and emotions so that they support our desires to unleash our genius en route to becoming more of who we really are.

Focus on What "Is"

You are not broken. You are not incomplete. You have everything you need inside of you. Nothing is missing. What you want, you already have. You cannot "make it happen," you only need to connect to what you want, act in a manner that supports what you want, and it will show up. The key is to focus your energies on what "is" in your life versus what you perceive to be lacking. Want better health? Focus on developing high-performing organs. Work out. Want better grades? Focus on greater comprehension and retention. Study. Want more sizzle in your relationships? Focus on exploring new and different ways to know your partner and to allow them to know you. Be loving, truthful, kind, open, and supportive and your relationship will be transformed.

Judge No More

Go on a judgment diet for life, but you can start by not judging anything or anyone for one entire day as I recommended earlier. Write down what you say each time you do judge something or someone, each time you condemn or ridicule someone. Each time you label someone, write it down. The enlightened warrior knows that there's no need to judge. Things just are. People are not bad or good. Through this exercise, you will become acutely aware of how much you judge yourself and those around you. Don't forget to record your judgments. The ultimate goal is to have a sheet that is empty. By replacing judgment with love and acceptance, you clear additional places in your heart to create more of what you want. By giving up your need to criticize and scrutinize, your genius will be fortified.

Maximize Now

Make a commitment to live in the now. When I'm juggling multiple projects, I must admit, this one is tough for me. Today while I was getting acupuncture, I was also making my to-do list in my head! That's not what you want to do, just in case you found yourself going, "Yeah, so?" You want to be present. You want to be fully available to maximize your nows. If your five-year-old's telling you about how much fun he had at playtime, be present. Listen and participate. If your spouse is sharing the details of her day, be there with her in that moment. If your aging father is reminiscing on one of his good-old-days stories, and you've heard it sixteen times in the last three days, stay in the now with him. When you are fully present, you open yourself up to amazing new insights and new levels of genius.

BE AWARE OF YOUR MAGNETISM

If there was a powerful magnet on your desk, and you got within a few feet of it with a paper clip, it would suck the clip up even if you tried to stop it because that's what magnets do. They attract metals to themselves. You and I are magnets, as well. Your thoughts and behaviors operate on a similar frequency. If you carry joy, you will attract joyous people (and those who want to be joyous people). If you carry negativity, don't be surprised when all of the negative people want to be your friend. If you want to know why you're attracting the people and circumstances in your life, take a long hard look at what you're putting into the world. Remember, genius loves company but so does misery.

IT'S NEVER TOO LATE TO UNLEASH YOUR GENIUS

It's true, we can never go back and redo what we did yesterday, but we can create a different today. I'm amazed by the people in my coaching practice who refuse to let yesterday be yesterday. I understand. I used to engage in the same behavior. They think it's too late for them to be whatever they wanted to be ten years ago, but in most cases, it's not.

My godbrother Charles is a prime example. He dropped out of college with so few credits to complete his degree that even he laughs about it. But that was then. This year, he enrolled in college because like most of us, he's got dreams. He knows that completing his degree will open up many doors for him as well as give him the completion he needs to take his life to the next level.

When we talk, it's always a spirited discussion about how different it is to be in college at thirty than at twenty, but overall, he's fired up about his decision to go back to school. I can feel the aspiration oozing out of him. I don't know what he'll do with what he's learning, but I believe that what Charles is experiencing is what many of you are experiencing. Your genius is dying to come out. Yet some of you are so sedated by your bills, weight, unhealthy relationships, six-figure incomes, fear, and illusions that you think you have no genius. You do!

As much as I'd like to be able to mail you a bottle of Genius Activation Pills, nothing is going to ignite your fire like truth. And the truth is that you are not living up to the potential of your genius, and you know it. How I wish we would stop using our age, gender, address, ethnicity, family name, GPA, relatives, and past transgressions as an excuse for not becoming the mega-watt bulb we were born to be.

Victor Hugo's words spring to mind: "No army is so powerful as an idea whose time has come." I say, "There's nothing like a star that's ready to shine. Nothing like a flower that's ready to bloom. Nothing like a genius who's ready to soar." It's your time. What are you waiting for?

BE THE REAL YOU

As we continue to evolve into more of our authentic selves, we open ourselves up to the wonders of the world. We immediately see things with a new set of eyes—eyes that twinkle with excitement. Our smiles glisten and invite people to smile more, too. Our high-voltage being lights up every room we enter. Being real and authentic doesn't require that you do anything. It's simply a state of you being exactly who you are.

When we let our guards down, suspend judgment of others and ourselves, and allow ourselves to be free from any limits, we are as real as we can get. When we love without the illusion of being hurt, dance because we love the music, and sing off-key at the top of our lungs, we are as real as we can get. When we leap joyfully into our purpose with passion and vigor, we are as real as we can get, and our genius is ripe for all seasons.

≈ REAL QUESTIONS, REAL ANSWERS ≈

I have many areas of genius, but I don't know how to harness them so that I can actually see some progress in my life. What should I do?

First, put your harness away! You don't need to harness your genius; you need to rejoice that at least you're embodying your gifts and talent. Authentic living requires that we gleefully step into our genius. It sounds like you're wondering how to put your genius to work in the world, and that, as you can imagine, does require some organization and discipline. I recommend that you buy a genius journal and record everything you want to do during your time on earth. Don't limit yourself. Don't censor your dreams. Just write.

Then I want you to organize your genius into a timeline. In other words, let's start to build a plan for making these dreams a reality. Decide what you want to "contribute" this year. Make a list and then break the list down into tiny action steps complete with tasks to be done and target dates. Do this for every year (or five years) on the timeline, and you should be on your way!

I'm afraid to be all that I can be. Success has meant leaving people in the past. I don't know how to break out of this mind-set.

If you're willing to see your success in a different frame, here's what I offer: The more successful we are, the more we can contribute to the world. And I'm not talking only about financial success. Success for me means actualized, whole, and complete. The more clarity we have about who we are, the more capable we are of helping to feed the world, strengthen the world, and heal the world. Your illusion about leaving people is based on fears that people have projected onto us by saying things like, "Don't forget where you came from." That's nothing more than fear that they will be forgotten, abandoned, or tossed away. Let that go. When we become our real selves, we leap into a power that allows us to elevate our human family to new levels of consciousness, love, wealth, and spiritual prosperity. And that's always a good (God) thing!

Conclusion
Live Now

Your time is right now. In this moment, you are creating what you want, as well as becoming who you are. The world is waiting for the debut of the real you. We're waiting on you to unleash your genius. No more sleeping through your classroom of life and asking for the notes in homeroom. No more sitting down when you should be standing tall. No more playing small when the world needs you to be a spiritual giant. You are now operating at new levels of awareness and alertness. We must always remind each other that the world we are living in is the world we're creating. What we wish to see in our world, we must first create in ourselves. What we want to see reflected in our children's eyes—hope, possibility, and love—we must also create in our own hearts. Only then will we become who we truly are and were meant to be.

I'll leave you with one of my favorite stories:

One day after class, one of Buddha's students asked, "Are you the Messiah?"

"No," answered Buddha.

"Then are you a healer?"

"No," Buddha replied.

"Then are you a teacher?" the student persisted.

"No, I am not a teacher."

"Then what are you?" asked the student, exasperated.

"I am awake," Buddha replied.

Be awake. Be real. Be you.

❧ For Further Information ❧

For additional information on Fran Harris's
appearances, books, products, lectures, classes, seminars,
and live events, visit www.franharris.com or
to inquire about having her speak to your organization, send your
request to info@franharris.com or call (310) 745-7762.
For information on the Real You Tour, as well as
a free gift from Fran, visit www.realyoutour.com.

Fran Harris Enterprises
P.O. Box 3594
Culver City, CA 90231
(310) 745-7762
info@franharris.com

*I*ndex